DECISIONS AT SECOND MANASSAS

BOOKS BY MATT SPRUILL

The U. S. Army War College Guide to the Battle of Chickamauga

Storming the Heights: A Guide to the Battle of Chattanooga

Echoes of Thunder: A Guide to the Seven Days Battles
with Matt Spruill IV

Winter Lightning: A Guide to the Battle of Stones River
Second Edition, with Lee Spruill

*Summer Thunder: A Battlefield Guide to
the Artillery at Gettysburg*

*Decisions at Gettysburg: The Nineteen Critical Decisions
That Defined the Campaign*

Summer Lightning: A Battlefield Guide to the Second Battle of Manassas
with Matt Spruill IV

*Decisions at Stones River: The Sixteen Critical Decisions
That Defined the Battle*
with Lee Spruill

*Decisions at Second Manassas: The Fourteen Critical Decisions
That Defined the Battle*
with Matt Spruill IV

DECISIONS
AT SECOND MANASSAS

The Fourteen Critical Decisions
That Defined the Battle

Matt Spruill III and Matt Spruill IV

Maps by Tim Kissel

Command Decisions
in America's Civil War

The University of Tennessee Press / Knoxville

Copyright © 2018 by The University of Tennessee Press / Knoxville.
All Rights Reserved. Manufactured in the United States of America.
First Edition.

Library of Congress Cataloging-in-Publication Data

Names: Spruill, Matt, author. | Spruill, Matt, IV, author.
Title: Decisions at Second Manassas: the fourteen critical decisions that defined the battle / Matt Spruill III and Matt Spruill IV; maps by Tim Kissel.
Description: First edition. | Knoxville: The University of Tennessee Press, 2018. | Series: Command decisions in America's Civil War | Includes bibliographical references and index. |
Identifiers: LCCN 2017027914 (print) | LCCN 2017029766 (ebook) | ISBN 9781621903819 (pdf) | ISBN 9781621903963 (Kindle) | ISBN 9781621903802 (pbk.)
Subjects: LCSH: Bull Run, 2nd Battle of, Va., 1862. | Command of troops—Case studies.
Classification: LCC E473.77 (ebook) | LCC E473.77.S669 2018 (print) | DDC 973.7/32—dc23
LC record available at https://lccn.loc.gov/2017027914

To our wives,
Kathy and Janet

and

To the memory of Cheryl Carson,
1969–2015,
marketing manager,
University of Tennessee Press

CONTENTS

Preface	xiii
Introduction	1
1. Before the Battle—June 26 to August 27, 1862	7
2. Contact is Regained—Thursday, August 28, 1862	31
3. Day of Battle—Friday, August 29, 1862	45
4. Day of Decision—Saturday, August 30, 1862	71
5. The Campaign Continues—Sunday, August 31 to Tuesday, September 2, 1862	97
6. Conclusions	107
Appendix I. Battlefield Guide to the Critical Decisions at Second Manassas	115
Appendix II. Union Order of Battle	209
Appendix III. Confederate Order of Battle	221
Notes	231
Bibliography	243
Index	249

ILLUSTRATIONS

Figures

President Abraham Lincoln, USA	8
Secretary of War Edwin M. Stanton, USA	9
Organizational chart of the Army of Virginia	11
Maj. Gen. John Pope, USA	12
Maj. Gen. Henry W. Halleck, USA	15
Gen. Robert E. Lee, CSA	20
Maj. Gen. Thomas J. Jackson, CSA	24
Maj. Gen. Irvin McDowell, USA	33
Brig. Gen. James B. Ricketts, USA	37
Longstreet's Right Wing marching through Thoroughfare Gap	38
Brawner Farm, August 28, 1862. View from position of Battery B/4th US Artillery	43
Terrain north of the Warrenton Turnpike and west of Sudley Road	49
Brig. Gen. John Buford, USA	53
Maj. Gen. James Longstreet, CSA	60
Maj. Gen. Fitz John Porter, USA	61
Center of Porter's Attack	76
Porter's Attack, Confederate view	77
Brig. Gen. Robert H. Milroy, USA	78
Brig. Gen. John F. Reynolds, USA	80
Position of Reynolds's division, south slope of Chinn Ridge	81

Warrenton Turnpike at the Sudley Road intersection	83
Col. Gouverneur K. Warren, USA	85
Col. Nathaniel C. McLean, USA	86
Col. Montgomery D. Corse, CSA	89
Col. Henry L. Benning, CSA	91
Sudley Road	92
Retreat over the Stone Bridge	96
Maj. Gen. Philip Kearny, USA	101
Brig. Gen. Isaac I. Stevens, USA	101
Brig. Gen. John Gibbon, USA	127
Lieut. Col. Edward S. Bragg, USA	129
Brig. Gen. Abner Doubleday, USA	131
Lieut. Col. J. William Hoffman, USA	133
Col. Wladimir Krzyzanowski, USA	139
Maj. Franz Blessing, USA	144
Sgt. Joseph Gould, USA	150
Col. Charles Roberts, USA	160
Col. Elisha G. Marshall, USA	163
Col. Leroy Stafford, CSA	166
S. D. Lee's Artillery Battalion in action	167
Col. Stephen D. Lee, CSA	168
Brig. Gen. Zealous B. Tower, USA	180
Maj. Gen. Franz Sigel, USA	190
Col. George T. Anderson, CSA	197
The fight at Thoroughfare Gap on August 28, 1862	201

Maps

Operational Situation, August 9–20, 1862	17
Lee's First Plan	21
The Turning Movement, August 25–26, 1862	25
Jackson Moves to the Stony Ridge, Night of August 27 and Morning of August 28, 1862	28
McDowell's Second Option, August 28, 1862	35
McDowell's Decision, August 28, 1862	36
Jackson Decides to Attack, Late Afternoon, August 28, 1862	42
Unit Locations at Sunrise, August 29, 1862	47
Attacks on August 29, 1862	54
Option 2: Possible Scenario, Afternoon, August 29, 1862	56
Porter Decides Not to Attack, August 29, 1862	65

Option 3: Possible Scenario, August 29, 1862	67
Situation in Early Afternoon, August 30, 1862	74
Situation at 3:45 p.m., August 30, 1862	82
Chinn Ridge, 4:30 p.m., August 30, 1862	88
Chinn Ridge, 5:15 p.m., August 30, 1862	90
Possible Scenario, Longstreet's Attack, Late Afternoon, August 30, 1862	93
Another Turning Movement, August 31 and September 1, 1862	100
Lee's Options, September 2, 1862	103
Critical Decisions Tour Map	114
Stop 2: Jackson Moves to the Stony Ridge, August 28, 1862	120
Stop 3, Position A: Initial Contact, Early Evening, August 28, 1862	123
Stop 3, Position B: Left of the Union Line, Late Evening, August 28, 1862	126
Stop 3, Position C: Center of the Union Line, Late Evening, August 28, 1862	130
Stop 4, Position A: Union Deployment, Morning and Early Afternoon, August 29, 1862	136
Stop 4, Position B: Krzyzanowski's Attack, Gregg's Defense, Mid- to Late Morning, August 29, 1862	140
Stop 4, Position C: Schimmelfennig's Attack, Barnes's Counterattack, Late Morning, August 29, 1862	146
Stop 4, Position D: Nagle's Attack, Late Afternoon, August 29, 1862	149
Stop 5, Position A: Porter's Attack Formation, Midafternoon, August 30, 1862	155
Stop 5, Position B: The Attack Begins, Midafternoon, August 30, 1862	158
Stop 5, Position C: Assault to the Unfinished Railroad, Midafternoon, August 30, 1862	162
Stop 7, Position A-1: McLean's Initial Position, Late Afternoon, August 30, 1862	173
Stop 7, Position A-2: McLean's Left Enveloped, Late Afternoon, August 30, 1862	174
Stop 7, Position B: McLean's Second Position, Late Afternoon, August 30, 1862	176
Stop 7, Position C: Tower Reinforces McLean, Late Afternoon, August 30, 1862	179
Stop 7, Position D: Stiles Reinforces Tower and McLean, Jenkins Joins the Attack, Late Afternoon, August 30, 1862	182

Stop 7, Position E: Koltes Defends, Benning Reinforces,
    Late Afternoon, August 30, 1862   185
Excursion Stop 1: Porter Decides Not To Attack, August 29, 1862   193
Excursion Stop 2, Position B: Fight for the Gap, Midafternoon,
    August 28, 1862   199
Excursion Stop 3: Jackson's March, August 31–September 1, 1862   203
Excursion Stop 3, Position B, Battle of Ox Hill (Chantilly),
    Late Afternoon, September 1, 1862   207

PREFACE

Our in-depth interest in the Battle of Second Manassas began when we were researching and writing *Summer Lightning: A Guide to the Battle of Second Manassas*. The logical next step was to make an even deeper study of the campaign and battle. We approached this examination with the critical-decision methodology. This method is designed to allow someone who has an understanding of "what happened" to move to the next level and ask, "Why did it happen, or what caused it to happen?" When the critical-decision concept is understood, it can be applied to any battle or campaign in any war.

We began by asking what had caused the campaign and battle to develop as it did. Were any actions or decisions so paramount that they influenced everything that followed? This question resulted in a list of critical decisions.

The chart on the next page shows the Decisions Hierarchy. At the bottom are various Decisions, above those is a lesser number of Important Decisions, and at the top are the very few Critical Decisions.

The criterion for a critical decision is that it is a decision of such magnitude that after it was made it shaped not only the events immediately following, but also the campaign or battle from thereafter. If these critical decisions had not been made, or a different decision made, the sequence of events for Second Manassas would have been significantly different.

The Second Manassas campaign and battle did not happen as a result of random chance. Events occurred as they did because of the decisions made at all levels of command on both sides. Some decisons were the normal

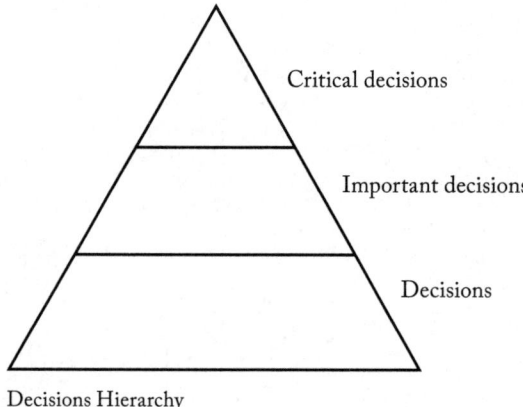

Decisions Hierarchy

ones made during any campaign or battle. Others were more important. A limited number of critical decisions shaped the way the campaign and battle unfolded.

It is important that you, the reader, understand the concept of a critical decision. Without this awareness, this book will appear to be only a short, selected narrative history of Second Manassas. Yet this book is not that. It is a work that explores the development of the battle and campaign and focuses on the "why" instead of the "what."

Critical decisions cover the entire spectrum of war: strategy, operational, tactics, organization, logistics, and personnel. Some decisions initially appeared to be minor, but are actually critical decisions that had a major impact on events.

The fourteen critical decisions for the Second Battle of Manassas are grouped into five specific time periods:

Before the Battle—June 26 to August 27, 1862
    Lincoln Decides to Create an Army
    Halleck Decides to Evacuate the Peninsula
    Lee Decides on a Turning Movement
    Jackson Moves to the "Stony Ridge"
Contact is Regained—Thursday, August 28, 1862
    Ricketts's Division Fights Alone
    Jackson Decides to Attack
Day of Battle—Friday, August 29, 1862
    Pope Decides to Attack
    Porter Decides Not to Attack
Day of Decision—Saturday, August 30, 1862
    Pope Decides to Attack Again

McDowell Decides to Reposition Troops
McLean Decides to Defend Chinn Ridge
Pope Decides to Retreat
The Campaign Continues—Sunday, August 31 to Tuesday, September 2, 1862
    Lee Decides on Another Turning Movement
    Lee Decides to Redeploy His Army

These critical decisions were chosen based upon our military background, extensive experience on the ground at Second Manassas, and close reading of primary and secondary material. Depending on their training and background, other historians might choose different decisions and interpret critical events in different ways. However, we firmly believe that the critical decisions enumerated in this book are the core decisions of the campaign and battle. Had they not been made, the character of the campaign, the battle, and the decisions that followed would have been different. This difference would have been of such magnitude as to alter events thereafter.

This is not to say that Maj. Gen. John Pope would have defeated Gen. Robert E. Lee. Although it might have happened that way, such speculation is beyond the scope of this book. We leave it to the reader to decide if the outcome would have been different. However, the sequence of events leading to the outcome would have altered, and the orientation of the opposing forces may have changed as well. Moreover, the battle could have been shorter or longer than it was, and it may have occurred at a different location.

The critical decisions at Second Manassas are grouped into five specific time periods. For each decision, the following topics are discussed: the situation, the options (courses of action) available to the decision-maker, the decision that was made, the results/impact of the decision, and, in some cases, other possible outcomes had another choice been made.

One should not rule out the possibility of chance, which can make apparently good decisions produce adverse results. Likewise, what seem to be bad decisions can sometimes produce positive results. Though our bias sometimes appears, we have attempted to refrain from calling a decision good or bad. Instead, we have concentrated on each decision's consequences or results and its effect on the campaign or battle.

This is not another history of all the events and decisions during the fighting at Second Manassas. Other books will provide the reader with a basic knowledge of the battle. Nor is it our purpose to offer a new interpretive history of Second Manassas. We have concentrated on the critical decisions to lay out some basic facts and present a relatively clear outline of a very complex situation. Without neglecting important details, this account presents a coherent and manageable blueprint as to why the battle developed as it did.

Preface

As you read you will notice the Union and the Confederacy used similar, but often different, methods to identify units. Therefore, some explanatory comments are appropriate.

Both sides used the same method to identify units at the company, battalion, and regimental level. Companies were identified by a letter—e.g., A Company. Regiments were identified by a number—e.g., Eighth (8th) New York, Ninth (9th) Virginia. Above the regimental level, the Union and Confederate armies diverged in their manner of identifying units.

The official designations of Union brigades, divisions, and corps were numeric and began with a capital letter. Some examples include First Brigade, First Division, Third Corps or Brig. Gen. John P. Hatch's First Brigade, Brig. Gen. Rufus King's First Division, and Maj. Gen. Irvin McDowell's Third Corps. Many publications use roman numerals to designate a corps—e.g., III Corps. However, this form of designation was not used in the Civil War. When referring to a brigade or division belonging to or commanded by an individual, lowercase letters are used. See, for example, Hatch's brigade, King's division, or McDowell's corps.

Early in the war the Confederacy used a numbering and a name system for unit designations. As the war progressed the numbering system was used less and the name system was most commonly used. The official designations of Confederate brigades, divisions, and corps were the commanders' names followed by Brigade, Division, or Wing (later Corps). Examples include Armistead's Brigade, Anderson's Division, and Longstreet's Right Wing—later Longstreet's Corps.

The Confederate system sometimes can be confusing. The unit officially designated Jackson's Division at Second Manassas had earlier been commanded by Maj. Gen. Thomas J. Jackson—hence its official designation. By the time of Second Manassas Jackson was a wing commander, and his old division was commanded by Brig. Gen. William B. Taliaferro. But the unit was not called Taliaferro's Division, as the designation had not been officially changed.

Lowercase letters are used when referring to a brigade, division, or wing (corps) belonging to or commanded by an individual. See, for example, Brig. Gen. Lewis A. Armistead's brigade, Brig. Gen. Armistead's brigade, Maj. Gen. Richard H. Anderson's division, Maj. Gen. Anderson's division, Maj. Gen. James Longstreet's wing (corps), or Maj. Gen. Longstreet's wing (corps). As with any matter pertaining to the Civil War, there are always exceptions.

There is value in being in close proximity to the place where a decision was made or carried out. Being on the ground provides you the opportunity to view the terrain and the tactical situation as the decision-maker did. In

Preface

some cases this is not feasible—for instance, if you are at Second Manassas and the decision was made in Washington or somewhere else away from the battlefield. However, many of the critical decisions were made and carried out on or near the Manassas Battlefield. We have, therefore, provided an appendix with a tour that will place you on the ground near or in the locations where critical decisions were reached or implemented. Included in the tour are excerpts from the *Official Records* or other primary source material. Some words are spelled differently today than they were in 1862—for example, *entrenchments* rather than *intrenchments*. We have left the spelling and grammar as it appears in the original documents.

Moreover, this brief guide has the specific, practical purpose of helping a reasonably well-informed reader get through the battle *on the ground* and gain further insights into the fighting and the effects of the critical decisions. The interpretive elements are specifically designed to support the appendix, which is more like a traditional guidebook.

We hope this book with its battlefield guide appendix will form a foundation for further reading, study, and reflection on the Battle of Second Manassas.

We wish to thank Ranger Jim Burgess of the Manassas National Battlefield Park for reading our manuscript and providing many valuable comments and suggestions. Thanks also to Scot Danforth, director of University of Tennessee Press, and his exceptional team who have guided and supported us through the publication and marketing process. Among them are Thomas Wells, Jon Boggs, Stephanie Thompson, and Tom Post; again, we extend our deepest thanks. A big thanks to Betsy Crowder for the excellent copy editing and refining of this book.

As always, our wives and best friends, Kathy and Janet, provided constant support and encouragement as this work developed from concept to book.

                              Matt Spruill III   Littleton, Colorado
                              Matt Spruill IV   Port Orange, Florida

INTRODUCTION

During 1862, the first full year of the Civil War, the pendulum of victory swung back and forth, first to the Union and then to the Confederacy. Brig. Gen. Ulysses S. Grant seized the initiative in the Western Theater, conducting a joint Army-Navy operation in February with Comdr. Andrew Foote and captured Fort Henry and Fort Donelson. The Cumberland and Tennessee Rivers were opened to the Union armies as routes of advance, supply, and communication into Tennessee, northern Alabama, and Mississippi. Grant's victories pierced the extended Confederate defensive line in the West that stretched from the mountains in southeastern Kentucky to Columbus on the Mississippi River, pushing the Confederate forward defenses back into central and southern Tennessee. In April the Confederate commander in the west, Gen. Albert S. Johnston launched a counteroffensive against Grant's Army of the Tennessee at Shiloh. Reinforced by Maj. Gen. Don Carlos Buell's Army of the Ohio, Grant fought a bloody two-day battle. The fighting on April 6 and 7 caused 23,746 casualties—21 percent of all troops engaged. The casualties at Shiloh exceeded the sum of all American losses in every war prior to the Civil War, and they were a harbinger of what was to come.[1]

Paralleling Grant's successes were those of the Union Army-Navy riverine force. These troops won several engagements while pushing south down the Mississippi River and capturing Memphis, Tennessee. Their operations secured the river from Cairo, Illinois, to Memphis.[2]

In the states west of the Mississippi River (the Trans-Mississippi), the Union victory at Pea Ridge (March 7–8) and the capture of New Orleans (April 25) did much to reverse the previous year's Confederate successes.[3]

In the far West a small Confederate army commanded by Brig. Gen. Henry H. Sibley marched from western Texas into New Mexico, then north toward Colorado. Halted by a Union force at Glorieta Pass, near Santa Fe, in late March, Sibley retreated back to Texas. This event ended the Confederacy's only serious attempt to expand its border on the southwestern frontier.[4]

In the Eastern Theater a force under Union Brig. Gen. Ambrose E. Burnside landed inside the North Carolina Outer Banks and secured a lodgment from which future operations into eastern North Carolina and southeastern Virginia could be conducted.[5]

The two main opposing armies in the East spent the winter of 1861–62 facing each other in northeast Virginia. In early March Confederate soldiers under Gen. Joseph E. Johnston abandoned their positions in the vicinity of Centreville and fell back to a defensive position on the natural barrier of the Rappahannock River.[5]

Almost simultaneously, Maj. Gen. George B. McClellan used sea power to conduct a turning movement against the Confederate army in northern Virginia. He landed his Army of the Potomac on the Peninsula and began a campaign up that landform to capture Richmond. Although movement was not as rapid as expected, McClellan's army was on the eastern outskirts of the city by the middle of June. It appeared that it was only a matter of time before the Confederate capital and a major manufacturing center would fall into Union hands.[6]

By late summer the euphoria from these victories was gone; Confederate armies went on the offensive and diminished early Union success. In the summer of 1862 the Confederacy was riding the crest of a wave that had the potential of fulfilling the dream of independence.

In the West Confederate forces launched a two-pronged offense into Kentucky. Maj. Gen. Edmund Kirby Smith led his Army of Kentucky north from Knoxville, Tennessee, reaching Lexington, Kentucky, on September 1. A second force joined Kirby Smith's on August 28, when Gen. Braxton Bragg led his Army of the Mississippi from Chattanooga, Tennessee, into Kentucky. Bragg's troops reached Bardstown, Kentucky, on September 23.[7]

Strong Confederate forces in Kentucky could have significant adverse strategic consequences for the Union. Maintaining an army or armies on the Ohio River would bring the South three major strategic advantages. First, Kentucky would become part of the Confederacy, if not through succession, then through occupation. Southern armies would then have access to large quantities of food, livestock, and horses. Secondly, a Confederate Kentucky would provide a buffer on Tennessee's northern border to protect the strategically and economically vital "Heartland." Thirdly, Confederate forces on the Ohio River would interdict the major river transportation route between the eastern and western

Union. However, before these advantages could be realized, Union and Confederate armies fought the Battle of Perryville on October 8, 1862. This battle caused Smith's and Bragg's armies to retreat back to Tennessee.

In Virginia, McClellan's turning movement forced the Confederate army under Gen. Joseph E. Johnston to move south from its positions along the Rappahannock River to protect the Confederate capital, Richmond. On May 31 Johnston was wounded at the Battle of Seven Pines (also called Fair Oaks), and he was replaced by Gen. Robert E. Lee.[8]

Throughout June, Lee concentrated his newly renamed Army of Northern Virginia in the trenches to the east and northeast of Richmond. Using part of his army to hold McClellan in position, Lee shifted the remainder to his left, brought Maj. Gen. Thomas J. "Stonewall" Jackson's force from the Shenandoah Valley, and on June 26 attempted a turning movement around McClellan's right, northern, flank. These actions initiated a series of battles (the Seven Days), culminating on July 1 at Malvern Hill, that drove McClellan's army away from Richmond. The casualties from the Seven Days Battles totaled 35,999—15,795 Union troops and 20,204 Confederates. For a complete study and tour of the Seven Days, see Matt Spruill III and Matt Spruill IV's *Echoes of Thunder: A Guide to the Seven Days Battles*, published by the University of Tennessee Press.[9]

Coming just three months after Shiloh, the casualties of the Seven Days Battles helped both sides realize that the Civil War would not be a short conflict decided by a victory in one or two battles. The battles during this period would show just how resilient large armies had become. They could now suffer large casualties and keep going as they recovered their strength and combat power.

With McClellan's army at Harrison's Landing on the James River, twenty-five miles southeast of Richmond, and a newly formed Union army in central Virginia, Lee considered a series of tactical options to confront a possible threat from McClellan and a developing threat from Maj. Gen. John Pope's Union Army of Virginia.[10]

After the Seven Days Battles, Lee organized his army into two commands under Maj. Gens. James Longstreet and Thomas J. "Stonewall" Jackson. The Confederate government did not authorize the formal organization of corps until October 1862 therefore, during the Second Battle of Manassas Longstreet's and Jackson's units were variously referred to as commands or as the Right Wing and the Left Wing respectively. They were corps for all practical purposes, but not in official designation. For ease of identification, we have chosen to use the terms Longstreet's Right Wing and Jackson's Left Wing.[11]

* * *

Introduction

Many consider the Campaign and Battle of Chancellorsville to be Lee's greatest offensive operation. However, the Campaign and Battle of Second Manassas ranks with Chancellorsville and maybe even above it. While the operations occurred within the same time period, however, the area of maneuver was larger and more significant for Second Manassas. Lee's victory at Chancellorsville resulted in the status quo. His success at Second Manassas moved the center of the war in the East from Richmond to just outside Washington, DC, and set the stage for his first incursion onto Northern soil.

The prelude to the Campaign and Battle of Second Manassas began when Lee shifted Jackson's Left Wing from Richmond to central Virginia. He acted in response to the creation and advance of the new Union Army of Virginia commanded by Maj. Gen. John Pope. Jackson fought the advance corps of this army at Cedar Mountain on August 9. With the inactivity of McClellan's Army of the Potomac on the Peninsula and its eventual evacuation, Lee shifted Longstreet's Right Wing and the army headquarters to join Jackson.

Lee realized that he had to engage and defeat Pope before significant reinforcement from McClellan could reach him. An unsuccessful attempt was made to trap Pope's army between the Rapidan and Rappahannock Rivers. Pope retreated to positions behind the Rappahannock, and Lee made several unsuccessful attempts to cross and attack him.

On August 25 Lee sent Jackson on a turning movement around Pope's right, through Thoroughfare Gap, and into the Union rear area at Bristoe Station. Arriving at Bristoe Station, Jackson severed Pope's supply line on the Orange and Alexandria Railroad. Jackson subsequently moved to Manassas Junction and destroyed Pope's forward supply base, and he then moved to the vicinity of the First Manassas battlefield. At this point, Jackson's location was unknown to Pope. On August 28, in the late afternoon, Jackson attacked one of Pope's divisions. Jackson's location was revealed, and Pope ordered his army to concentrate.

On August 26 Longstreet's Right Wing, with Lee in accompaniment, commenced marching along Jackson's previous route. The wing passed through Thoroughfare Gap, and during the morning hours of August 29 its troops arrived and deployed on Jackson's right.

A two-day battle was fought on August 29 and 30. On the first day, Pope concentrated on attacking Jackson's Wing and either ignored or miscalculated Longstreet's arrival on the battlefield. Pope continued to ignore Longstreet's arrival on the second day, attacking Jackson instead. This mistake resulted in a counterattack by Longstreet's Wing on Pope's exposed left flank. The result was the near destruction of the Union army.

Pope retreated to Centreville. Lee unsuccessfully attempted another turning movement that was stopped at Chantilly (Ox Hill). Pope then retreated farther to Washington, and Lee ended the campaign. Lee's army redeployed to Leesburg in preparation for crossing the Potomac River into Maryland.

The events of Second Manassas were not a random happening, but the result of a few critical decisions. These critical decisions determined the sequence of events that gives us the campaign and battle as we know it.

CHAPTER 1

BEFORE THE BATTLE—
JUNE 26 TO AUGUST 27, 1862

If you have bypassed the preface, please return there and read the definition of a critical decision to fully understand the presentations in this book.

The decisions made prior to the Battle of Second Manassas concerned organization and maneuver. They created the conditions that brought Gen. Robert E. Lee's Army of Northern Virginia and Maj. Gen. John Pope's Army of Virginia to fight a decisive battle. This fighting would change the character of the war in Virginia and position Lee to cross the Potomac River and conduct a campaign in Union territory.

Lincoln Decides to Create an Army

Situation

In the spring of 1862 four significant Union field forces were in Virginia. The largest was the Army of the Potomac, with four corps. Maj. Gen. George B. McClellan had used naval power to transport this army to the Peninsula with the intent of capturing Richmond. However, McClellan's plans had been completely wrecked by Gen. Robert E. Lee during the Seven Days Battles, and McClellan had retreated to Harrison's Landing on the James River.[1]

Maj. Gen. Irvin McDowell's thirty-thousand-man First Corps (detached from the Army of the Potomac) was at Fredericksburg. McDowell's corps

President Abraham Lincoln.
Library of Congress.

was supposed to march overland, threaten Richmond from the north, and unite with McClellan. However, because President Abraham Lincoln did not think McClellan had left sufficient troops to defend Washington, McDowell's corps was detached and positioned to cover the southern approach to the Union capital. The other two Union field forces were led by Maj. Gens. John C. Fremont and Nathaniel P. Banks. Fremont's newly created Mountain Department consisted of fifteen thousand soldiers stationed west of the Shenandoah Mountains. Banks's twenty-three thousand troops were positioned in the Shenandoah Valley.[2]

During Maj. Gen. Thomas J. "Stonewall" Jackson's brilliant Shenandoah Valley Campaign in May and June 1862, an attempt was made to maneuver the forces of McDowell, Fremont, and Banks to trap Jackson. The Union commanders' uncoordinated and inept operations caused Lincoln and his secretary of war, Edwin M. Stanton, to consider reorganizing these forces.[3]

Edwin M. Stanton was born in 1814 in Steubenville, Ohio. Prior to the Civil War he was a lawyer, and his most famous case was the defense of Daniel E. Sickles, who was charged with the murder of his wife's lover. In this trial, Stanton was the first person to successfully use the insanity defense. In 1860 he was appointed United States attorney general. In January 1862 Lincoln appointed Stanton secretary of war, a position he held until his re-

Secretary of War Edwin M. Stanton.
Library of Congress.

turn to private law practice in 1868. He was appointed to the Supreme Court shortly thereafter, but he died in 1869 prior to taking the oath of office.[4]

Options

Lincoln and Stanton had three options. They could do nothing about the three separate field forces, they could combine two of these forces into an army, or they could combine all three into an army.

Option 1

Lincoln and Stanton could choose to make no decision concerning the three separate field forces. They would maintain the status quo as a result, and the three units would continue to operate with seperate chains of command back to the War Department. There were no advantages to this option and several disadvantages. First, continued separation would dissipate the total strength of these organizations. An inefficient and disjointed command structure would continue to exist in central and western Virginia. While divided, these units of potentially sixty-seven thousand troops could not effectively support McClellan's Peninsular Campaign. Finally, continued separation would provide Lee, after defeating McClellan, the opportunity to engage each of the Union units separately. With his superior numbers at the point of contact, Lee could then defeat or destroy one or more of these commands in isolation.

Option 2

Alternatively, two of the three separate field forces could be combined into an army. McDowell's and Bank's commands were the most likely candidates for this arrangement. Merging two units had the benefit of creating an army with a potential strength of fifty-three thousand soldiers. A force of this size could maneuver in central Virginia and the area south toward Richmond. These troops would support McClellan's Peninsula Campaign by drawing some of the Confederate units away from defending the capital. In addition, the Mountain Department would still provide a Union troop presence in western Virginia. The disadvantages included the fact that the total troop strength in central and western Virginia would not be used to maximum effect. While merging two field forces into one unit would be better than doing nothing, an inefficient command structure with two separate commanders would continue to exist in central and western Virginia. This circumstance would place the new army at a considerable disadvantage in engaging Lee's Army of Northern Virginia.

Option 3

The third option was to combine all three separate commands into one army. This arrangement would create one organization providing organizational structure and command and control. It would also eliminate the cumbersome process of trying to coordinate the actions of three separate commands from Washington. Moreover, the resulting army would be strong enough to realistically protect the southern and western avenues of approach to Washington. In maneuvering south through central Virginia, this force would create a viable second threat to the Confederate capital, a threat that Lee could not ignore.

Decision

Ultimately, all three forces were combined into one army, the Army of Virginia. Fremont's command became the First Corps. Rather than serve under a junior-ranking officer, as determined by date of rank, Fremont resigned and was replaced by Maj. Gen. Franz Sigel. Banks's command became the Second Corps, and McDowell's corps was redesigned the Third Corps.[5]

The new army needed a commander. None of the three corps commanders had any tactical success that would recommend them for the position. Although Sigel had contributed to the Union victory at Elkhorn Tavern

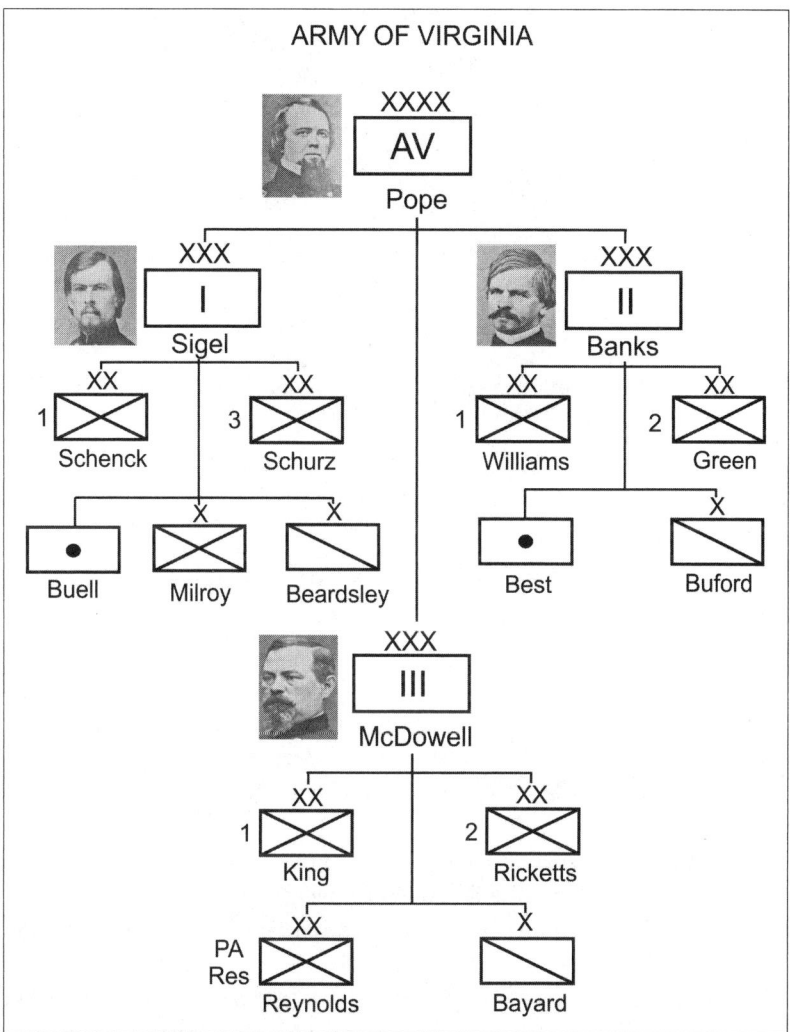

Organizational chart of the Army of Virginia.

(Pea Ridge), he did not possess the attributes for army command. Moreover, Banks had performed poorly during the Valley Campaign, and McDowell had been defeated at First Manassas. After Second Manassas, these three officers were assigned to relatively less important positions.[6]

Searching for an army commander, Lincoln and Stanton turned to the Western Theater, where one officer seemed to hold promise. Kentuckian John Pope had graduated from West Point in 1842 and served in the Mexican War. He was appointed a brigadier general of volunteers on June 14, 1861, and then

Major General John Pope, USA, Commanding Army of Virginia. U. S. Army Military History Institute (USAMHI).

promoted to major general in March 1862. Supported by the navy's riverine flotilla, Pope opened the upper Mississippi River almost to Memphis with the capture of New Madrid and Island Number 10. In May his forces constituted the left wing of Maj. Gen. Henry W. Halleck's force in the advance to Corinth.[7]

Pope's political views on the war included the beliefs that slavery must be done away with and that the fighting must be conducted by harsher means. Many in the Lincoln administration considered Pope's views on slavery and the prosecution of the war, which were in line with their own views, as one of his greatest attributes. Pope was ordered east, and on June 24 he arrived in Washington. On June 26, 1862, an order signed by Lincoln created the Army of Virginia and appointed Pope its commander. Pope was forty years of age when he assumed leadership of the Army of Virginia.[8]

Results/Impact

Lincoln's creation of the Army of Virginia is the first critical decision for Second Manassas; everything else flows from it. Had he chosen differently, there would have been no unit by that name and no Second Manassas, at least not as we know it. The three separate field commands would have remained as such. If past results were an indicator, any concentrated action against Lee would have been improbable. Events may have gone so far that Lee would have defeated, if not destroyed, each of these forces separately. Had that happened in July or early August, with the Army of the Potomac still being redeployed to the Washington area, the course of the war in Virginia would have been drastically different.

On June 26, 1862, Abraham Lincoln signed an executive order bringing the Army of Virginia into existence and assigning Pope as its commander. Pope and his army were given three broad objectives: protect Washington, defend the Shenandoah Valley, and disrupt the Virginia Central Railroad in the vicinity of Charlottesville and Gordonsville. In threatening this vital railroad it was thought that Lee would be compelled to draw off part of his army from the defense of Richmond, a move that would support McClellan's operation. The commands that now formed the Army of Virginia required a period of reorganization and resupply. It was not until mid-July that Pope was able to tentatively commence moving his soldiers into central Virginia. By that time, Lee had driven McClellan away from Richmond and to a defensive enclave on the James River.[9]

However, the Army of Virginia, under Pope's command, had been created. Other critical decisions and events followed into July and August as the Campaign and Battle of Second Manassas unfolded.

Halleck Decides to Evacuate the Peninsula

Situation

After the Union's disastrous defeat at First Manassas, Maj. Gen. George B. McClellan was brought from western Virginia to Washington and given command of all Union forces around the capital. During the winter of 1861–62 he reorganized these soldiers into the Army of the Potomac.[10]

The primary Confederate army in Virginia wintered just outside of Washington near Centreville and Manassas. Gen. Joseph E. Johnston, the army commander, worried that his force was overextended and vulnerable to being enveloped by McClellan. In February he decided to move farther south. In early March Johnston's army withdrew forty miles to new positions along the Rappahannock River.[11]

From mid-to late March, McClellan used superior Union naval power to sidestep Johnston's defenses, conduct a turning movement, and transport his army down the Chesapeake Bay to Fort Monroe at the tip of the Peninsula. By early April the majority of his forces were assembled. McClellan was located the same distance southeast of Richmond that Johnston was positioned north of the city. However, McClellan allowed this advantage to slip away during his slow and tedious campaign up the Peninsula.[12]

Just outside of Richmond, Johnston engaged McClellan in the inconclusive battle of Seven Pines (Fair Oaks) on May 31 and June 1. Johnston was wounded during the first day of battle, and President Jefferson Davis replaced him with Gen. Robert E. Lee. Lee withdrew his army into the Richmond defenses, began to strengthen the defenses, and planned to go on the offense. Lee began offensive operations and initiated the Seven Days Battles on June 26, when he attacked at Beaver Dam Creek (Mechanicsville). In a series of offensive maneuvers and battles he forced McClellan to retreat across the Peninsula to the James River. After the last of these battles, Malvern Hill, McClellan retreated to Harrison's Landing, and Lee moved closer to Richmond to reorganize, refit, and resupply his army.[13]

Early in July Abraham Lincoln visited McClellan at Harrison's Landing. Lincoln wanted to see the Army of the Potomac and discuss McClellan's next move. Nothing definitive came from this meeting. Upon returning to Washington, Lincoln appointed Maj. Gen. Henry W. Halleck general-in-chief.[14]

Halleck was born in Westernville, New York, in 1815. In 1839 he graduated third in his class at the United States Military Academy, and in 1844 he toured French fortifications. Halleck later presented a series of lectures published as *Elements of Military Art and Science* that was read widely by army officers. He served in California during and after the Mexican War, and he resigned his commission in 1854 in order to practice law. With the commencement of the Civil War, Halleck was appointed a major general in the regular army. His initial service was in the Western Theater. In July 1862 Lincoln brought Halleck to Washington and appointed him general-in-chief, a position he held until Ulysses S. Grant replaced him in March 1864. Halleck served the rest of the war as Grant's chief of staff. After the war he commanded the Department of the Pacific and then the Department of the South. While serving in the latter position Halleck died in 1872.[15]

Options

Maj. Gen. Henry W. Halleck, the Union general-in-chief, had to decide what the Army of the Potomac would do. He had three options to choose from: order McClellan to resume the offense and maneuver against Lee's army and Richmond, send McClellan across the James River to maneuver against Petersburg and the railroad junction there, or command the Army of the Potomac to evacuate from the Peninsula and return to the Washington-Alexandria area.[16]

June 26 to August 27, 1862

Major General Henry W. Halleck, USA, Union General in Chief. USAMHI.

Option 1

Remaining north of the James River and maneuvering against Lee's army with the intent of capturing Richmond was a viable option. The Army of the Potomac was already in a defensible lodgment area at Harrison's Landing and had a secure naval line of supply on the James River. At this location McClellan could resupply his army and then commence another offensive against Richmond, only 25 miles away. Lee would have to maneuver and attack or defend against this threat.

Pope's army was in central Virginia and moving toward Richmond and the vital railroads from the Shenandoah Valley and other areas in the western Confederacy. Pope would also present a second threat that Lee could not ignore. The simultaneous maneuvering by McClellan and Pope against Richmond would present Lee with a difficult tactical situation.

The disadvantage to this option was that both Union armies would have to develop and maintain coordinated operations. If one force stopped or went on the defense, Lee would have the opportunity to focus on, isolate, and attack the other army.

Option 2

McClellan could also cross to the south side of the James River and maneuver toward Petersburg, as Grant did in 1864. Richmond and the Army of Northern

Virginia were supplied by railroads from the south and west. South of Richmond three railroads came into Petersburg: the Southside Railroad, the Weldon Railroad, and the Norfolk and Petersburg Railroad. The Richmond and Petersburg Railroad went north from this junction to Richmond. The Virginia Central Railroad and the Richmond and Danville Railroad came into Richmond from the western part of the state. Connected to the southern, central, and western Confederacy by other railroads, these were vital communication and supply lines for the Army of Northern Virginia and the Confederate capital.[17]

Capturing Petersburg would sever the railroad supply lines from the south and severely reduce the capability of supplying Lee's army and the capital. Pope's simultaneous capture of any section of the Virginia Central Railroad, leaving only the Richmond and Danville Railroad open, would significantly reduce the amount of supplies and equipment coming from the Shenandoah Valley and the western Confederacy. One railroad would be insufficient to supply Lee's army. He could not ignore the threat to or the loss of these railroads, and he would be forced to maneuver against one or perhaps both of the Union armies. Once Petersburg was captured, McClellan would be able to move directly against Richmond, just twenty miles away.

As with Option 1, the maneuvering of both Union armies would have to be coordinated lest Lee create the opportunity to decisively engage them separately. So far, no Union command structure had demonstrated such coordination capability.

Option 3

McClellan could abandon his Peninsula Campaign, move his army to the Fort Monroe area, and then sail to the Washington-Alexandria area. Such a move, once completed, would place McClellan's and Pope's armies in close proximity to each other. Their combined strength would give the Union commanders a distinct advantage over Lee.[18]

There were disadvantages to this option. Primarily, McClellan's army would be unable to operate with or reinforce Pope's while it was at the southern tip of the Peninsula or in transit by ship. Lee would then have the opportunity to maneuver against and attack Pope's army while it was isolated.

A Union withdrawal from the Peninsula would give up all the gains that had been made since April and remove the near threat from Richmond. In turn, the two-army threat confronting Lee would be eliminated for a short period of time. The return of the Army of the Potomac to the Washington-Alexandria area would bring the Union operational situation full circle in Virginia. The forces would be where they had been in March.

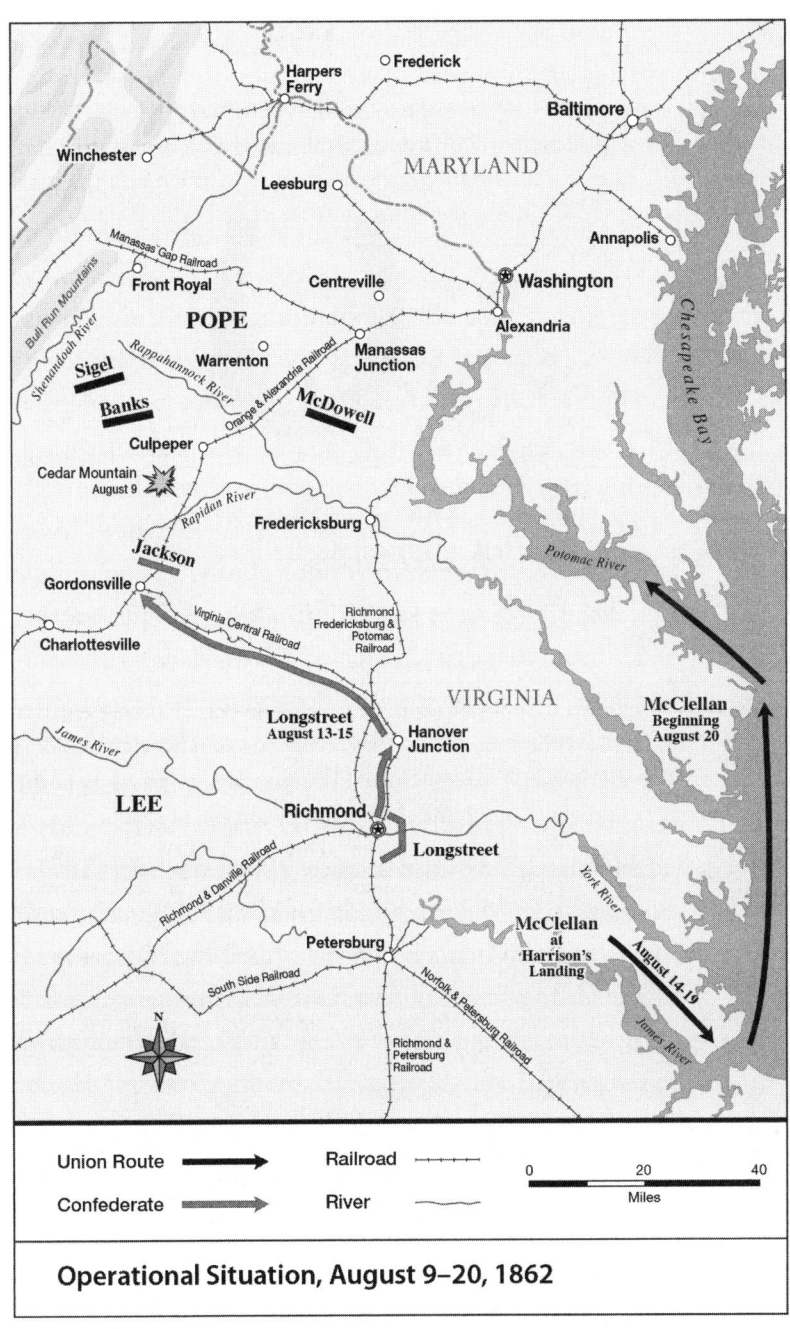

Operational Situation, August 9–20, 1862

Decision

On July 25 Halleck visited McClellan at Harrison's Landing. During this meeting the two generals discussed McClellan's next move. McClellan favored crossing the James River and relocating to Petersburg. Halleck found this choice inadvisable, but he offered a reinforcement of twenty thousand troops if McClellan commenced operations against Richmond on the north side of the river. If McClellan could not do that, then Halleck thought his army should be removed from the Peninsula.[19]

Halleck returned to Washington believing McClellan would accept the additional man power and recommence operations north of the river. Instead, McClellan asked Halleck for a reinforcement of sixty thousand troops before moving on Richmond.[20]

Supported by Lincoln, Halleck ordered McClellan to move his army to Fort Monroe, on the tip of the Peninsula, then return to the Washington-Alexandria area by ship.

Results/Impact

This critical decision had far reaching effects for both the Army of Northern Virginia and the Army of Virginia. It kept Lee from having to face two Union armies simultaneously. He had already sent three divisions under "Stonewall" Jackson to central Virginia to confront one of Pope's corps as it moved south, while the remainder of the army watched McClellan. With the Army of the Potomac's redeployment, Lee was able to move the other five divisions under Maj. Gen. James Longstreet's command to join Jackson. With his army reunited and only one Union army, though perhaps temporarily, able to maneuver against him, the stage was set for the Second Manassas Campaign. Without Halleck's critical decision the entire situation confronting Lee would have been different. The events of the Second Manassas can be traced back to this decision.

The next critical decision would result in one of Lee's most audacious maneuvers and fighting, Chancellorsville notwithstanding. Some consider Lee's next actions his finest campaign and battle.

Lee Decides on a Turning Movement[21]

Situation

In the first three weeks of August, a series of events led Lee to order Jackson's turning movement around Pope's right (west) flank. On August 3, Halleck ordered McClellan to evacuate his Army of the Potomac from the Peninsula and return to the vicinity of Washington, DC, and Alexandria, Virginia. McClellan reluctantly marched his army to the southern tip of the Peninsula. His troops sailed north back up the Chesapeake Bay from August 20 to August 25.[22]

Pope's Army of Virginia was formally constituted on June 26. Although Pope's units did not move until early August, Lee saw the need for a force between it and Richmond. With McClellan static at Harrison's Landing and giving no indications of recommencing offensive operations, on July 13 Lee took a calculated risk. Lee sent Jackson to Gordonsville with two divisions. Two weeks later, he reinforced him with Maj. Gen. Ambrose P. Hill's division.[23]

On August 2 Pope's army began to move south. By August 8 Bank's Second Corps had reached Culpeper. Jackson immediately responded, marched north, and fought the Battle of Cedar Mountain on August 9. Jackson was the victor, but he was unable to take advantage of his success. With Union reinforcement arriving on August 11, he withdrew to Gordonsville.[24]

After Cedar Mountain, Pope deployed his army astride the Orange and Alexandria Railroad, his major supply line, with its front facing the Rapidan River. On August 13 Lee ordered the remainder of his army from Richmond to Gordonsville, where he moved his headquarters two days later. With his army reunited, Lee began planning to maneuver against Pope.[25]

When Pope advanced his army to the Rapidan River, he placed it in a precarious position. The Rapidan and the Rappahannock to its north both flow on convergent courses to the southeast. Just west of Fredericksburg, the Rapidan flows into the Rappahannock, forming a triangle of terrain in which the two rivers are the sides. This area had limited maneuvering space. If Lee could trap Pope between the two rivers, he could force him into a decisive battle.

Robert E. Lee was born in 1807 and was fifty-five years old at the time of Second Manassas. In 1829 he graduated second in his class from the United States Military Academy. Before the Mexican War he performed various engineering duties. During that conflict he served on the staff of Winfield Scott, performing admirably. At the war's end Lee continued with engineering assignments, then served as superintendent of West Point and with the cavalry in Texas. He commanded the detachment of marines that captured John Brown at Harpers Ferry in 1859.[26]

With the outbreak of the Civil War, Lee refused an offer to command US forces. He resigned his commission in the army, subsequently accepting a commission in Virginia and then the Confederate service. Lee spent 1861 and early 1862 commanding troops in the Allegheny counties of Virginia,

General Robert E. Lee, CSA, Commanding Army of Northern Virginia. Library of Congress.

examining the defenses on the South Atlantic coast, and acting as military advisor to President Jefferson Davis. When Gen. Joseph E. Johnston was wounded at the Battle of Seven Pines (Fair Oaks) on May 31, 1862, Lee was made the commander of what became the Army of Northern Virginia. He would command this army throughout the war until its surrender at Appomattox in April 1865. After the war Lee was the president of Washington College (later renamed Washington and Lee University) in Lexington, Virginia. He died in Lexington on October 12, 1870.[27]

Lee decided to take advantage of the favorable terrain situation the two rivers provided him and attack Pope. His plan was for Confederate cavalry to pass east around Pope and advance rapidly to capture the major crossing over the Rappahannock River. With Pope's main avenue of retreat severed, Jackson and Longstreet would envelop and attack Pope's left (east) flank. Trapped between the two rivers, Pope would be forced into a decisive battle. Lee designated August 18 as the day to commence the operation. However, other events postponed the offensive until August 20.[28]

In the intervening time, a reconnaissance by two Union cavalry regiments captured Maj. Norman Fitzhugh, a member of J. E. B. Stuart's staff who was in possession of document containing Lee's plan. Forewarned, Pope immediately withdrew his army north of the Rappahannock. His army now occupying a strong position with a major obstacle (the Rappahannock River)

June 26 to August 27, 1862

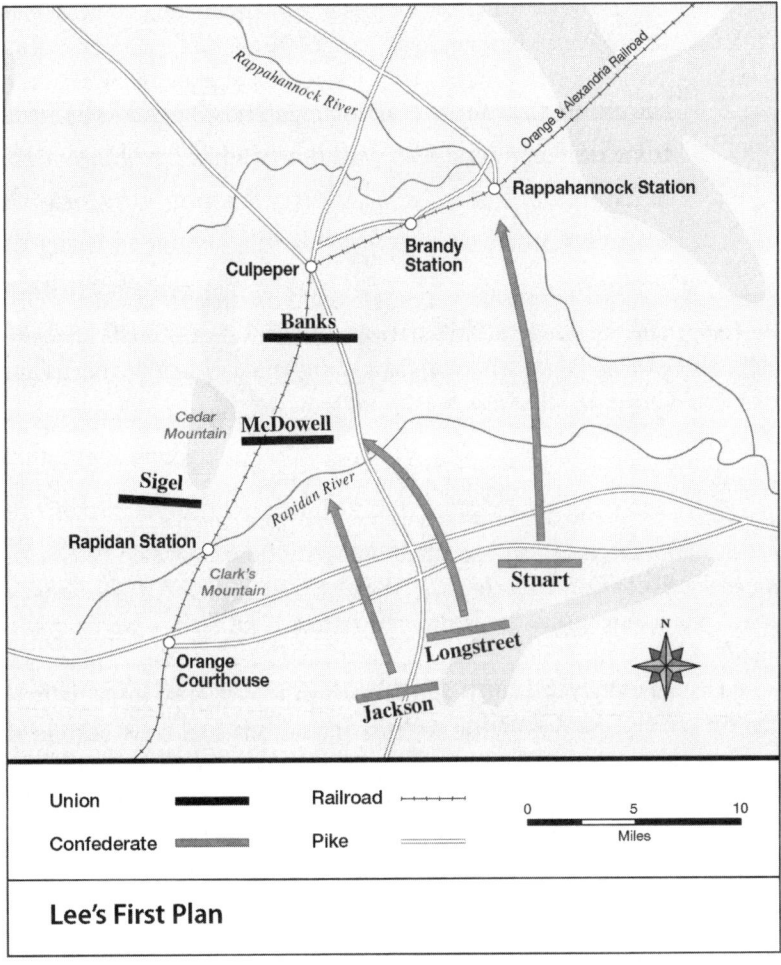

Lee's First Plan

between it and Lee's forces, Pope decided to remain on the defense and await the arrival of the Army of the Potomac. The joining or close positioning of the Army of Virginia and the Army of the Potomac would greatly outnumber Lee's Army of Northern Virginia.[29]

Lee understood that with every passing day McClellan's Army of the Potomac was closer to completing its move from the Peninsula and joining Pope's army. With this in mind, Lee moved his army to the Rappahannock River. The water was high, thwarting several attempts to cross the river and envelop Pope's right (west) flank.[30]

A raid by Stuart's cavalry, which began on August 22, captured some of the wagons of Pope's headquarters. The attack turned up correspondence revealing that Pope was going to hold his positon and await the arrival of McClellan. Realizing that time was running short and he had to do something before McClellan's army arrived, Lee began to rethink his operational choices.[31]

Options

Several options were available to Lee. He could continue to attempt to cross the Rappahannock River and attack Pope. Alternatively, Lee could maneuver and try to envelop Pope's left (east) flank, or he could make a bold maneuver that would penetrate deep into Pope's rear area.

Option 1

The option for Lee to remain where he was, wait for favorable conditions, and attack across the river had several advantages. His army would be concentrated south of the Rappahannock. This river was a natural major obstacle, and it would strengthen Lee's position as he waited for the water level to recede. Lee's army would be between any Union force and Richmond and would have a good and secure supply line using the Virginia Central Railroad and the Orange and Alexandria Railroad.

A major disadvantage of this plan was that Lee, by waiting, would provide additional time for all or a significant part of McClellan's army to reinforce Pope's. Lee would also have to conduct a frontal attack across a major river obstacle.

Option 2

Lee's second option, an envelopment of Pope's left flank, had potential for success. The two wings of his army would be in close proximity to each other, and one could reinforce the success of the other. A successful envelopment could compel Pope to fight on two fronts. It might also cut his the Orange and Alexandria Railroad supply line.

But there were several disadvantages. Before crossing the river the enveloping force would have to move east to ensure it was on Pope's left flank. Farther east the Rappahannock River became wider and therefore more difficult to cross. Pope again might succeed in retreating to a new position closer to reinforcements. In addition, Lee would expose his right flank to attack from the arriving corps of the Army of the Potomac.

Option 3

Lee's third option was to conduct a turning movement around Pope's right (west) flank and into his rear area. This option had several significant advantages. The maneuvering force would cross the Rappahannock River near its headwaters, where the river would not be a major obstacle. A successful turning movement would position a significant enemy force across Pope's line of supply and communication, the Orange and Alexandria Railroad. In this event, Pope would be forced to abandon his position on the Rappahannock and fight in another direction. In doing so, he would commence a campaign of maneuver rather than one of position. Such a operation would provide Lee the opportunity to destroy the Army of Virginia or render it combat ineffective before the Army of the Potomac arrived in significant force.

This option's major disadvantage was that the two wings of Lee's force would be too far apart to support each other during the turning movement. If Pope realized what was happening, he might maneuver his army to successfully attack one of the two separate parts of Lee's army. In addition, once the turning movement was complete, Lee's supply line would be doubled in length. As the bridges across the rivers had been destroyed, the railroads could only bring supplies about half the distance to Confederate troops. Wagons, of which Lee had an insufficient quantity, would have to be used for the remainder of the journey. However, a rapidly executed turning movement and the defeat of Pope's army would lessen this disadvantage.

Decision

For the first time, but not the last, Lee decided to divide his army and maneuver to gain an operational advantage and the element of surprise against his foe. Jackson conducted the turning movement with three divisions. Longstreet and his five divisions occupied Pope's attention along the Rappahannock River, then marched to join Jackson. Jackson proved to be the ideal commander for the turning movement.

Born in 1824, Thomas J. Jackson was thirty-eight years old when he fought in the Second Battle of Manassas. He graduated from West Point in 1846, fought in the Mexican War, and then resigned his commission to become a professor at the Virginia Military Institute. At the Civil War's commencement, Jackson was a colonel of Virginia militia. He was promoted to brigadier general in June 1861, to major general in October 1861, and to lieutenant general in October 1862. Jackson received his nickname, "Stonewall," at the Battle of First Manassas. His Valley Campaign in the spring of 1862 brought him instant fame, and he participated in all of the battles of the Army of

Major General Thomas J. "Stonewall" Jackson, CSA, Commanding Jackson's Left Wing, Army of Northern Virginia. Library of Congress.

Northern Virginia from June 1862 to May 1863. Jackson was wounded at the Battle of Chancellorsville on May 2, 1863. He had an arm amputated and died eight days later of pneumonia.[32]

Results/Impact

Lee's turning movement met all expectations. Jackson's Left Wing departed from the vicinity of Jeffersonton on August 25 and marched twenty miles to Salem (present-day Marshall). The wing bivouacked there overnight. The next day the troops turned east, marched eleven miles through Thoroughfare Gap, and then traveled an additional sixteen miles to Bristoe Station on the Orange and Alexandria Railroad. Bristoe Station's capture cut Pope's main supply line. Jackson then followed the railroad northeast for five miles, captured Pope's main supply base at Manassas Junction, and destroyed it.[33]

Once Pope realized the size of the force in his rear area and across his supply line, he began withdrawing from the Rappahannock River position. Lee sent Longstreet's command on the same route used by Jackson. In the late afternoon of August 28, Longstreet's Right Wing arrived at the western entrance to Thoroughfare Gap. Longstreet was then only a short march from Jackson.[34]

After the Seven Days, Lee moved the focus of the war in the East to central Virginia. His critical decision to conduct a turning movement shifted the center of the fighting to northern Virginia and threatened Washington, DC. This decision and its successful implementation reversed all the previous Union gains in Virginia and set the stage for one of Lee's greatest battles.

Jackson Moves to the "Stony Ridge"

Situation

Jackson captured Bristoe Station on the Alexandria and Orange Railroad late on August 26. This placed him twenty-five miles into Pope's rear area and across his major line of communication and supply. Learning of a large supply depot five miles north at Manassas Junction, Jackson sent a force to capture it that night. The remainder of Jackson's troops, minus a rear guard, followed the next morning.[35]

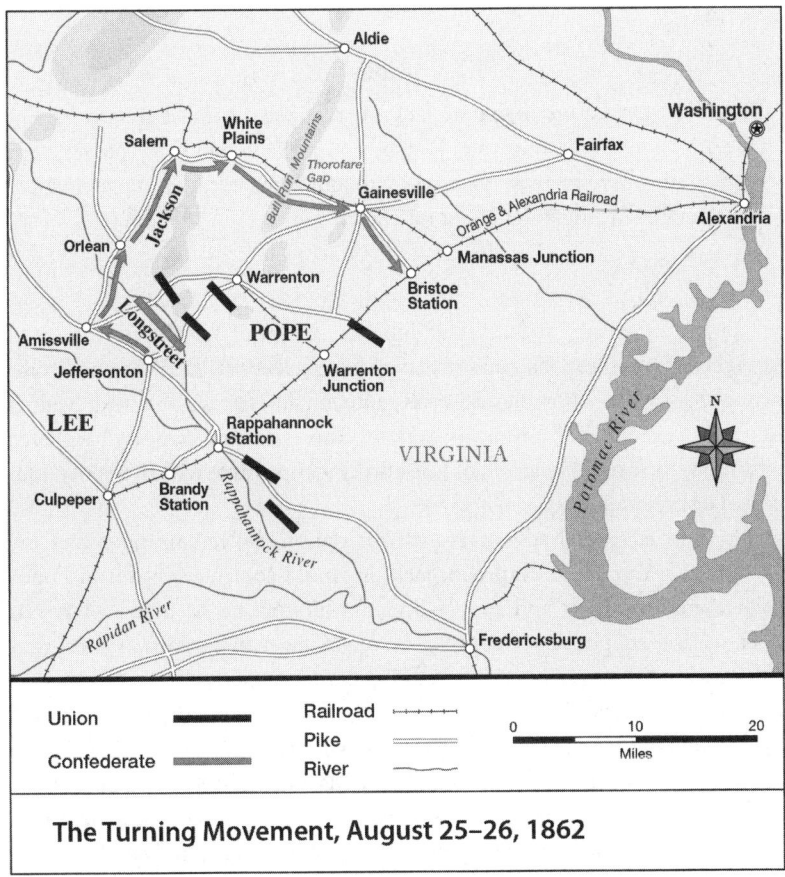

The Turning Movement, August 25–26, 1862

Once he learned that Jackson had cut his line of communication and captured his main supply depot, Pope turned his army north to engage Jackson and reopen his direct communications with Washington, DC. At the same time, Maj. Gen. Henry W. Halleck, the Union army general-in-chief, saw an opportunity to trap Jackson between two forces. Halleck ordered Maj. Gen. William B. Franklin's Sixth Corps (Army of the Potomac), recently arrived from the Peninsula, to march south and engage Jackson. However, Maj. Gen. George B. McClellan, typically seeing insurmountable dangers where others saw opportunity, countermanded this order and kept Franklin's corps at Alexandria.[36]

August 27 witnessed an engagement between Jackson's rear guard and advance units of Pope's army. On that same day, a brigade of Union infantry fought elements of Maj. Gen. Ambrose P. Hill's division north of Manassas Junction. Both of these incidents alerted Jackson to the approach of Union forces.[37]

Options

With this information in hand, Jackson realized he must determine his course of action until Longstreet joined him. Jackson had three possible options: remain where he was, march west to join Longstreet, or move north to a location where Longstreet could join him.

Option 1

Jackson could remain at Manassas Junction and wait for the remainder of the Army of Northern Virginia to arrive. Longstreet's Right Wing had commenced its march, following Jackson's route, on August 26. The next evening the troops were at White Plains, west of Thoroughfare Gap, and eighteen miles from Jackson. A reunion of Lee's army was possible within twenty-four to thirty-six hours.

There were several advantages to this option. By remaining across the Orange and Alexandria Railroad, Jackson would continue to control Pope's major communication and supply line. As long as he occupied Manassas Junction, the supply depot could provide for Jackson's troops. When they joined Jackson, Longstreet's men could get provisions as well.

One disadvantage was that Jackson might face a superior-size enemy if Pope could concentrate before Longstreet arrived. In addition, if Pope could separate Jackson's and Longstreet's commands, he might defeat each of them one at a time. This outcome would be possible if Pope used a sufficient part of his force to block Longstreet's route through Thoroughfare Gap. (The next chapter contains more information about this prospect.)

Option 2

Jackson's troops could depart Manassas Junction and march west toward Gainesville and Thoroughfare Gap. With Longstreet marching east and Jackson west, their units would probably link-up in the Haymarket-Gainesville vicinity late on August 28.

There were numerous advantages to this option. It would reunite Lee's army late on August 28 and allow him to choose the terrain on which to initiate battle. The Bull Run Mountains to the west would limit Pope's avenues of approach and the maneuver space needed to conduct an envelopment or turning movement. Marching west away from Washington and Alexandria would increase the distance the Army of the Potomac's units must travel to reinforce Pope. In addition, a position in the vicinity of Haymarket or Gainesville would provide Lee a large area to the east where he could carry out offensive maneuvers and select the time and place to engage Pope.

Among this option's disadvantages was the fact that Pope could continue to consolidate his army near Manassas Junction, block the routes to Washington, reopen his communication and supply line, and await the arrival of the Army of the Potomac. The longer Pope could do so, the stronger he would become as units from the Army of the Potomac would reinforce him. Pope could also select the terrain where he would engage Lee's army. As time went by, Lee would have to attack Pope on this terrain before the entire Army of the Potomac arrived from the Peninsula. Once the entire Army of the Potomac arrived, it would be able to maneuver against Lee through the other mountain passes while Pope held Lee in position.

Option 3

Jackson could leave Manassas Junction and march north to a position near the site of the Battle of First Manassas. There, he would find a position that would provide concealment, and he could then wait for the arrival of Longstreet's Right Wing. From this location, Jackson could conduct offensive or defensive operations as the situation required.

There were several advantages to marching north. Pope would naturally think Jackson would remain at Manassas Junction or retrace his route back west. Pope's orders for his subordinate units to converge on Manassas Junction were based on that assumption, as were the routes these soldiers used. Thus a move north would be unexpected and would confuse Pope as to Jackson's whereabouts. At the same time, Jackson would move out of a potential trap and a battle against a superior enemy force. A location near the old battlefield would provide several routes of escape if needed. Jackson could march west to Haymarket, then continue west until he met Longstreet coming east. If this route was not feasible, Jackson's men could march north and then west to Aldie, march through a pass in the Bull Run Mountains, then turn south and march to Longstreet's location. Jackson would be able to choose the location of the fighting. He would also be in a position to intercept Union forces moving along the Warrenton Turnpike, disrupt a Union concentration, confuse Pope as to Lee's intentions, and occupy a position along a major route that would facilitate Longstreet's movement to his location.

The disadvantages of this option included the fact that the Army of Northern Virginia would be divided for at least one additional day. This day would lengthen the time in which Pope could keep Jackson and Longstreet separated and attack each in turn. In addition, Jackson would have to destroy or leave behind a large amount of captured supplies that his troops and the rest of the army needed.

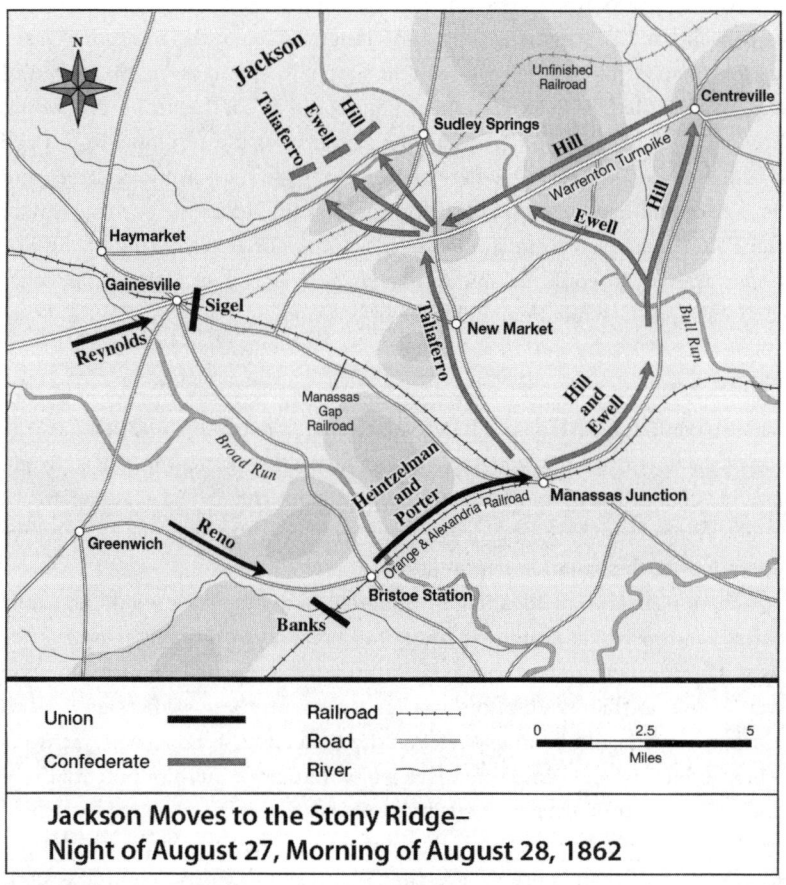

**Jackson Moves to the Stony Ridge–
Night of August 27, Morning of August 28, 1862**

Decision

Jackson decided to depart from Manassas Junction on the night of August 27 and march north to a position near the First Manassas battlefield. The first division to leave, Taliaferro's, marched north on the Sudley Road to that road's intersection with the Warrenton Turnpike. A. P. Hill's Division marched northeast, crossed Bull Run at Blackburn's Ford, and continued on to Centreville. The next morning this division marched west on the Warrenton Turnpike to the old battlefield. Ewell's Division, the last to depart, also crossed Bull Run at Blackburn's Ford, then followed the north bank to the bridge on the Warrenton Turnpike. There, it turned west and marched on the pike to the old battlefield. By noon on August 28, Jackson's divisions were reunited in the vicinity of the Warrenton Turnpike and Sudley Road intersection. From the intersection they moved northwest a short distance to positions on "Stony Ridge."[38]

Results/Impact

This critical decision had far-reaching effects on the forthcoming battle. Jackson had escaped a possible trap and attack by a superior-size enemy force. In doing so he had moved a possible battle away from Manassas Junction. He was in a concealed position that allowed him to observe and if necessary interdict an enemy force marching on the Warrenton Turnpike. The location of the position near the turnpike facilitated reuniting with Longstreet's Right Wing. Most importantly, Jackson's selection of the position along the unfinished railroad decided where the Battle of Second Manassas would be fought. Combat forces from both armies were drawn into this area and into a bloody three-day (August 28, 29, and 30) struggle.

This was the last of the critical decisions prior to the battle. This decision and the other three had set the stage for the battle that followed. The next two critical decisions would initiate the Battle of Second Manassas.

CHAPTER 2

CONTACT IS REGAINED— THURSDAY, AUGUST 28, 1862

This day was one of movement for the major commands of both armies. Jackson had departed Manassas Junction and moved his Left Wing to a position that overlooked a major turnpike near the old First Manassas battlefield. Longstreet was marching to join Jackson, and he was at Thoroughfare Gap by the evening of August 28. Meanwhile, Pope's army concentrated toward Manassas Junction, where it was believed they would trap and destroy Jackson. Not finding Jackson there, Pope then ordered his army to Centreville. A late afternoon engagement revealed the location of Jackson's Wing, drawing both armies to this area.

Ricketts's Division Fights Alone

Situation

Maj. Gen. Irvin McDowell, commander of the Army of Virginia's Third Corps, made two of the critical decisions during the Second Manassas campaign and battle. Both choices were extremely poor, and both led directly to Lee's victory on August 30. This decision is McDowell's first one.

Jackson began the turning movement on August 25. He marched through Amissville and Orlean to Salem, just west of Thoroughfare Gap, where his Left Wing spent the night. On August 26 Jackson's column passed through

Thoroughfare Gap, then marched sixteen miles and captured Bristoe Station on the Orange and Alexandria Railroad. The troops subsequently turned north and marched five miles to capture Manassas Junction. Seizing Bristoe Station and Manassas Junction positioned Jackson deep in Pope's rear area, effectively cut his supply line, and destroyed his supply base. Jackson then moved from Manassas Junction to the "Stony Ridge" near the old First Manassas battlefield to wait for the arrival of Longstreet's Right Wing. Although he had been extremely successful, Jackson was in a potentially precarious situation.[1]

The quickest, most direct route for Longstreet to join Jackson was through Thoroughfare Gap, then to Gainesville, and then east on the Warrenton Turnpike. Pope was concentrating his army. If Pope realized what the actual situation was, he could block Longstreet's march (the best place being the gap) and concentrate superior force against Jackson. Moreover, he might severely damage or even destroy this isolated part of Lee's army. Such a success would void the success of the turning movement and leave Longstreet to confront Pope's army alone.

Once Pope realized the extent of Jackson's turning movement, he began repositioning his force. His army was ordered to march generally northeast, away from the line of the Rappahannock River. Pope's two westernmost corps, the First and Third, had marched northeast, and on August 27 they were just shy of Gainesville.[2]

Gainesville was the hub of several operationally and tactically important roads. The forces who controlled them could rapidly move large troop formations east or west and north or south. The Warrenton Turnpike came northeast from Warrenton, passed through Gainesville, crossed the future battlefield, then crossed Bull Run and continued on to Centreville. From the west a major road extended east through Thoroughfare Gap to Gainesville. There, it diverged into two roads that continued on to Bristoe Station and Manassas Junction. A sufficient Union force at or west of Gainesville could cut the line of communication and march between Jackson's and Longstreet's commands.

On August 27 McDowell had a significant force under his command: the two divisions (Brig. Gens. Rufus King's and James B. Ricketts's) of his Third Corps and Brig. Gen. John F. Reynolds's attached Pennsylvania Reserve Division. Maj. Gen. Franz Sigel's First Corps (two divisions and one independent brigade) was also under McDowell's operational control.[3]

Irvin McDowell was forty-three years old at the time of Second Manassas. He graduated from the US Military Academy in 1838, worked as a tactics instructor, and served as an aide-de-camp to Gen. John E. Wool during the Mexican War. After the war he served in the office of the adjutant general

Thursday, August 28, 1862

Major General Irvin McDowell, USA, Commanding Third Corps, Army of Virginia. Library of Congress.

until 1861. In May of that year McDowell was promoted to brigadier general and given command of the Union army at the Battle of First Manassas, a Confederate victory. Relieved of that command, he was promoted to major general in March 1862 and given command of a corps in the Army of the Potomac. When the Army of Virginia was organized, McDowell's corps became its Third Corps. He commanded this unit at the Second Battle of Manassas, another Confederate victory. McDowell lost command of his corps when the Army of Virginia was absorbed into the Army of the Potomac. In July 1864 he was given command of the Department of the Pacific. After the Civil War he commanded the Departments of the East and South. Returning west in 1876, McDowell commanded the Division of the Pacific until his retirement in 1882. He died in 1885.[4]

After Jackson's successful turning movement on August 26, Lee ordered Longstreet to follow Jackson's route, pass around the Union forces, march through Thoroughfare Gap, and join Jackson's Wing, thereby reuniting the Army of Northern Virginia. Longstreet's command reached White Plains, just west of the gap, the next day. He planned to reach and march through the gap on August 28. The same day, Jackson established positions on the "Stony Ridge."[5]

Longstreet's march had not gone unnoticed. As his cavalry brigade had been operating along Longstreet's right flank, Brig. Gen. John Buford was monitoring the Confederate movement and providing information to McDowell. McDowell must have realized he was in a position to completely disrupt Lee's maneuver plans, and perhaps to inflict grave damage to the Confederate army. During the 11:00 p.m. hour on August 27, McDowell chose to take advantage of his position near Gainesville. He ordered Sigel's First Corps and Reynolds's division to march to Haymarket. From this location their units could block and engage Longstreet's Wing as it emerged from Thoroughfare Gap. The two divisions of McDowell's Third Corps would march to Gainesville, turn southeast, and then march toward Manassas Junction to engage Jackson. These moves would isolate the two wings of Lee's army from each other, and make it possible for McDowell's forces to disrupt Lee's maneuver plan. However, before McDowell could implement his plan, events transpired that changed his situation and forced him to make a critical decision.[6]

By nightfall on August 27, Pope realized that Jackson was at Manassas Junction. What he did not know was that Jackson was departing Manassas Junction. Pope thought that Longstreet might still be south of the Rappahannock River, but he was concerned by reports that a significant-size force was west of the Bull Run Mountains. On August 27 Pope's army was moving toward Manassas Junction, and he thought he had an opportunity to trap, attack, and defeat Jackson. At 9:00 p.m. that night, Pope directed his army to concentrate at Manassas Junction against a nonexistent enemy position.[7]

McDowell was ordered to march his Third Corps and Sigel's First Corps southeast from the vicinity of Gainesville toward Manassas Junction. At the junction, they would join the rest of the Union corps in attacking Jackson. McDowell realized that complying with this order would uncover Thoroughfare Gap and the road leading east from it. Longstreet would then have an unopposed direct route to Jackson's location.[8]

Options

The receipt of Pope's order created a difficult situation for McDowell and presented him with three possible courses of action. He could comply with the order in its entirety, he could ignore the order and proceed with his previous plan, or he could comply with the order in a modified version.

Option 1

McDowell could comply with the order as he received it. Doing so would turn his Third Corps and Sigel's First Corps away from Thoroughfare Gap and Longstreet's Wing, which was in a position to pass through the gap.

This option would bring maximum force against Jackson. But if McDowell marched to Manassas Junction, he would allow Longstreet complete freedom of movement.

Option 2

Alternatively, McDowell could ignore Pope's order and continue on with his plan to block Longstreet's approach. While Sigel's corps and Reynolds's division would establish themselves in the Gainesville-Haymarket vicinity, McDowell's Third Corps would march to Manassas Junction. This decision could be justified by the fact that McDowell, as the commander on the scene, had more accurate and updated information as to Longstreet's location and possible intentions. McDowell would have to provide Pope with proactive,

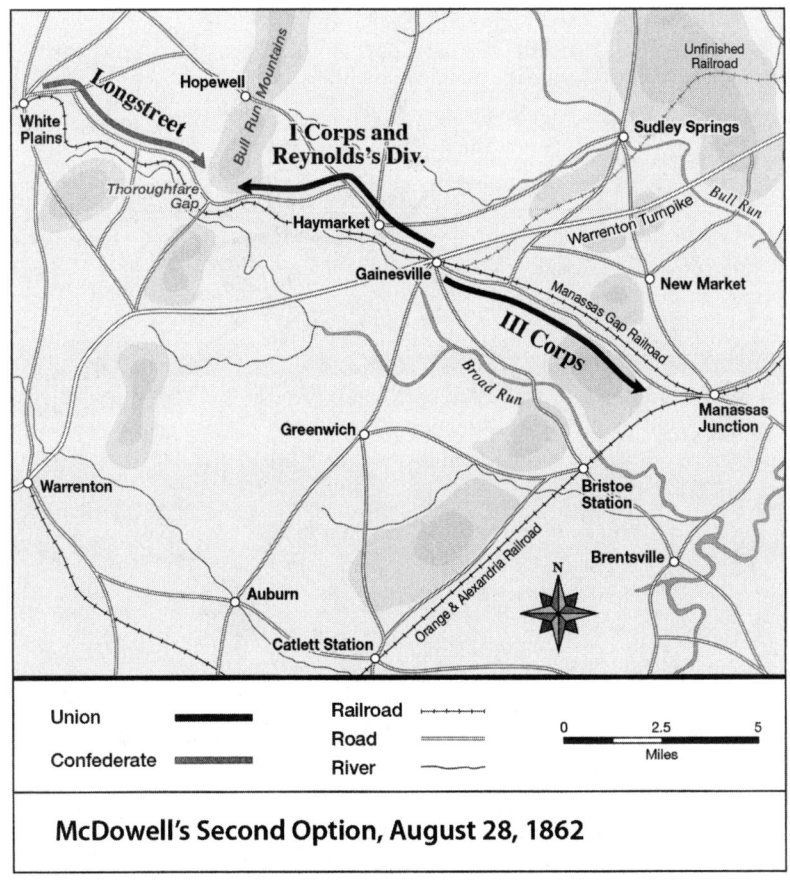

McDowell's Second Option, August 28, 1862

detailed communications explaining his actions. This option would place a three-division force in a position to intercept and delay Longstreet's march and provide Pope timely information with which he could modify his plans and prevent the Army of Northern Virginia's reunification.

Option 3

McDowell's third option was to comply with a modified version of Pope's order. He could march the two corps southeast toward Manassas Junction, then detach a division to watch Thoroughfare Gap and the egress road leading east from it. The detached division could provide early warning of Longstreet's approach. While it would not have the strength to stop Longstreet's Right Wing, it could delay its progress. The early warning and delay could provide Pope important information upon which to develop his plans for the next day.

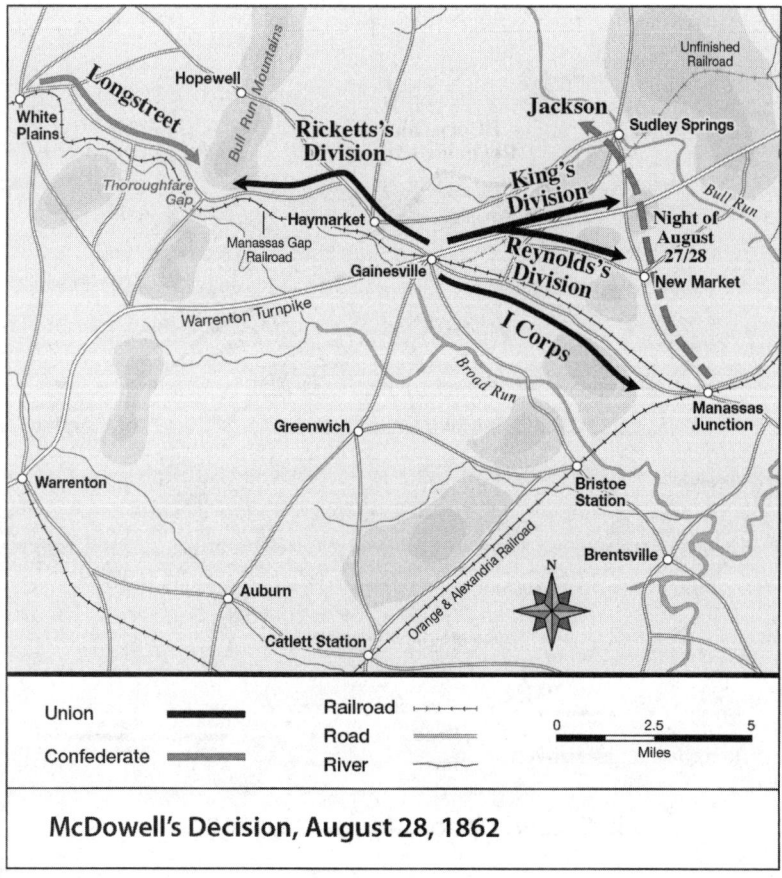

McDowell's Decision, August 28, 1862

Thursday, August 28, 1862

Brigadier General James B. Ricketts, USA, Commanding Second Division, Third Corps, Army of Virginia. Library of Congress.

Decision

McDowell's critical decision implemented option three. He detached Ricketts's division from his own corps with instructions to watch the road from Thoroughfare Gap. Ricketts was directed to resist any enemy force coming through the gap while the remainder of McDowell's command marched to Manassas Junction.[9]

Results/Impact

As the rest of McDowell's Third Corps and Sigel's First Corps marched eastward from Gainesville, Brig. Gen. James B. Ricketts's division turned west and marched to Thoroughfare Gap. There, it attempted to stop Longstreet's Left Wing in the late afternoon. Ricketts did not have the combat power to block Thoroughfare Gap and other secondary routes Longstreet could use. After he was driven back from the gap and confronted with superior enemy strength, Ricketts fell back to Gainesville. He subsequently marched to Bristoe Station, arriving early the next morning, and then to Manassas Junction.[10]

After driving Ricketts's division back, part of Longstreet's wing proceeded through the gap and camped on its east side. Longstreet resumed his march the next day, arriving on Jackson's right flank by late morning. The Army of Northern Virginia was reunited.[11]

Longstreet's Right Wing Marching Through Thoroughfare Gap. Library of Congress.

McDowell's critical decision would help shape the next two days of battle. It allowed Longstreet to march the last twelve miles separating his and Jackson's wing rapidly and unopposed. The day after that, Longstreet found himself in an advantageous position for launching a devastating attack.

Alternate Decision and Scenario

It is interesting to speculate on the outcome if McDowell had chosen the second option and ignored Pope's order. A three-division Union force either just east of Thoroughfare Gap or slightly farther back could have seriously delayed, if not defeated, Longstreet's movement through it. Such an action would have left Jackson's Left Wing exposed for an excessive amount of time. Pope then would have had sufficient time to concentrate combat power in front of the "Stony Ridge" position and either defeat Jackson or force him to retreat northwest to Aldie. At Aldie, Jackson could pass back through the Bull Run Mountains and join Longstreet. In any case, the entire flow of the campaign and battle from August 29 onward would have been different.

Jackson Decides to Attack

Situation

Jackson completed his turning movement on August 26, when he captured Bristoe Station and cut Pope's direct line of supply and communication with

Alexandria and Washington. Learning of a major supply depot just five miles away at Manassas Junction, Jackson then marched his command there and captured it. During the night of August 27 Jackson destroyed the supplies his troops could not take with them. He then marched the three divisions of his Left Wing north from Manassas Junction to the vicinity of the Warrenton Turnpike and Sudley Road intersection on the old First Manassas battlefield. From the crossroads Jackson's divisions moved northwest 2,000 yards (1.1 miles) to the "Stony Ridge" area.[12]

Jackson's new location, twelve miles east of Thoroughfare Gap, overlooked the Warrenton Turnpike. This covered and concealed position on key terrain gave him several tactical advantages. An unfinished railroad grade that could be used as a defensive trench or breastwork ran parallel to this position. Situated here, Jackson could avoid enemy reconnaissance, conduct a defense, or attack any Union force marching on the Warrenton Turnpike. Located near the turnpike, his right flank could easily tie in with Longstreet's wing when it arrived from Thoroughfare Gap. If a large Union force positioned itself between Jackson and Longstreet, Jackson had two routes he could use to march to Longstreet's location. He could march directly west to Haymarket, then continue on west until he met Longstreet. If this route was not feasible, he could march north then west from his present position to Aldie, march west through a gap in the Bull Run Mountains, then turn south and march to Longstreet's location.[13]

By late afternoon Jackson's troops were in position on the "Stony Ridge." A Union division was observed marching along the Warrenton Turnpike. Its appearance was the result of Pope's continual attempts to close with Jackson's force and engage it. This sighting would precipitate the next critical decision.

Pope had ordered the dispersed corps of his army to Manassas Junction, believing that Jackson would remain there and could be trapped and destroyed. However, when the lead elements of Maj. Gen. Samuel P. Heintzelman's Third Corps (Army of the Potomac) reached the junction, they discovered Jackson had departed. Reports then indicated Jackson was in Centreville. Pope ordered his army there.[14]

Heintzelman was ordered to march his corps to Centreville. Maj. Gen. Jesse L. Reno's command followed Heintzelman's corps upon reaching Manassas Junction. Maj. Gen. Franz Sigel's First Corps had earlier been ordered to Manassas Junction from Gainesville. While in route, Sigel he was ordered to march to Centreville. When he discovered Jackson was not there, Sigel marched his corps to Henry Hill, which overlooked the Warrenton Turnpike–Sudley Road intersection on the site of the Battle of First Manassas. Sigel missed Jackson at the road intersection by four or five hours.[15]

While Union units were approaching Manassas Junction and Centreville from the southwest, other forces were marching from the west. Brig. Gen. John F. Reynolds's Pennsylvania Reserve Division had marched east from Gainesville along the Warrenton Turnpike. Just before reaching the vicinity of Jackson's position, it turned southeast and proceeded toward Manassas Junction. Following Reynolds, Brig. Gen. Rufus King's First Division of Maj. Gen. Irvin McDowell's Third Corps marched toward Centreville along the Warrenton Turnpike. It was this division that the Confederates on "Stony Ridge" saw. McDowell's Second Division, commanded by Brig. Gen. James B. Ricketts, had marched from Buckland and through Gainesville to a position west of Haymarket. This unit was charged with stopping any enemy force coming through Thoroughfare Gap (the previous critical decision).[16]

Options

As the four brigades of King's division marched along the Warrenton Turnpike, their presence was observed and reported to Jackson. Jackson had two tactical options when he received word of King's division: remain in his present concealed position or take aggressive action against the enemy as they crossed in front of him.

Option 1

Since departing Manassas Junction, Jackson had successfully hidden his location from Pope and his major subordinate commanders. Jackson could possibly confuse the enemy for a while longer by remaining concealed on the "Stony Ridge." He expected Longstreet's wing to arrive the next morning. The reuniting of the Army of Northern Virginia would allow Lee to maneuver and attack an unaware Pope. However, as Union units were coming nearer Jackson's location, he probably thought discovery was not too far away. If discovered first he would lose any tactical advantage.

Option 2

Jackson's other option was to take the initiative and attack King's division as it marched east on the turnpike. This attack would reveal his location and bring a concentration of the remainder of Pope's force against him. If Pope could move fast enough, he could assemble considerable force against Jackson.

Two considerations offset this threat. Jackson had received a message by courier that Longstreet's Right Wing was at Thoroughfare Gap and would reach his right flank the next day. In addition, Jackson fully understood Lee's intentions and campaign objectives. Lee worried that McClellan's Army of the Potomac would complete its redeployment from the Peninsula to northern Virginia and join Pope's Army of Virginia. Some of McClellan's army (Third and Fifth Corps and elements from other corps) had completed the move and had been attached to Pope. If this were to happen, Lee would be faced with a foe of much superior strength. Another of Lee's campaign objectives was defeating Pope before the complete Army of the Potomac could join him. As Pope's units marched east and northeast, the distance the remainder of McClellan's army had to travel to reach Pope's troops decreased.

Decision

Jackson made the critical decision to attack. His larger force could cause enough casualties to render King's four-brigade division combat ineffective, thereby decreasing Pope's strength. Attacking King would reveal Jackson's position and bring Pope's army to his location. If Union units that had marched east retraced their steps westward, McClellan's troops would have a longer journey to join Pope. The concentration of Union forces at Jackson's position and the arrival of Longstreet the next day would bring the reunited Army of Northern Virginia close to the Army of Virginia. This proximity would let Lee fight the decisive battle he wanted before McClellan could fully reinforce Pope.

Results/Impact

As King's division reached the small village of Groveton in the late afternoon, Jackson commenced artillery fire on the first two Union brigades (Brig. Gen. John P. Hatch's First Brigade and Brig. Gen. John Gibbon's Fourth Brigade, which within a month would be named the Iron Brigade). Hatch and Gibbon initially responded with their artillery batteries. Gibbon then maneuvered one of his regiments against the Confederate artillery. By this time Jackson's infantry had moved from its positions and engaged the Union troops. Gibbon committed the rest of his brigade, more Confederate infantry joined the fight, and Brig. Gen. Abner Doubleday reinforced Gibbon with two regiments from his Second Brigade. Neither Hatch nor Brig. Gen. Marsena R. Patrick, commanding the Third Brigade, committed any infantry to the fight.[18]

Reinforced by Doubleday, Gibbon's brigade engaged the infantry regiments of four Confederate brigades in a bloody stand-up fight until darkness brought it to an end. After nightfall Jackson's troops withdrew to the vicinity of the unfinished railroad. Gibbon's and Doubleday's troops recovered on the pike and established aid stations to treat their wounded. Facing a larger

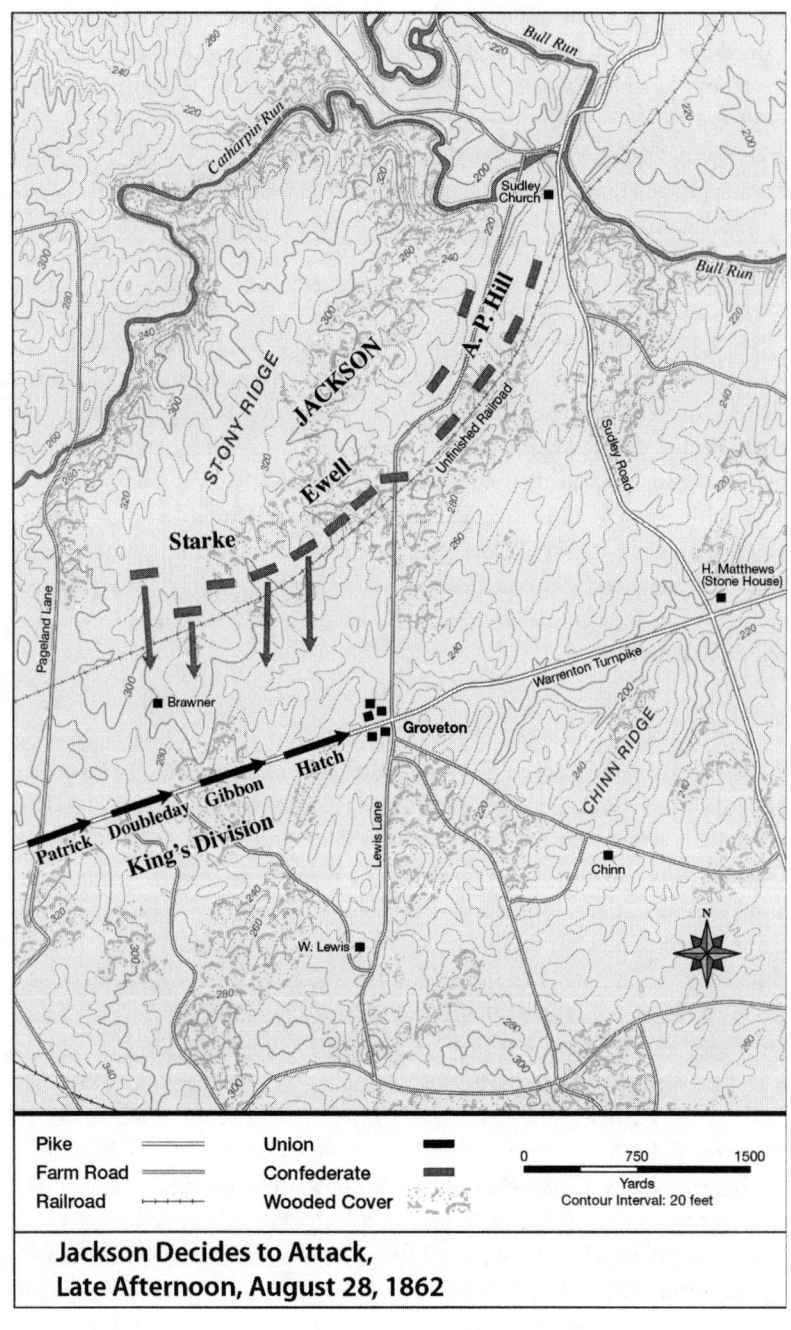

Jackson Decides to Attack, Late Afternoon, August 28, 1862

Thursday, August 28, 1862

Brawner Farm, August 28, 1862. View from the position of Battery B, 4th US Artillery. Confederate Infantry attacked from the far wood line. The Union center was where the lone tree is in the middle distance. Photo by the authors.

enemy force, King's division withdrew during the night and marched to Manassas Junction.[19]

Jackson's critical decision to attack King's division as it marched east on the Warrenton Turnpike had the desired effect. When the contact was reported to Pope, he ordered his commanders to change their direction of march and to move to Groveton and the old Manassas battlefield. He intended to hold Jackson in position, attack, and destroy the Confederates.

Jackson's decision initiated the Second Battle of Manassas. Had he chosen differently, Pope's force would have continued to search for Jackson. In addition, Longstreet would have joined up with Jackson the next day. With his army reunited and no major contact between the two forces, Lee would have had to conduct additional maneuvering to bring Pope to battle. As a result, the battle might have been fought at some other location. Furthermore, Pope might have been reinforced with even more units from McClellan's army. Such events would have changed the actual events of the next two days.

CHAPTER 3

DAY OF BATTLE— FRIDAY, AUGUST 29, 1862

August 29 was the first full day of combat between the armies. On the Union side, the day was one of misunderstanding the actual tactical situation, and of confusion and lost opportunities. From the Confederate perspective, August 29 witnessed a courageous defense by Jackson's Left Wing along the unfinished railroad position. Under the misapprehension that Jackson was retreating, Pope committed much of his combat power in uncoordinated piecemeal attacks. Longstreet's Right Wing completed its march from Thoroughfare Gap and moved into position on Jackson's right during the late morning and early afternoon. Pope did not realize Longstreet had arrived on the battlefield.

Pope Decides to Attack

Situation

This critical decision by Maj. Gen. John Pope set the tempo and focus of the fighting on August 29.

When the sun rose at 5:36 a.m. Friday morning, Lee's army was in two separate locations. Jackson's Left Wing was on the "Stony Ridge," where all three divisions were deployed in a defensive position. The left of the line was occupied by Maj. Gen. Ambrose P. Hill's six-brigade division. Hill deployed four of his brigades in the defensive line and retained two in reserve. On Hill's right Ewell's four-brigade division, commanded by Brig. Gen. Alexander R. Lawton, was deployed with two brigades in the defensive position. The other two units were held in reserve and covering the right of Jackson's position until the arrival of Longstreet's Right Wing. On Lawton's right was Jackson's four-brigade division, commanded by Brig. Gen. William E. Stark. All four brigades were deployed along the defensive position, with no reserve. Jackson's position was 3,200 yards (1.8 miles) long.[1]

At sunrise Longstreet's Right Wing at Thoroughfare Gap was twelve miles from Jackson. Longstreet put his command on the road at 6:00 a.m. Throughout the morning Longstreet's four divisions, one separate brigade, and the Washington Artillery Battalion of his reserve artillery marched east on the Manassas Gap Road to Gainesville, then on to the Warrenton Turnpike until its intersection with Pageland Lane. Passing through Gainesville at 8:45 a.m., Brig. Gen. John B. Hood's two-brigade division arrived on the battlefield and deployed at 10:00 a.m. Hood was followed by Brig. Gen. Nathan G. Evans's brigade, which deployed in a supporting position at 10:30 a.m. Brig. Gen. James L. Kemper's three-brigade division arrived at 11:00 a.m. and was followed an hour later by Brig. Gen. David R. Jones's three-brigade division and Col. James B. Walton's artillery battalion. Brig. Gen. Cadmus M. Wilcox's three-brigade division arrived and deployed between 1:00 and 2:00 p.m.[2]

Maj. Gen. Richard H. Anderson's three-brigade division was the last major Confederate unit to reach the battlefield. Anderson's Division and Col. Stephen D. Lee's artillery battalion of Longstreet's reserve artillery had been detached to conduct deception operations. These soldiers made it appear that Lee was still in force along the Rappahannock when the rest of the army left. Departing their position on the river on August 28, the two commands marched for nineteen hours and arrived at 3:00 a.m. on August 30.[3]

On the morning of August 29, Maj. Gen. John Pope's combat forces consisted of thirteen infantry divisions, four separate infantry brigades, forty-one batteries of artillery, and three calvary brigades grouped into six corps. Three of these corps were organic to his Army of Virginia; the other three corps were attached from the Army of the Potomac (Reno's Ninth Corps had just been assigned). Pope's forces were spread out over a forty-nine-square-mile area represented by an inverse scalene triangle. The three points of this triangle were at Gainesville, Centreville, and Bristoe Station. Concentration of these forces at the point of contact with Jackson's wing required some time.

At dawn Pope's Army of Virginia and the attached corps from the Army of the Potomac were positioned at the following locations:

Maj. Gen. Franz Sigel's First Corps, Army of Virginia (two divisions and two attached brigades) was in position on the battlefield between the

Friday, August 29, 1862

Warrenton Turnpike and the Sudley Road. The corps was deployed and prepared to engage Jackson's Left Wing to develop intelligence on the enemy position.[4]

Maj. Gen. Nathaniel P. Bank's Second Corps, Army of Virginia (two divisions) was camped at Bristoe Station, ten miles from the battlefield. Bank's corps remained in this location for the next two days.[5]

Maj. Gen. Irvin McDowell's Third Corps, Army of Virginia (three divisions) occupied two separate locations. The First Division (King's) was at Manassas Junction, six miles from the battlefield. The Second Division (Ricketts's) was at Gainesville, but it marched to Bristoe Station, arriving at 7:00 a.m., then marched to Manassas Junction. The Pennsylvania Reserves

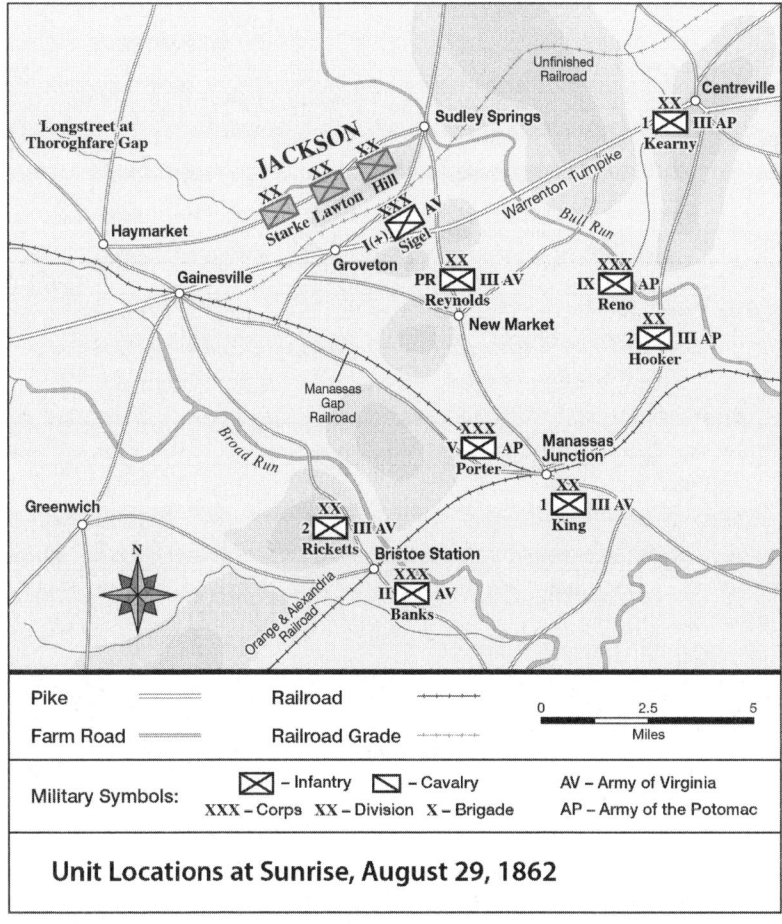

Unit Locations at Sunrise, August 29, 1862

Division (Reynolds's) was positioned south of Henry Hill, along the Manassas-Sudley Road, and was ready to deploy.[6]

Maj. Gen. Samuel P. Heintzelman's Third Corps, Army of the Potomac (two divisions) was positioned in two separate locations. The First Division (Kearny's) camped at Centreville, six miles from the battlefield. The Second Division (Hooker's) was at Union Mills, nine miles from the battlefield by way of Centreville.[7]

Maj. Gen. Fitz John Porter's Fifth Corps, Army of the Potomac (two divisions and one brigade) spent the night at Bristoe Station. At dawn the Fifth Corps marched to Manassas Junction, arriving there at 8:30 a.m., and was six miles from the battlefield.[8]

Maj. Gen. Jesse L. Reno's Ninth Corps, Army of the Potomac (two divisions) was situated near Union Mills, nine miles from the battlefield by way of Centreville.[9]

Early in the morning three Union divisions and one independent brigade were in close proximity to Jackson's position. Sigel's First Corps was deployed with his First Division (Schenck's) in the vicinity of Groveton. From this location the unit conducted limited reconnaissance to the west to locate Confederate positions. On Schenck's left (south) flank Reynolds's Pennsylvania Reserve Division, positioned along Lewis Lane, also reconnoitered to discover enemy positions.[10]

The First Corps' Second Division (Schurz's) was positioned astride the Sudley Road. These troops were probing the left of Jackson's defenses to determine the identity and strength of the forces there. The division also established whether those enemy soldiers were defending or retreating.[11]

Milroy's Independent Brigade occupied the area between Schenck's and Schurz's divisions. Milroy had used offensive action to discover a strong Confederate position where the Groveton-Sudley Road crossed the unfinished railroad.[12]

The Union forces ordered to the battlefield arrived throughout the morning and early afternoon. The first to arrive were the two divisions of Third Corps, Army of the Potomac. Kearny's division marched from Centreville and arrived at 9:00 a.m., followed by Hooker's division at 11:00 a.m. The Ninth Corps began to arrive at 11:30 a.m., when Stevens's division reached the battlefield. Reno's division followed and arrived shortly after 11:30 a.m. Although only six miles from the battlefield, Hatch's (King's) division was not ordered to march until early afternoon. It reached the Sudley Road–Warrenton Turnpike intersection at 3:30 p.m.[13]

On the central part of the battlefield, Union strength early in the morning totaled nine brigades. The force increased to fifteen brigades by midmorning,

Friday, August 29, 1862

Terrain north of Warrenton Turnpike and west of Sudley Road. Photo by the authors.

owing to the arrival of Kearny's and Hooker's divisions. At noon the arrival of the Ninth Corps improved the Union strength to 20 brigades. The last upsurge in strength was at 3:30 p.m., when the three brigades from Hatch's four-brigade division arrived. This brought the brigade total to twenty-three.

During most of the day, the two divisions of the Fifth Corps and Ricketts's division (ten brigades) were involved in an operation on the south flank along the Manassas-Gainesville Road. They were not ordered to march to the central part of the battlefield until it was too late for them to impact the day's fighting against Jackson. The two divisions (five brigades) of the Second Corps remained in the vicinity of Bristoe Station and did not contribute any combat power to the battle.[14]

Ever since Jackson had arrived at Bristoe Station on August 26 and cut his supply line, Pope had been attempting to attack him. However, Jackson had managed to stay one step ahead of Pope, and he even disappeared when he took position on the "Stony Ridge" on August 28. Only Jackson's attack on King's (later Hatch's) division late that afternoon revealed his location. Having finally discovered Jackson's whereabouts, Pope was determined to engage him. Jackson's continual movements made Pope think he was retreating west to unite with Longstreet. Pope intended to prevent the reuniting of Lee's army by severing Jackson's direct line of retreat. To accomplish this, Pope would have to hold Jackson in position with attacks, then envelop his right flank. Isolated from Lee, Jackson would then be destroyed.[15]

The best opportunity to keep the two Confederate forces separated was lost when insufficient Union combat power was sent to Thoroughfare Gap on

August 28. On the morning of August 29, when Pope published what became known as the "Joint Order," he estimated that Longstreet would join Jackson, and that both commands would reach his position that night or the next day. The position Pope referred to was not the Manassas battlefield, which he did not reach until early afternoon. Rather, it was Centreville, his location at the time the order was written. After Pope reached the Manassas battlefield he may have revised the estimated time of Longstreet's arrival. He may also have stayed with his original estimate, as Centreville was only six miles away, about a two- to three-hour march. Whatever his opinion on Longstreet's arrival time, we do know that Pope was in error. Longstreet arrived much sooner than he anticipated.[16]

The nine brigades (First Corps and Reynolds's division) that were on the battlefield in the early morning conducted limited objective attacks and reconnaissance in force to discover Jackson's location and intentions. By midmorning these tasks had been accomplished. The locations of the Confederate position were fairly understood, and it was obvious to the division and brigade commanders in contact that Jackson was not planning a retreat. Pope did not grasp Jackson's real objectives, instead operating under his own invalid assumptions for the rest of the day. One question led to Pope's critical decision: What should he do with the remaining fourteen brigades as they arrived?

Options

Pope had three options to consider. First, he could bring his separated forces to the battlefield, assume a defensive position, and wait for the rest of Lee's army to arrive. Secondly, once most or all of the remaining fourteen brigades arrived, Pope could use them in a coordinated attack against Jackson. Finally, Pope could commit all or part of these brigades in attacks against Jackson as soon as they arrived on the battlefield or shortly thereafter.

Option 1

The terrain at Second Manassas offered Pope several good positions for a defense. Just east of the Sudley-Manassas Road, the north-south high ground of Matthews, Buck, and Henry Hills offered good terrain upon which to anchor a position. Perhaps even better was the ground just east of Bull Run. This area provided not only suitable defensive positions but also the natural obstacle of a watercourse.

The defensive option was beneficial in that the longer it took Lee to bring his army together and decide to maneuver or attack, the stronger Pope's position would become. Maj. Gen. William B. Franklin's Sixth Corps and Maj. Gen. Edwin V. Sumner's Second Corps of McClellan's army had arrived from the Peninsula and were at Alexandria. Advance Sixth Corps units had already moved toward Pope, and they would be followed by the remainder of the corps. The Second Corps followed on August 30.[17]

Lee's operational intention was to attack the Army of Virginia and destroy or render it combat ineffective before the Army of the Potomac could strongly reinforce it. If Pope went on the defense, Lee would have to attack or maneuver to Pope's flank and then attack. It was imperative that he defeat Pope before more reinforcements arrived from McClellan's army. A major disadvantage of this option was the fact that Pope would be surrendering the initiative to Lee. Lee would have the advantage of deciding when and where to strike.

Option 2

To conduct a coordinated attack, Pope would have to wait until all or most of the fourteen marching brigades reached the battlefield. Eleven of those brigades (Kearny's, Hooker's, Stevens's, and Reno's divisions) would be in position on the battlefield by 1:00 p.m. With the units already there, these troops would provide Pope with a powerful force to conduct a coordinated attack. A main attack by part of this force might penetrate Jackson's defenses. A properly positioned reserve could then exploit this success while other units conducted supporting attacks to keep Jackson from moving reserves to the point of Union penetration.

The last three brigades (Hatch's division) arrived at 3:30 p.m. They could be committed to reinforce anywhere on the battlefield. Alternatively, Pope could wait for their arrival to commence his attack, which would make it even more powerful.

Option 3

Pope had committed Sigel's First Corps' divisions to attacks that confirmed Jackson was still on the "Stony Ridge." Five divisions were marching to join him. Pope could commit the brigades of these five divisions as soon as they arrived. This option would make three brigades available to Pope shortly after 9:00 a.m., then three more two hours later. These six units would be followed by another three just before noon and an additional two brigades between noon and 1:00 p.m. No further reinforcements would be available until the three brigades from Hatch's division arrived at 3:30 p.m.

The advantage of immediately committing all or some of these brigades as they arrived would be continuous pressure on Jackson. It would be difficult for Jackson to move to a different position or retreat west to join Longstreet. The disadvantage was that uncoordinated attacks would be a piecemeal commitment of Pope's combat power. They would not have the strength of a coordinated attack, which could be launched after waiting for most of the brigades to arrive. In addition, if Pope did not engage the Confederates across their entire defensive position, Jackson and his division commanders could move units to threatened sectors to stop or drive back penetrations.

Decision

Pope ordered a series of attacks against Jackson's defensive position as soon as units arrived (Option 3).

Pope failed to realize that time was on his side. The longer it took Lee to reunite his army and maneuver against him, the stronger Pope became. Yet for two days Pope clung to the idea that Jackson was attempting to retreat to join Longstreet. Therefore, Jackson had to be held in position while other units of Pope's army maneuvered to cut him off. (More on this concept appears later.) Pope also believed that holding Jackson in position would give him sufficient time to destroy or severely damage Jackson's Left Wing before Longstreet's Right Wing reached the battlefield.

The conclusions upon which Pope formulated his August 29 orders were incorrect. However, once he believed that Jackson was retreating and that Longstreet was farther away than he actually was, Pope was not receptive to modifying his concept of operations. The piecemeal commitment of his units continued even after it was apparent to the attacking commanders that Jackson was not going anywhere.

From late morning on, the Union units on and south of the Warrenton Turnpike began making contact with a strong skirmish line. These forces suspected that there was a much larger enemy force behind the skirmishers. This was Longstreet's Right Wing going into position on Jackson's right.

Covering the withdrawal of Ricketts's division, Brig. Gen John Buford's cavalry brigade near Gainesville observed part of Longstreet's Wing as it marched east toward Jackson's position. Buford sent a sighting report to Ricketts at 9:30 a.m., and it was then forwarded to McDowell. Buford stated, "Seventeen regiments, one battery, five hundred cavalry passed through Gainesville three quarters of an hour ago [at 8:45], on the Centreville road [Warrenton Turnpike]. Please forward this." The aforementioned troops were Hood's Division, Evans's Brigade, and the lead element of Kemper's Division. This information that a Confederate force was approaching from the west was extremely important. Since Jackson's position was known, who could the advancing soldiers be but Longstreet's? The report reached McDowell, who for some unexplained reason did not give it to Pope until that evening. This intelligence might have influenced Pope's decisions on August 29, or it might

Friday, August 29, 1862

Brigadier General John Buford, USA, Commanding Cavalry Brigade, Army of Virginia. Library of Congress.

not have. The next day, after he had had Buford's report for over twelve hours, Pope still did not understand the large enemy threat just to the west.[18]

Results/Impact

As a result of this critical decision, separate uncoordinated attacks—seven brigade size and one division size—were made against the three Confederate divisions on the "Stony Ridge." In addition, a division attack occurred west along the Warrenton Turnpike. The first three attacks were launched by Krzyzanowski's brigade (10:00 a.m.), Milroy's brigade (10:15 a.m.), and Schimmelfennig's brigade (10:45 a.m.). Although Kearny's and Hooker's divisions arrived at 9:00 and 11:00 a.m., only one brigade from Kearny (Robinson's) and one from Hooker (Grover's) attacked at 3:00 p.m. These brigade attacks were not coordinated or mutually supporting. Stevens's and Reno's divisions began arriving at 11:30 a.m. A brigade from each division attacked at 4:00 p.m. (Nagle's) and 5:30 p.m. (Leasure's). The only attack approaching a coordinated effort was a 5:00 p.m. effort by two brigades of Kearny's division, supported by Leasure's brigade.

Several of these offensives managed to penetrate the defenses, but no follow and support units or designated reserves were available to exploit success.

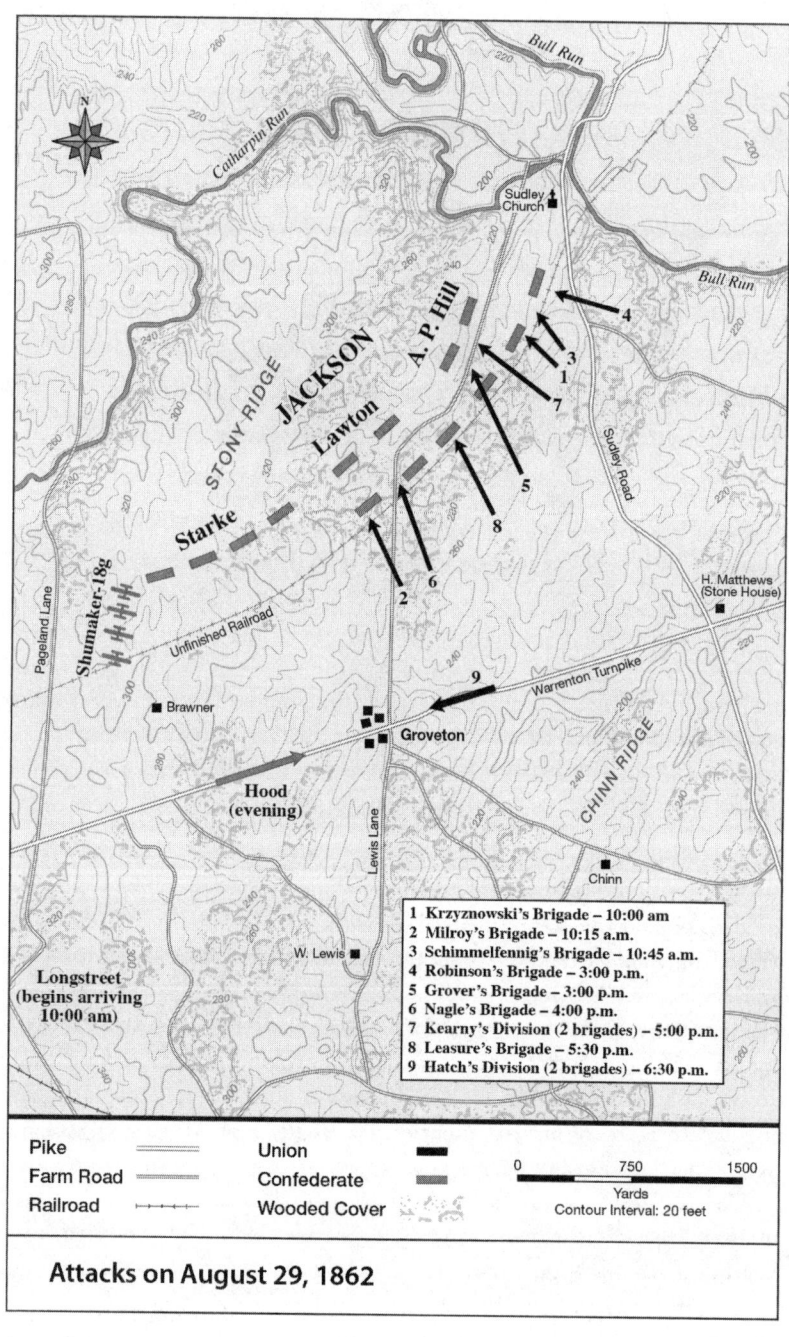

The uncoordinated attacks allowed many unengaged Confederate brigades to counterattack at the point of penetration and restore the defenses.

The last Union offensive effort began at 6:30 p.m. Two brigades of Hatch's division were ordered west on the Warrenton Turnpike in the mistaken belief that they were pursuing a retreating enemy. Before they reached Groveton, a counterattack by Hood's Division drove them back.

The repeated attacks hitting strong defenses and the information that suggested a large force was deploying near Pageland Lane should have convinced Pope to review his earlier assumptions and conclusions. Such a review might have made him modify the commitment of his combat power. This was not the case. Pope's faulty decision-making process continued into the next day with disastrous results.

Alternate Decision and Scenario

It is interesting to explore how the fighting might have developed had Pope chosen the second option. This decision would have had him wait to attack until the arrival of all or most of the units he had ordered to join him. In this scenario the offensive operation would have been a two-corps attack. The main attack could have consisted of Schurz's Third Division, First Corps, Army of Virginia and Kearny's First Division and Hooker's Second Division, Third Corps, Army of the Potomac. Kearny's and Schurz's divisions could have deployed in the attacking echelon, with Hooker's division as the reserve. Maj. Gen. Samuel P. Heintzelman, Third Corps commander, might have commanded this attack. The objective of this attack would be the center and left sectors of A. P. Hill's defensive position.[19]

The supporting attack, consisting of the Ninth Corps' two divisions, would have maneuvered to the left of the main attack. One division would have been in the attacking echelon, followed by the other one, as the corps reserve. The objective of this attack would have been the right of A. P. Hill's Division and the left of Lawton's Division. Blocking positions would have protected the left flank of these attacks. Milroy's brigade and Schenck's First Division, First Corps, Army of Virginia might have established two such positions along the Groveton-Sudley Road north of the Warrenton Turnpike. South of the turnpike, Reynolds's Pennsylvania Reserves Division could have established a blocking position along Lewis Lane.[20]

After 3:30 p.m. Hatch's First Division, Third Corps, Army of Virginia would have been in position near the Sudley Road–Warrenton Turnpike intersection to serve as the army's reserve. From this intersection Hatch could have reinforced the main or supporting attacks, or any one of the blocking positions.

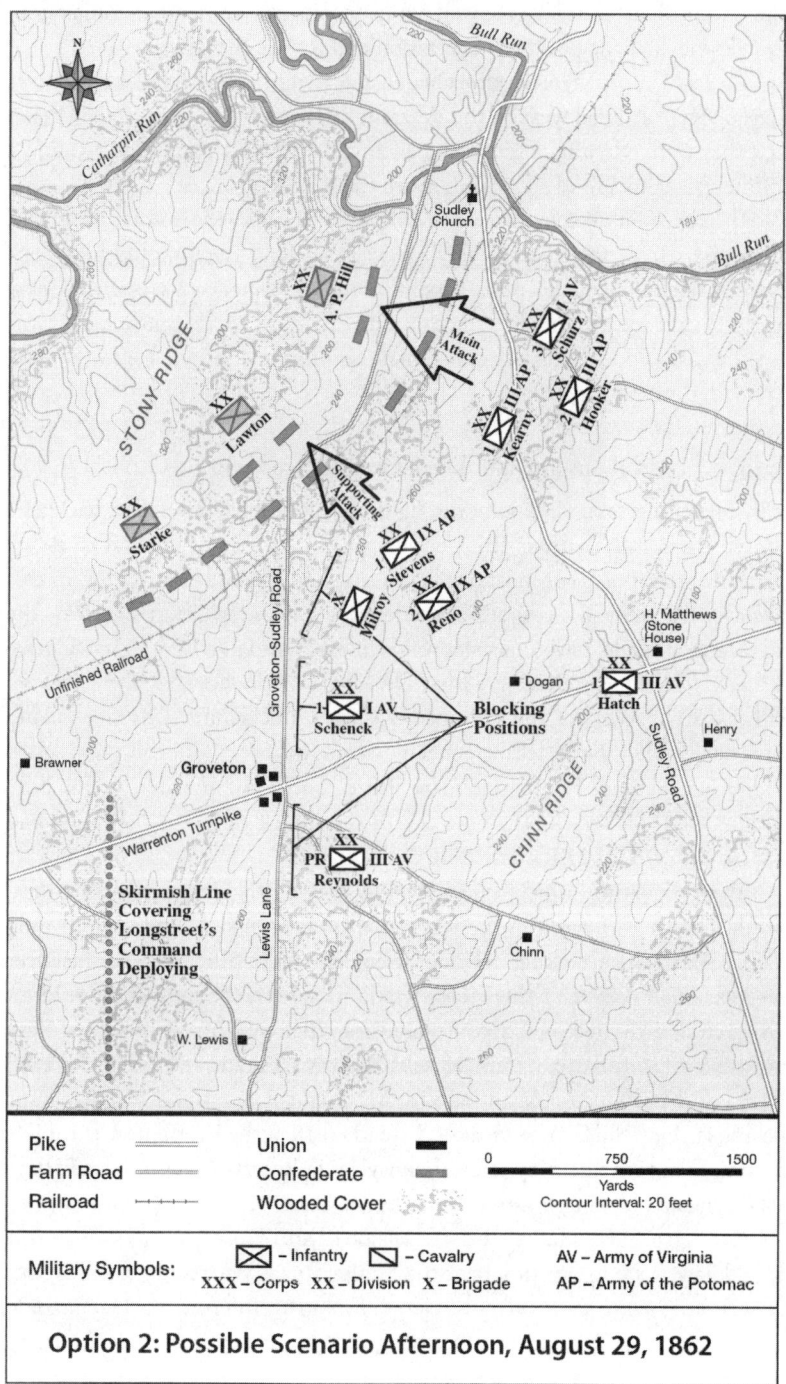

Option 2: Possible Scenario Afternoon, August 29, 1862

Although nothing in combat is a certainty, this option might have provided the coordinated combat power to penetrate and disrupt Jackson's defenses. Attacking across a broad front would have made it difficult to commit other Confederate brigades to reinforce threatened sectors. Any Confederate reinforcement could have been countered by the division-size reserves supporting the attacks. The flank would have been protected. A sufficiently large reserve would have been available at the corps and army level to exploit the success of any penetration.

However, Pope did not select this option. Instead, he committed much of his formidable combat power to numerous brigade-level attacks in a piecemeal fashion. This critical decision as to how his available combat power would be used set the fighting for August 29 and even carried into the next day. One of the other options might have given Pope better tactical results, but the one he chose gives us the history of the battle on August 29 and sets the stage for the following day.

Porter Decides Not to Attack

Situation

While the combat at the unfinished railroad was in progress, other events were occurring on Pope's left flank, three and a half miles south, that would cause the next critical decision. This critical decision would not only affect the events of that Friday, but also carry forward with major consequences on the following day (August 30). To develop this critical decision it is necessary to follow the movements and deployments of three major commands: Maj. Gen. James Longstreet's Right Wing (Army of Northern Virginia), Maj. Gen. Fitz John Porter's Fifth Corps (Army of the Potomac), and Maj. Gen. Irvin McDowell's Third Corps (Army of Virginia).Longstreet's wing had spent the previous night in the vicinity of Thoroughfare Gap. Early that morning it commenced marching east to join Jackson's Left Wing in a defensive position along the "Stony Ridge" and the unfinished railroad. This position was about to receive the first in a series of Union attacks. When Longstreet's advance unit, Hood's Division, reached Gainesville, it turned onto the Warrenton Turnpike and proceeded toward Groveton. Prior to reaching this crossroads hamlet, Hood's Division went into position astride the turnpike and connected with Jackson's right (southwest) flank. Evans's Independent Brigade followed Hood and deployed into a supporting position.[21]

Brig. Gen. Beverly H. Robertson's cavalry brigade of Maj. Gen. J. E. B. Stuart's cavalry division was positioned near Gainesville as Longstreet's Wing began to pass through and onto the turnpike. Accompanied by Stuart,

Robertson's cavalry brigade commenced a flank guard mission on Longstreet's right. Robertson's cavalry proceeded southeast along the Gainesville–Manassas Junction Road for approximately three miles, reaching high ground that overlooked a small stream, Dawkin's Branch. Robertson was then positioned on the right of Longstreet's deploying divisions. He and his troops blocked the road from Manassas Junction, seven miles farther southeast, to Gainesville.[22]

While Longstreet's wing was marching through Gainesville and deploying on Jackson's right, two Union corps in the vicinity of Manassas Junction began to reposition. McDowell's Third Corps (Army of Virginia) had been divided the previous afternoon. Believing Jackson was still at Manassas Junction, Pope ordered McDowell to march his Third Corps and the First Corps (temporarily under his operational control) from the vicinity of Gainesville southeast toward Manassas Junction. Earlier, Buford had informed McDowell of a sizeable Confederate force (Longstreet) marching toward Thoroughfare Gap. McDowell realized that complying with this order would uncover Thoroughfare Gap and the road east from the gap. As a result, Longstreet would be able to move rapidly and unopposed to join Jackson.[23]

McDowell sent Sigel's corps on toward Manassas Junction and ordered King's (Hatch's) division to march on Sigel's left and along the Warrenton Turnpike. Concerned about Thoroughfare Gap, McDowell ordered Ricketts's division to march from Buckland to Gainesville, and then to a position west of Haymarket to cover the eastern egress from Thoroughfare Gap. (See chapter 2 for a discussion of this critical decision.)[24]

Jackson attacked King's division as it marched on the Warrenton Turnpike. After heavy fighting, the division withdrew towards Manassas Junction during the night. It arrived there about 7:00 a.m. the next morning (August 29). Ricketts's division, having been forced back from Thoroughfare Gap, spent the night in the vicinity of Gainesville. The division marched to Bristoe Station at daylight, arriving there at 7:00 a.m.[25]

Porter's Fifth Corps (Army of the Potomac) began to move from its overnight location at Bristoe Station. Porter received an order from Pope at 5:20 a.m. to march to Centreville. After breakfast the Fifth Corps was on the road, and by 8:30 a.m. its leading elements were passing through Manassas Junction. Here, Porter received a communication from Pope ordering him to attach King's (Hatch's) Division to his corps and march to Gainesville. Hatch's division was attached because Pope did not know where McDowell or Ricketts were located.[26]

In the meantime, McDowell had joined Porter, learned of the detachment of Hatch's division from his corps, and appealed to Pope by messenger for the unit's return to his command. McDowell now had Hatch's division (still attached to Porter) at Manassas Junction, Ricketts's division at Bristoe Station, and Reynolds's division just south of the Warrenton Turnpike protecting the left of Sigel's corps. With this situation and disposition of troops, Porter, along with his two divisions and Hatch's, marched northwest on the connecting road from Manassas Junction to Gainesville. After ordering Ricketts to march from Bristoe Station to Manassas Junction, McDowell followed Porter.[27]

Around 11:00 a.m. another order arrived from Pope. He had written it at 10:00 a.m., while his headquarters was at Centreville. The directive was addressed to Porter and McDowell, and by inference it returned Hatch's division to McDowell's command. Known as the "Joint Order," this communication was supposed to clarify Porter's and McDowell's mission on the Manassas Junction–Gainesville Road. Pope stated in part, "You (Porter and McDowell) will please move forward with your joint commands towards Gainesville. . . . Heintzelman, Sigel, and Reno are moving on the Warrenton turnpike, and must now be not far from Gainesville. . . . As soon as communication is established between this force and your own the whole command shall halt. . . . It may be necessary to fall back behind Bull Run at Centreville to-night. I presume it will be so on account of our supplies. . . . If any considerable advantages are to be gained by departing from this order it will not be strictly carried out."[28]

The order was based upon the incorrect assumption that Jackson was attempting to retreat westward and rejoin Lee and Longstreet. Poorly written, the document contained contradictions and further confused Porter's situation. From reading the order, Porter and McDowell understood they were supposed to continue toward Gainesville. There were no specific instructions as to what they were to do once they reached Gainesville, or as to what they should do before reaching the town. If they established communications (made flank contact) with the rest of the army, the troops were merely to halt.[29]

However, from the previous order they had received and from the sentence about the other corps proceeding on the Warrenton Turnpike, Porter and McDowell could have made some inferences. The order implied missions to block Jackson's retreat, to attack any enemy force in front of them, and to strike the south or western flank of the Confederate army, wherever it might be.

In addition, Pope addressed the army's supply situation. As many units were low on food and other items, the time was rapidly approaching when resupplying would be necessary. It could be done by having the army move east back to Centreville. If Pope was thinking along these lines, then he probably believed that Jackson could be cut off, destroyed, or severely damaged, thereby allowing the army to fall back to Centreville. There, the troops could resupply while waiting for Longstreet's wing to make an appearance.

Pope's assumptions about Jackson's intentions and Longstreet's location were faulty. To the north of Porter, the divisions of Sigel's, Heintzelman's, and Reno's corps were on the battlefield or arriving. Moreover, the piecemeal attacks were in progress.

After marching a little over four miles, Porter's lead division (Morell's), with Griffin's brigade as the advance guard, reached the small stream of Dawkin's Branch. At this location they observed enemy troops on the higher ground, astride the road in front of them. These soldiers were from Robertson's cavalry brigade, which had also observed the Union march. Stuart ordered brush to be cut and dragged along the road, creating dust clouds to give the impression of an approaching Confederate force. Porter halted the march and deployed Morell's division.[30]

At the same time, the remainder of Longstreet's Right Wing approached the battlefield. Kemper's Division arrived at 11:00 a.m., and Kemper deployed two brigades so as to extend Hood's line farther south of the turnpike. Longstreet ordered Kemper to send Col. Montgomery D. Corse's brigade to reinforce Robertson's cavalry. An hour later (noon) Jones's Division arrived, and it was deployed to protect Kemper's right and support the blocking force astride

Major General James Longstreet, CSA, Commanding Longstreet's Right Wing, Army of Northern Virginia. National Archives.

Friday, August 29, 1862

the Manassas Junction–Gainesville Road. In the early afternoon Wilcox's Division arrived and was positioned north of the turnpike as a reserve. Later that afternoon it was moved south of the turnpike to support Jones's division.[31]

With Porter's movement toward Gainesville confronted by a Confederate force and the arrival and deployment of Longstreet's wing, the stage was set for the next critical decision. Events would unfold in such a manner that Maj. Gen. Fitz Jon Porter, commanding the Fifth Corps, was the decision-maker.

Born in 1822, Fitz John Porter was one day shy of his fortieth birthday at the battle of Second Manassas. He graduated from the US Military Academy in 1845, fought in the Mexican War, was an instructor at West Point, and then served as Albert Sidney Johnston's adjutant in the Utah Expedition. After the war's outbreak, Porter was promoted to brigadier general of volunteers in August 1861. He joined McClellan in Washington to help train the new troops of the Army of the Potomac. During the Peninsula Campaign Porter commanded a division, then the Fifth Corps, and was promoted to major general. His corps was attached to Pope's Army of Virginia, with which it fought in the Second Battle of Manassas.[32]

After the battle, Pope brought charges of disobedience and misconduct against Porter. Following the Maryland Campaign, Porter was relieved of command and court-martialed. Found guilty, he was dismissed from the

Major General Fitz John Porter, USA, Commanding Fifth Corps, Army of the Potomac. Library of Congress.

army. In 1879 a board of officers exonerated Porter, but it was not until 1886 that President Cleveland returned him to the army's officer rolls with the rank of colonel. Porter died in 1901.[33]

Part of the decision process to comply with an operational order (which the "Joint Order" was) is to determine the tasks to be accomplished. The stated tasks in the order were as follows: Move along the axis of the Manassas Junction–Gainesville Road toward Gainesville. Halt as soon as communication was established with Heintzelman, Sigel, and Reno, who were moving west on the Warrenton Turnpike axis of advance. Be prepared to fall back (east) behind Bull Run to Centreville for resupply. The implied tasks were: If possible, attack any enemy force on the road to Gainesville and develop information as to its size and composition. Capture and control the crossroads intersection at Gainesville. Cut Jackson's line of retreat and prevent him from reuniting with Longstreet. If Jackson remains in position, after reaching Gainesville attack so as to envelop his right flank.

Both Porter and McDowell had received the "Joint Order" from Pope and had met to discuss its implications. Porter's advanced units had reached Dawkin's Branch and made contact with Robertson's cavalry. Simultaneously, Longstreet's divisions continued marching east on the Warrenton Turnpike, deploying to Jackson's right, and then extended Longstreet's (and the army's) right flank south.[34]

Options

Porter had three options: reposition along the Manassas Junction–Sudley Road, remain in position and develop the situation, or move aggressively northwest on the road to Gainesville.

Option 1

Porter and McDowell could move from their current locations and take up positions on the Manassas Junction–Sudley Road. This shift would help open communications (make contact) with the corps to their right (north), and it would provide Pope with a secure left (south) flank. This measure would also facilitate the withdrawal behind Bull Run to Centreville, as stated in the "Joint Order."

There were several disadvantages to this option. Porter and McDowell would have to break contact with the enemy in their front without determining exactly who they were and in what strength. This action would not comply with Pope's intent for aggressive action on his south flank. Breaking contact would also allow this enemy force the freedom of maneuver. A position along the Manassas Junction–Sudley Road would be a defensive position, and it would surrender the initiative on the south flank, if they should take it, to Lee and Longstreet.

Option 2

Having made contact with a Confederate force of unknown size, Porter could remain in position and conduct reconnaissance to determine its strength and composition. At the same time, McDowell could march his corps north on the Sudley Road to a point where it could turn west and move into the space between Porter's right flank and the remainder of the army's left flank.

The advantages of this option included Porter's remaining in contact with the enemy to his front. This measure would hold the Confederates in place, as they needed to block the farther movement of Porter's corps. It might also result in additional Confederate units being deployed to the south flank, which would disperse Lee's combat power. At the same time, a redeployment of McDowell's corps to Porter's right would facilitate establishing communication with the corps to the north and add an additional threat to Longstreet's right. Such a positioning of Porter's and McDowell's corps would provide Pope with a substantial position north and south of the Warrenton Turnpike.

Based on Buford's earlier communication, Porter and McDowell should have expected the arrival of additional Confederate units. Aggressive reconnaissance from their positions could have further developed the information that Longstreet's Right Wing was present on the battlefield. Lee and Longstreet would be confronted with a substantial two-corps Union force south of the Warrenton Turnpike. If they were still there the next day, this would have an effect on Lee's plans. This option would also facilitate withdrawing behind Bull Run to Centreville.

The option's disadvantages included the time that would be required for McDowell to move to a new location, as well as the minimization of Porter's aggressive action and development of the enemy situation while McDowell moved into position. This option did not provide for sustained aggressive action toward Gainesville as Pope desired.

Option 3

Porter and McDowell would remain together and aggressively move along the axis of the Manassas Junction–Gainesville Road, engage the enemy force to their front, and develop the tactical situation. Porter's Corps would be the leading element, with McDowell's Third Corps following in a supporting role. The two corps would have the strength of Porter's two divisions, six brigades, with the addition of Piatt's attached brigade (soon to arrive) and six artillery batteries and McDowell's two divisions, eight brigades, and eight artillery batteries.

One advantage of this option would be a formidable Union force maneuvering northwest on the axis of advance toward Gainesville. Neither Lee nor Longstreet would be able to disregard a force of this size maneuvering on their right and right front. Porter and McDowell would engage the right of Lee's army, requiring much of Longstreet's wing to reposition to defend or counterattack against this threat. In addition, this option would provide creditable intelligence about Longstreet's arrival and location. This course of action would comply with the intention of Pope's order to march to Gainesville, although the troops probably would not get there. As the situation developed, it would also provide Pope with better tactical alternatives than the ones he had been following.[35]

Primary among the disadvantages of this option was the gap between Porter and McDowell and the remainder of the army, which Longstreet might exploit to attack their right. It would also be difficult for Union forces to break contact and withdraw behind Bull Run, if Pope chose to do so. However, with success on this flank, Pope probably would not order such a withdrawal.

Decision

Porter decided to remain in position and develop the situation. In making this critical decision Porter's corps and McDowell's (for a short period of time) essentially remained where they were along the road to Gainesville. Several attempts were made, though not very aggressively, to determine the strength and composition of the enemy to Porter's front. Porter's decision essentially removed the combat power of four divisions (his two and McDowell's two) from the battle on August 29.

Results/Impact

In response to Porter's presence on his flank, Longstreet shifted a significant part of his force to the Confederate right throughout the afternoon. Initially, this was Corse's Brigade, and they reinforced Robertson's cavalry. They were followed in the early afternoon by the three brigades of Jones's Division, and later by the three brigades of Wilcox's Division. A total infantry force of seven brigades with supporting artillery was shifted to Longstreet's south flank.[36]

McDowell's corps departed and marched north on the Sudley Road toward the sound of the combat. McDowell told Porter he would deploy one of his divisions as a connection between Porter's right and the rest of the

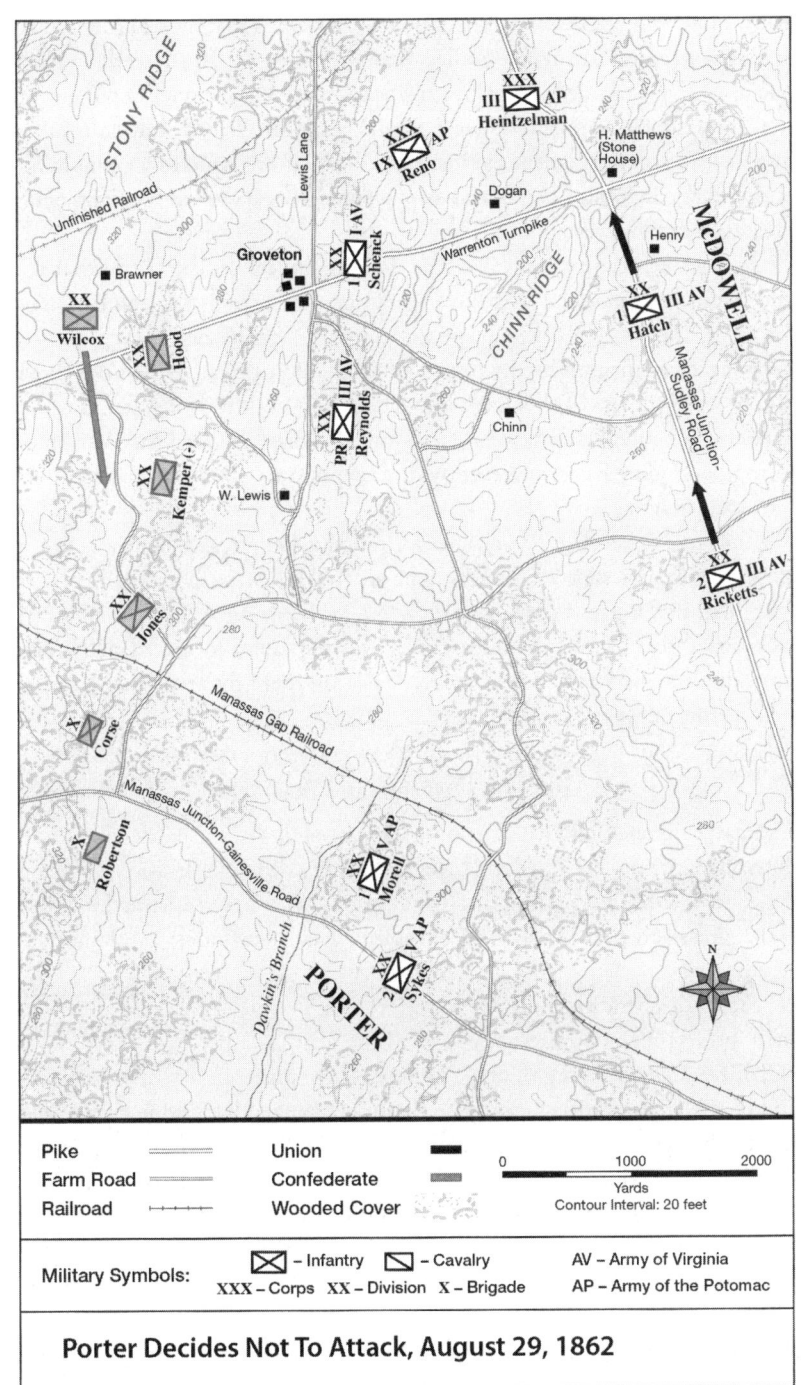

Porter Decides Not To Attack, August 29, 1862

army. However, McDowell did not do this; his corps marched to the vicinity of the Warrenton Turnpike–Sudley Road intersection. In the early evening one of McDowell's divisions (Hatch's) was ordered to conduct "a pursuit" of the "retreating" Confederates west on the turnpike. This operation resulted in a disastrous engagement against Hood's Division, which was simultaneously advancing east. Only darkness prevented Hatch's casualties from being greater than they were.[37]

Porter's critical decision had far-reaching effects on the battle that day and the next. It ensured that there would be no aggressive action by Union forces on the south flank. Longstreet initially repositioned a large part of his wing to confront what he perceived as a Union threat. When the threat didn't develop, part of this force was redeployed back to Longstreet's center and left. When Hatch's division (McDowell's corps) reached the Warrenton Turnpike–Sudley Road intersection, it was sent on a poorly conceived offensive operation to the west.

That night, because Porter had not produced any results and was not in close contact with an enemy force, Pope ordered his corps to march north and join the army. Porter's corps was therefore available on August 30 to attack Jackson's right. Finally, because Porter was not there to hold Longstreet's units in place, he was able to favorably position them for an offensive operation the next day.

Alternate Decision and Scenario

Again, it is interesting to explore how the sequencing of the battle might have developed, or not developed, if Porter had made a different decision. In accordance with Option 3, Porter and McDowell would have remained together and aggressively moved along the axis of the Manassas Junction–Gainesville Road.

Had this operation been conducted, the Union forces available for it were the four divisions (fourteen brigades) of the Third Corps, Army of Virginia and Fifth Corps, Army of the Potomac, their fourteen artillery batteries, and possibly one additional brigade that was attached but had not yet joined the Fifth Corps. As of noon the available Confederate forces astride and south of the Warrenton Turnpike were Robertson's Cavalry Brigade, Hood's, Kemper's, and Jones's Divisions (eight brigades), and Evans's Independent Brigade, for a total of nine infantry brigades. Artillery with these units totaled eight batteries plus the four batteries of Col. James B. Walton's Washington Artillery Battalion. In midafternoon this force was increased by three more brigades and three more batteries with the arrival of Wilcox's Division.[38]

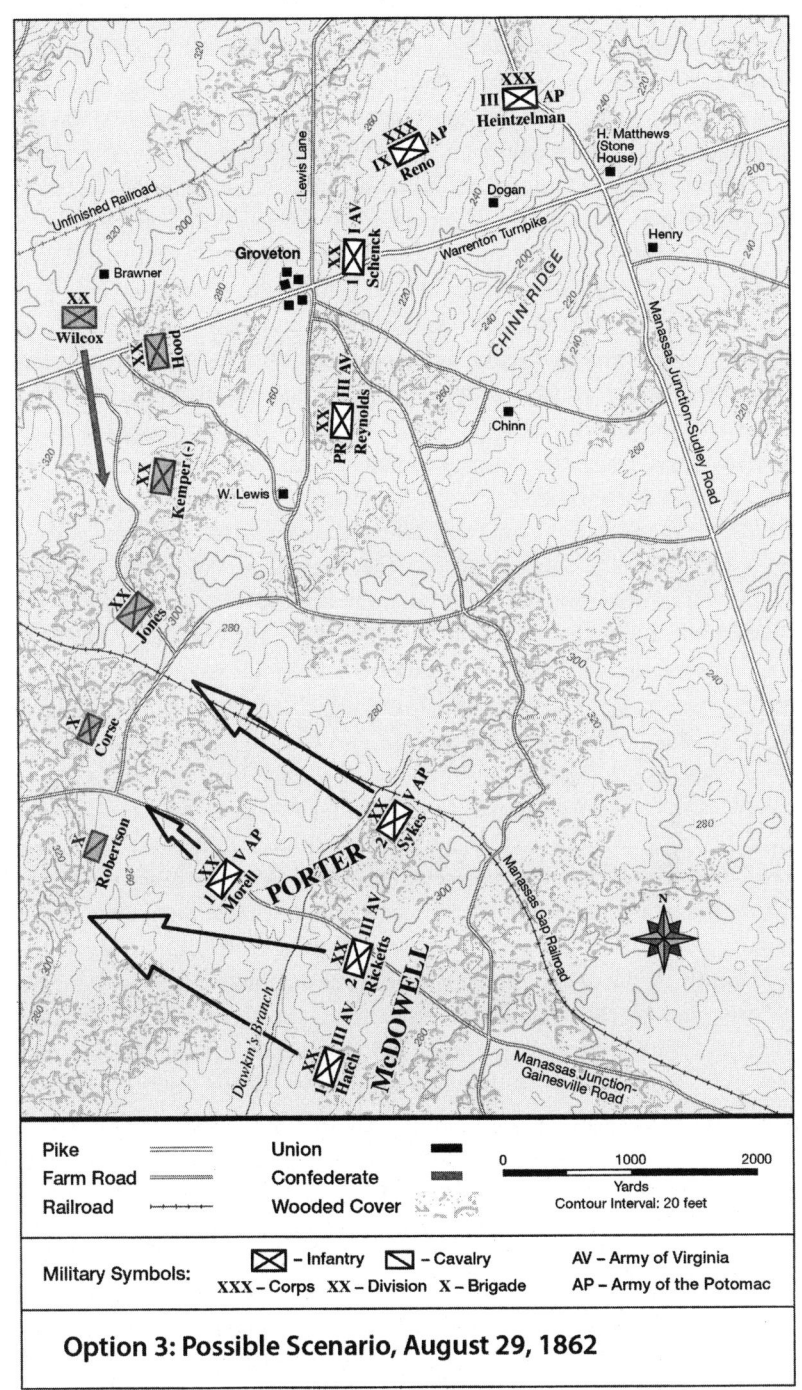

Option 3: Possible Scenario, August 29, 1862

However, this entire force would not have been available to defend against Porter and McDowell. Hood's Division of two brigades and Evans's Brigade were deployed astride the Warrenton Turnpike to block this vital road. Two brigades of Kemper's Division, on Hood's right, were in contact and skirmishing with Reynolds's division. Thus five brigades were subtracted from Longstreet's deployable force, initially leaving him four brigades to defend the south flank. This number increased to seven when Wilcox arrived.[39]

A possible scheme of maneuver for Porter and McDowell would have been for Porter to attack with McDowell held in reserve. Porter could have had Morell's three brigades attack northeast astride the Gainesville Road, with Sykes's three brigades in a follow-and-support role. As soon as Morell had developed the situation or met strong resistance, Sykes could have been committed on Morell's right (or left if necessary). This arrangement would have developed into a two-division coordinated attack, with Sykes protecting the right flank. In the event of a breakthrough, McDowell's two divisions could have been committed to exploit the success and attack into Longstreet's rear area. If Porter was unable to break the Confederate defenses to his front, McDowell's corps could have been committed on Porter's left to envelop the defenses and attack into the enemy rear area. Even if Longstreet was able to hold the south flank, the presence of Porter and McDowell would have continued to pose a significant threat. It is unlikely that Pope would have ordered Porter or McDowell to break contact and march north on the Sudley Road to his location.

The effects of Porter making this decision would have been far reaching. Essentially, a large part of the battle that day and the next day would have followed a different sequence. Concerned with defeating or stopping the attack on his south flank, Longstreet would have committed a significant amount of his combat power to that area. Even if successful, he would not have had the freedom to position his force as he did for an attack the next day. If Porter and McDowell were successful, Longstreet's divisions might have been pushed back north to just south of the Warrenton Turnpike, and then oriented to the south and southeast. In an extreme case, they might have been regrouped and redeployed on Jackson's right so as to extend that position to the southwest. Faced with attacks against Jackson and Longstreet, Lee would have had to rethink his tactical plan for the next day. Lee would have had to attack, reposition, or temporarily withdraw to gain maneuvering space with which to re-engage Pope. This measure in itself would have provided additional time for the remaining two corps (Second and Sixth) of the Army of the Potomac to come forward and reinforce Pope. The arrival of these two corps would have completed the uniting of Pope's and McClellan's armies—

exactly what Lee wanted to prevent. Or Lee might have moved farther north toward the Potomac River and commenced some version of the Maryland Campaign.

With Porter's corps decisively engaged on the south flank, it would not have been practical for Pope to bring it north and conduct the attack against Jackson's right the next day. Without this attack, and the events that immediately followed, there would have been no counterattack by Longstreet. As McDowell's corps, supporting Porter's, would also have been decisively engaged, it would not have been available to move north in the afternoon. Subsequently, Hatch's division would not have been available for the "pursuit" (attack) west on the Warrenton Turnpike.

However, none of these possible events transpired because Porter did not choose this more aggressive option. Porter's critical decision resulted in part of the battle scenario for that day and set the stage for the following day.

CHAPTER 4

DAY OF DECISION— SATURDAY, AUGUST 30, 1862

This day saw both armies concentrated and in close proximity to each other. Although heavy combat would not begin until the afternoon, once it commenced it continued with unabated fury until darkness ended the fighting. The critical decisions made on August 30 would result in a major attack, a dangerous exposure of one army's flank, a counterattack, and the near destruction of an army.

Pope Decides to Attack Again

Situation

During the night the last major units of the Army of Northern Virginia, Lieut. Col. Stephen D. Lee's artillery battalion and Maj. Gen. Richard H. Anderson's three-brigade division, reached the battlefield. Anderson's Division marched too far east on the Warrenton Turnpike, placing itself in an exposed location forward of the army. At dawn it retraced its steps and went into position behind Longstreet's left flank.[1]

Lee's army now occupied a position 7,850 yards (4.5 miles) long. On the left, Jackson's three-division Left Wing continued to hold a defensive position extending from the vicinity of the Sudley Road southwest along the "Stony Ridge" and the unfinished railroad for 3,600 yards (2.1 miles). A. P.

Hill's, Lawton's, and Starke's Divisions were situated from Jackson's left to his right. Longstreet's Right Wing, consisting of five divisions and one separate brigade, was deployed on Jackson's right. Longstreet's position reached south from just north of the Warrenton Turnpike for 4,250 yards (2.4 miles). From Longstreet's left to right, were positioned Hood's Division astride the turnpike with Evans's Brigade just behind it. Farther behind Hood and Evans were Wilcox's and Anderson's Divisions in a reserve position. To Hood's right were Kemper's Division and then D. R. Jones's Division. In the area between Jackson's right and Longstreet's left were five of the eight artillery batteries of Starke's Division under the command of Maj. Lindsay M. Shumaker, three of the six batteries of Lawton's Division, and five of the six batteries of S. D. Lee's Artillery Battalion. Jackson's and Longstreet's positions formed an obtuse angle of approximately 115 degrees.[2]

The previous day (Friday), Pope's forces were concentrated in two areas of the battlefield. Part of his army was in the northwest area formed by the intersection of the north-to-south Sudley Road and the west to east Warrenton Turnpike. The other part, Porter's Fifth Corps and McDowell's Third Corps, was located farther south astride the Manassas Junction–Gainesville Road and the Manassas Gap Railroad. That afternoon McDowell moved his two divisions (Hatch's and Ricketts's) north to the vicinity of the Warrenton Turnpike–Sudley Road intersection and joined the rest of the army. Early Saturday morning Porter was ordered to march north and rejoin the army. By 8:00 a.m. the Fifth Corps (Morell's and Sykes's divisions) began to arrive in the area of the Warrenton Turnpike–Sudley Road intersection.

Porter's and McDowell's moves concentrated the majority of Pope's army in the area north and west of the Sudley Road–Warrenton Turnpike intersection. The troops in this area were from the Army of Virginia: the two divisions of Sigel's First Corps, two of the three divisions of McDowell's Third Corps, and Milroy's Independent Brigade. The following units were attached from the Army of the Potomac: the two divisions of Heintzelman's Third Corps, two divisions of Porter's Fifth Corps, and two divisions of Reno's Ninth Corps. A division and two other brigades were just south of the Warrenton Turnpike. The two divisions of Banks's Second Corps remained near Bristoe Station and added no combat power to the fight. Although the Second and Sixth Corps from the Army of the Potomac were marching west from the vicinity of Washington and Alexandria, they would not reinforce Pope before the battle was over.[3]

By noon Pope's forces occupied a 4,200-yard-long position (2.4 miles) that made a slight arc from east of the Sudley Road southwest and south to the south side of the Warrenton Turnpike. Pope's right flank, east of the

Sudley Road, was Kearny's three-brigade division. To Kearny's left and west of the Sudley Road were two brigades of Ricketts's division. To Ricketts's left were the three brigades of Stevens's division. To Stevens's left were Reno's two-brigade division and then the two brigades of Schenck's division. Schenck's left flank touched the Warrenton Turnpike. Behind Schenck were the two brigades of Schurz's division. Porter's reinforced Fifth Corps was forward of Schenck's and Reno's position. In addition to his two divisions (Morell's and Sykes's), Porter was reinforced with Hatch's division. Porter was initially on Dogan Ridge, but he later moved forward to just east of the Groveton-Sudley Road. Porter's units were north of the turnpike, except for Warren's brigade of Sykes's division, which was south of the turnpike. Also south of the turnpike, initially along Lewis Lane (an extension of the Groveton-Sudley Road), were the three brigades of Reynolds's division. In pushing one of his brigades forward in reconnaissance, Reynolds had met so much resistance that he had withdrawn to more easily defensible terrain east of Lewis Lane.[4]

Pope's position provided him with an interior line. He was on the inside of an arc, whereas Lee was occupying the outside of an arc—an exterior line. To move units from one flank to another, Pope would travel a shorter distance than Lee. Depending on his decision as to what to do, Pope could have a distinct advantage. However, we do not know if Pope recognized this advantage or considered using it.

Throughout the morning, units from Kearny's, Ricketts's, Stevens's, and Reynolds's divisions made contact with units from Jackson's and Longstreet's Wings and met with stiff resistance. All four of these commanders reported to Pope that the Confederates were in position and in strength. The strong resistance to the Union forward moves should have indicated to Pope that Jackson was not retreating, and that Longstreet had arrived earlier than he had calculated. Moreover, Buford's report from the previous morning, which McDowell finally gave to Pope the previous night, indicated that a substantial Confederate force was moving east through Gainesville. Finally, there was the repulse of Hatch's westward "pursuit" on the Warrenton Turnpike the evening before.

While Pope decided on his course of action, the troops were positioned as described above, and he received the aforementioned information from his subordinates in contact with the enemy.

Options

As Lee had yet to take the initiative and maneuver against him, Pope had three possible courses of action. He could defend, retreat (withdraw), or attack.

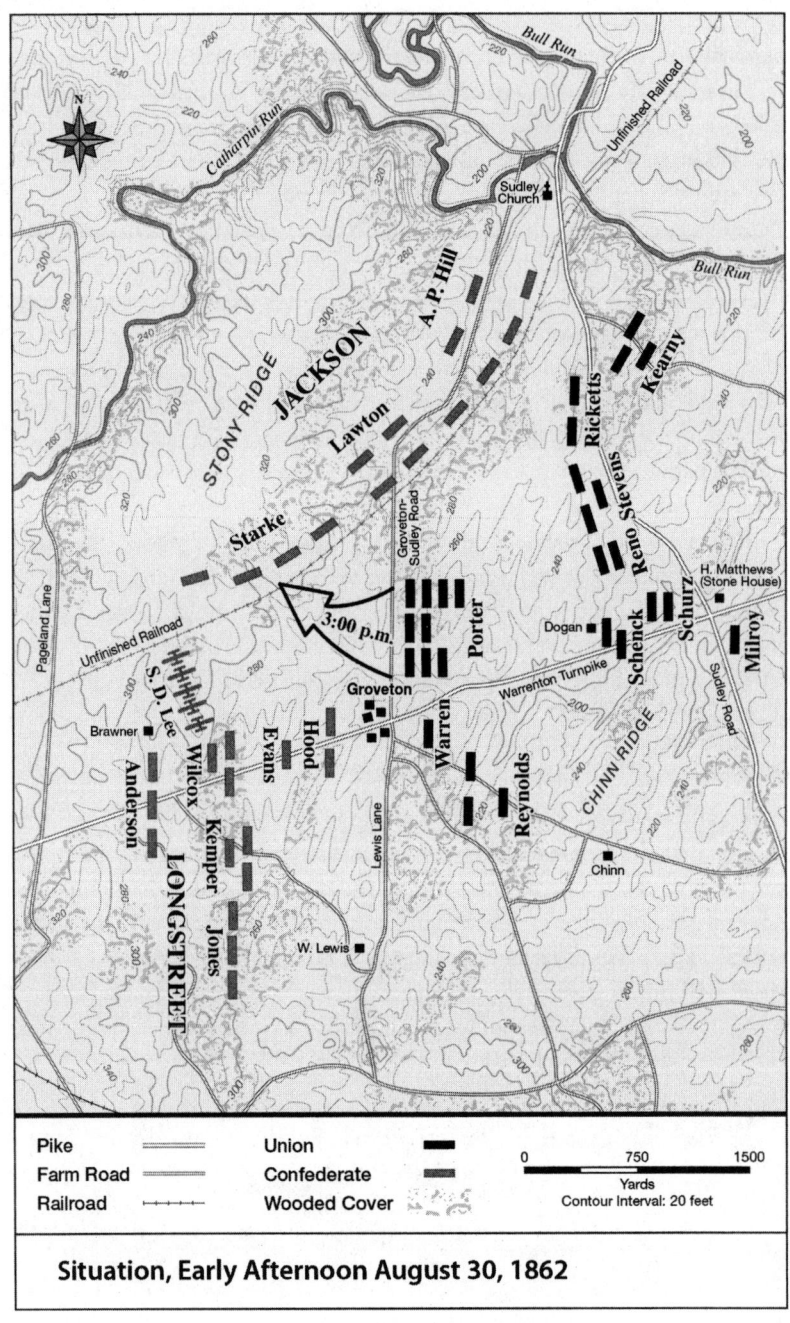

Situation, Early Afternoon August 30, 1862

Saturday, August 30, 1862

Option 1

Pope could shift from the offense to the defense. He could remain in his current position, or he could withdraw a few miles east and defend along the east side of Bull Run. This option had several advantages. Bringing his army together, except for Banks's Second Corps, had given Pope a relatively powerful force to conduct a defense. The terrain where he was positioned and the terrain just east of Bull Run provided good defensive positions. Time was on Pope's side, not Lee's. Lee's operational concept involved defeating Pope before McClellan's army joined him. A successful defense would buy Pope additional time for the remaining corps of the Army of the Potomac to reach his position and reinforce it, just what Lee was trying to prevent.

However, this plan had a major disadvantage. If Pope went over to the defense, he would give the tactical initiative to Lee. Lee might use this initiative to neutralize Pope's defense by executing another turning movement.

Option 2

Retreat (withdrawal) was another viable alternative. In the "Joint Order" issued the previous day, Pope had alerted commanders to the possibility of withdrawing east to the vicinity of Centreville to resupply the army.[5]

This option would position Pope's army that much closer to the Second and Sixth Corps (Army of the Potomac) that were marching to reinforce him. If he withdrew to Centreville, Pope would probably be reinforced late that day (Saturday, August 30) by Franklin's Sixth Corps. Sumner's Second Corps could reinforce the next day. In addition, Bank's corps at Bristoe Station would have to march northeast to Centreville to keep from being isolated, and this unit would further increase Pope's combat strength. Pope could also resupply his troops with food, ammunition, and other supplies at Centreville. As a result, Lee would be confronted by an enemy force that greatly outnumbered his army. Such a situation would mostly negate his original concept of operations and the success of the turning movement.

A disadvantage of retreat was that Pope would lose contact with Lee's army. Lee would then have the capability to maneuver in any direction and manner he wished to gain an advantage for future operations. Also, the Northern population and politicians might perceive Pope's withdrawal as an admission of defeat, a sign that his troops had been driven from the battlefield.

Option 3

Pope's last option was to attack, and he had several choices as to location. An attack against A. P. Hill's, and the army's, left flank had the potential to

View of the center of Porter's attack on the afternoon of August 30, 1862. Note the lone monument on the higher ground in the center of the photograph. Photo by the authors.

overrun the defenders and roll up Hill's brigades and others. Attacking with his right would require blocking positions on the army's left. Pope's interior line would give him an advantage in moving additional troops for the attack and to blocking positions. This interior line would also facilitate the placement and commitment of a reserve. Though it was less desirable, an attack could be made in the center or right center of Jackson's position to attempt a breakthrough.

Pope would have the initiative if he attacked, and he might severely disrupt Lee's defensive position. However, Lee might be able to take advantage of his longer position and effectively counterattack. Additionally, many of Pope's brigades and divisions had taken serious casualties the day before, and sufficient combat power might not be available for a successful attack.

Decision

Pope decided to resume offensive operations with an attack followed by a pursuit. He made this decision based upon the incorrect assumption that the enemy in his front was retreating or preparing to retreat. Four separate reports that the Confederates were still occupying a strong position were discounted or ignored by Pope. Pope fixated on the idea that Jackson had been attempting to retreat the previous day and the morning of this day. Nothing could change his mind. In addition, despite information to the contrary, Pope

Saturday, August 30, 1862

View of Porter's attack on August 30, 1862 as seen from the positions of Johnson's and Stafford's Brigades along the unfinished railroad. Photo by the authors.

completely discounted the possibility that Longstreet's Right Wing had arrived and Lee's army was now reunited.

Results/Impact

To implement this decision, Pope ordered Porter and his reinforced Fifth Corps to attack the right and right center of Jackson's position along the unfinished railroad. Porter's forces for this attack were the three brigades of Sykes's division, two brigades of Morell's division commanded by Brig. Gen. Daniel Butterfield, and the four brigades of Hatch's division from McDowell's Third Corps. This critical decision by Pope sent Porter's units into a poorly conceived, unsupported attack against a strongly defended position. The results were disastrous.

At 3:00 p.m. on August 30, Porter ordered his troops, who were on the north side of the Warrenton Turnpike, forward to attack the right and right center of Jackson's defensive position. The brigades (Weeks's, Roberts's, and Sullivan's) in the forward line of attack came out of the woods, crossed the Groveton-Sudley Road, and began to cross the 525-yard field separating them from the Confederate defenses along the unfinished railroad. Once in this exposed position, they were subjected to deadly, sustained enfilading fire from Col. Stephen D. Lee's artillery battalion and other artillery batteries 1,300 yards to their left. As they approached the unfinished railroad position,

Porter's men were then subjected to a heavy volume of fire from the defending infantry. Under this combined fire and with supporting units unable to move forward, the attack faltered then collapsed.[6]

The failure of Porter's attack and the subsequent confusing but short retreat set in motion a chain of events that would deny Pope the victory and nearly cost him his army.

McDowell Decides to Reposition Troops

Situation

As a result of the previous critical decision, Porter's reinforced Fifth Corps attacked the right and right center of Jackson's position along the unfinished railroad. Frontal and flanking Confederate fire broke up and repelled this attack. The repulse of the attack forced the forward attacking brigades on a confusing retreat across the open ground they had just crossed. Once again, these soldiers were under sustained enfilading fire from the Confederate artillery. Along the Groveton-Sudley Road what should have been supporting units for the attack were deployed to stop the retreat. The retreating troops went through this position and continued east across open fields to the main

Brigadier General Robert H. Milroy, USA, Commanding Independent Brigade, First Corps, Army of Virginia. Library of Congress.

Union position. There, they were eventually stopped. Porter's remaining units along the Groveton-Sudley Road drove back a limited Confederate counterattack and then withdrew eastward.[7]

During Porter's attack on the north side of the turnpike, the area to the south of the turnpike was occupied by six Union brigades. Farthest west and closest to Longstreet's Right Wing was Col. Gouverneur K. Warren's two-regiment Third Brigade of Sykes's division. Four brigades were positioned nine hundred yards east on Chinn Ridge: the three brigades of Brig. Gen. John F. Reynolds's Pennsylvania Reserves Division, with four batteries of artillery, and Col. Nathaniel C. McLean's four-regiment Second Brigade of Schenck's division, with one battery of artillery. Brig. Gen. Robert H. Milroy's four-regiment Independent Brigade was stationed 1,300 yards northeast of Chinn Ridge, at the base of Henry Hill.[8]

Maj. Gen. Irvin McDowell was able to observe much of Porter's attack. He saw the soldiers as they were driven back, the flight eastward of the disorganized units that had crossed the open field under artillery and infantry fire, and the limited counterattack by some of the Confederate defenders. He apparently did not see the repulse of the counterattack and the stabilization of the retreating units along the main Union position near the Sudley Road. McDowell was concerned that the Confederate counterattack, closely following the retreating Fifth Corps troops, would drive into the Union position north of the Warrenton Turnpike and create an even worse situation.

Options

In response to the situation as he viewed it, McDowell had two options: take no action or redeploy units.

Option 1

McDowell had the option of not doing anything. A closer analysis of the situation might show him that while the situation north of the turnpike was chaotic, it was being brought under control. This choice would keep Reynolds's division in the Chinn Ridge defensive position or, if necessary, send it to attack north across the Warrenton Turnpike into the flank of any Confederate counterattack during Porter's retreat.

Option 2

McDowell's other option was to redeploy troops from the south side of the turnpike to the north side. Additional combat power would then be positioned to stop any Confederate counterattack that continued beyond the

Groveton-Sudley Road. However, a limited number of units were located south of the turnpike. Shifting any of these troops north would appreciably weaken the minimal combat power on Pope's left flank. Considering the strength and location of Longstreet's Right Wing, this action would be extremely dangerous.

Decision

Acting impulsively and forgetting that a large enemy force (Longstreet's) might be south of the turnpike, or, like his commander, possibly not believing these troops were there, McDowell decided to take action. Analysis of the situation might have convinced McDowell that he did not need to do anything; the situation north of the turnpike was being controlled. However, McDowell decided to shift troops to the north side of the turnpike. Among the critical decisions made during the campaign and battle, this one had the potential to destroy Pope's army.

Results/Impact

McDowell ordered Reynolds to move his division north of the Warrenton Turnpike. Reynolds's division immediately began moving north along Chinn

Brigadier General John F. Reynolds, USA, Commanding Pennsylvania Reserve Division, Third Corps, Army of Virginia. Library of Congress.

Saturday, August 30, 1862

Position of Reynolds's division on the south slope of Chinn Ridge at midafternoon August 30, 1862. Photo by the authors.

Ridge and crossed the turnpike. Though this division's departure removed three brigades and four batteries from the defense of this area, one brigade and a battery would return. When Longstreet ordered the five divisions, totaling fifteen brigades, of his Right Wing forward, there were only three, later four, Union brigades and two artillery batteries south of the Warrenton Turnpike. None of these brigades was in coordinated or supporting positions with the others.[9]

Henry Hill was the terrain objective of Longstreet's attack. It was one of the most important pieces of key terrain on the battlefield, maybe even the most important one. This hill, where the visitor center is today, overlooked the Warrenton Turnpike and Sudley Road, the intersection of these roads, and the section of the turnpike that extended east from that intersection to Bull Run, the Stone Bridge, and on to Centreville. As such, Henry Hill controlled a north-south road that continued along the Union position and a vital intersection. More importantly, it controlled Pope's major route of retreat. If this hill was occupied by a sizeable Confederate force, much of Pope's army would be cut off and susceptible to capture or destruction.[10]

When McDowell moved Reynolds's division to the north side of the Warrenton Turnpike, he reduced the defensive capability on the south side to almost nothing. With an overwhelming force, Longstreet now commenced an attack in this area that was designed to capture and control Henry Hill, just 3,600 yards (2.04 miles) from his forward units. The attack began at 3:45 p.m. Longstreet's troops had three and one-half hours to capture Henry Hill.[11]

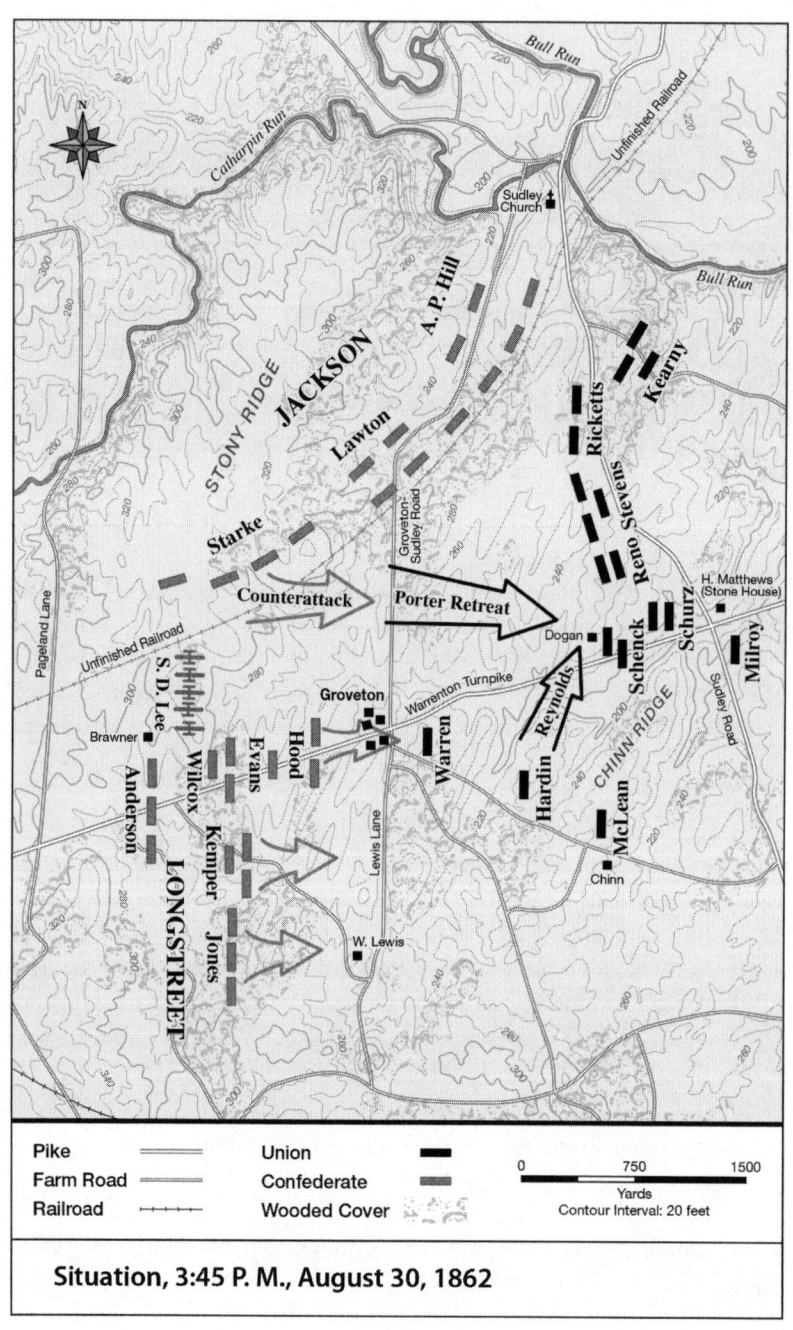

Situation, 3:45 P.M., August 30, 1862

View east along the Warrenton Turnpike at the Sudley Road intersection. From left to right: Stone House, the intersection, and north slope of Henry Hill. Photo by the authors.

The sequence of events for the remainder of the afternoon would flow from this critical decision.

McLean Decides to Defend Chinn Ridge

Situation

Throughout the morning, Reynolds's Pennsylvania Reserves had conducted reconnaissance south of the turnpike. Skirmishers deployed along Lewis Lane and probing west had revealed the presence of a strong enemy force. At midday Reynolds decided his forward position was too vulnerable and withdrew east to Chinn Ridge.[12]

On the night of August 29 and the morning of August 30, Col. Nathaniel C. McLean's Second Brigade of Schenck's First Division from the Army of Virginia's First Corps occupied a position three hundred yards east of the Warrenton Turnpike–Sudley Road intersection. The brigade's left flank rested on the turnpike. At noon McLean was ordered to send one regiment (Fifty-fifth Ohio) south of the turnpike to form a connection with Reynolds's division. At 2:00 p.m. McLean was ordered to follow with the reminder of his brigade (Twenty-fifth, Seventy-third, and Seventy-fifth Ohio) and the four 10-pound Parrott Rifles of Capt. Michael Wiedrich's Battery I, First New York Artillery. The Ohio regiments and New York artillery crossed the turnpike and joined the Fifty-fifth Ohio on Chinn Ridge. The Union position on Chinn Ridge then consisted of four brigades and five artillery batteries. This force could be expected to conduct a defense that could stop any initial Confederate attack and protect Pope's left flank from an envelopment.[13]

Two other brigades were established south of the Warrenton Turnpike. Nine hundred yards forward of the Chinn Ridge position, Warren's two-regiment brigade, the left flank brigade of Sykes's division, occupied an exposed position. Milroy's Independent Brigade was at the base of Henry Hill, 1,300 yards northeast of (and behind) Chinn Ridge. Neither of these brigades was coordinated with or supporting the troops on Chinn Ridge.[14]

Prior to Porter's attack, Longstreet's Right Wing was formed and prepared to strike Pope's position south of the Warrenton Turnpike. Longstreet was on Jackson's right, with an open obtuse angle between the two wings. In the forward units was Brig. Gen. John B. Hood's two-brigade division, which was astride the turnpike. Brig. Gen. Nathan G. Evans's Independent Brigade was positioned just behind Hood for support. To Hood's right was Brig. Gen. James Kemper's three-brigade division. To Kemper's right was Brig. Gen. David R. Jones's three-brigade division. Brig. Gen. Cadmus M. Wilcox's three-brigade division occupied a reserve position just north of the turnpike. An additional reserve, Maj. Gen. Richard H. Anderson's three-brigade division, was positioned farther back. Longstreet's attack formation had a frontage of 4,250 yards (2.4 miles).[15]

As discussed with regard to the two previous critical decisions, Porter's attack began at 3:00 p.m. and within 45 minutes had been defeated and driven back. Brigades on Jackson's right conducted limited counterattacks but were stopped. In response to Porter's repulse, McDowell ordered Reynolds to move his division from Chinn Ridge to the north side of the turnpike.

At 4:00 p.m. Longstreet ordered his Right Wing, south of the turnpike, to attack. Two events then occurred almost simultaneously. Warren's brigade was attacked by Hood's Texas Brigade, and McDowell tried to return Reynolds's division back to Chinn Ridge. In a short period of time Warren was outflanked and overrun, and the survivors fled to the east. Casualties in this brigade were 299 out of 490 troops in one regiment and 115 in the other regiment of comparable size.[16]

McDowell realized his mistake and went in search of Reynolds to return his division to the south side of the turnpike. But it was too late. Two of the brigades and three of the artillery batteries had already crossed the turnpike. McDowell was able to intercept Reynolds's Third Brigade, commanded by Col. Martin D. Hardin, and Capt. Mark Kerns's Battery G, First Pennsylvania Artillery, and he ordered them into a position between Warren and McLean. Hardin's four regiments and Kerns's four 10-pound Parrotts occu-

Saturday, August 30, 1862

Colonel Gouverneur K. Warren, USA, Commanding Third Brigade, Second Division, Fifth Corps, Army of the Potomac. Library of Congress.

pied their new position just in time to be violently struck by Hood's Brigade. Hardin's brigade was driven off its position with 321 casualties and the loss of all of Kerns's guns.[17]

After overrunning Hardin's position, three regiments of the Texas Brigade continued their attack toward Chinn Ridge. They were closely followed and reinforced by Evans's Brigade.[18]

The only force between the attacking Confederates and Henry Hill, other than Milroy's brigade on Henry Hill, was McLean's brigade on Chinn Ridge. Nathaniel C. McLean, forty-seven years old at the time of Second Manassas, was born in 1815 in Ridgefield, Ohio. After graduating from Harvard in 1838, he moved to Cincinnati and practiced law. In 1861 McLean was commissioned the colonel of the Seventy-fifth Ohio. Prior to Second Manassas he had fought with his regiment in the engagement at McDowell, Virginia. McLean was promoted to brigadier general in November 1862. He then fought at Chancellorsville, received an assignment to the Department of the Ohio, and participated in the Atlanta Campaign and the later part of Sherman's campaign in North Carolina. He resigned his commission in April 1865 and returned to his law practice in Cincinnati. McLean died in 1905.[19]

Colonel McLean's brigade had been ordered to Chinn Ridge to support Reynolds and connect Reynolds's right with the remainder of the army north

Colonel Nathaniel C. McLean, USA, Commanding Second Brigade, First Division, First Corps, Army of Virginia. USAMHI.

of the Warrenton Turnpike. He was surprised by the sudden departure of Reynolds's division, which negated the original purpose of his brigade's being sent to Chinn Ridge.

Options

After Reynolds's departure McLean had three options: he could move his brigade with Reynolds's division, move to a less exposed location, or remain in position.

Option 1

McLean could move with Reynolds's division. As he had received no additional orders from his division commander or from Reynolds, McLean could assume that a situation north of the turnpike required reinforcements his men could provide. If they followed Reynolds, McLean's troops would be north of the turnpike and possibly used to reinforce the defense of Henry Hill. However, McLean's movement across the turnpike would also remove the last Union force interposed between the attacking Confederates and Henry Hill. As a result, Longstreet's Wing would have an interrupted avenue of approach to this piece of key terrain and its weak defenses. In addition, there probably would not be sufficient time to adequately reinforce the Henry Hill defenders.

Option 2

Alternatively, McLean could move his brigade back east to Henry Hill and join Milroy's brigade. This measure would initially position two brigades to defend Henry Hill. They might successfully perform this task until reinforced. However, this option again abandoned defensible terrain on Chinn Ridge and provided the Confederates an uncontested avenue of approach to key terrain. It also would have allowed the right units of Longstreet's attack freedom of maneuver to envelop the defenses on Henry Hill.

Option 3

Finally, McLean could keep his brigade in position on Chinn Ridge. This would keep an organized force between the Confederate attack and Henry Hill. Defending on Chinn Ridge would buy some valuable time so that the one brigade on Henry Hill, Milroy's, could be reinforced. The additional time would also allow McLean to be reinforced on the Chinn Ridge position. Continued defense on this ridge would delay enemy forces' arrival at Henry Hill and reduce the daylight hours available for attack. In addition, any Confederate force that the defense held up and disorganized, if only temporarily, might not have sufficient strength to successfully attack the Henry Hill defenses.

The weakness of this option was that McLean's brigade would initially be in an exposed and unsupported position until reinforcements arrived, if they ever did. A strong first attack against his position might overrun the brigade or drive it off the ridge. In this case, the attacking force might reach Henry Hill before the Union reinforcements. Furthermore, McLean's defensive frontage was not as wide as Longstreet's attack. Therefore, Confederate units on the right of the attack could easily bypass the defenses, isolate McLean, and strike Henry Hill from the south rather than the west.

Decision

Col. McLean decided to defend from his position on Chinn Ridge to buy time for the Henry Hill defenses to be reinforced. From 4:30 to 6:00 p.m. this position was like a magnet drawing Union reinforcements and Confederate attacking units into the fight.

Results/Impact

The first attacks were frontal attacks by parts of Hood's and Evans's Brigades against the west-facing defenders. When Longstreet's attack commenced, Kemper's Division was deployed to Hood's right (south). The division was

Day of Decision

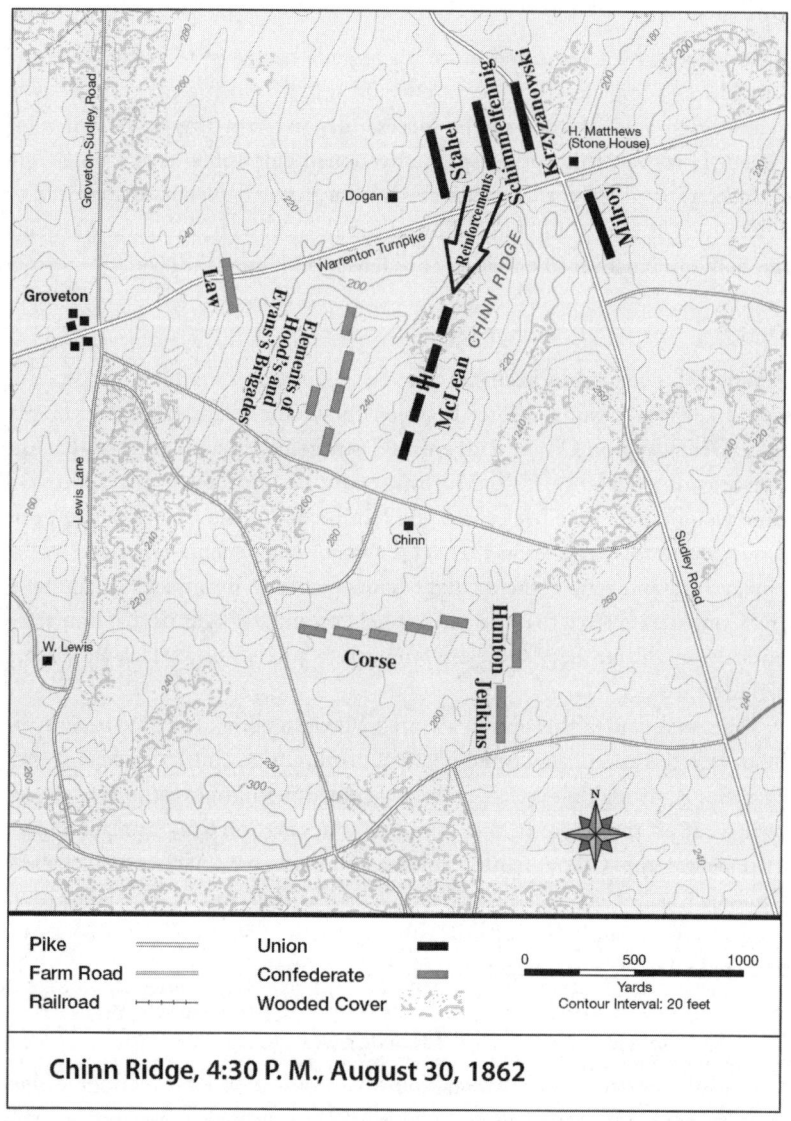

Chinn Ridge, 4:30 P. M., August 30, 1862

in a two-line formation with Col. Eppa Hunton's brigade (on the left) and Brig. Gen. Micah Jenkins's brigade (on the right) in the first line. The second and supporting line was Col. Montgomery D. Corse's brigade. Kemper's Division's avenue of approach should have passed south of Chinn Ridge to the Sudley Road, then turned north and struck Henry Hill from the southwest. No Union force directly blocked this division's route of attack. When

Saturday, August 30, 1862

Colonel Montgomery D. Corse, CSA, Commanding Kemper's (Corse's) Brigade, Kemper's Division, Longstreet's Right Wing, Army of Northern Virginia. National Archives.

Kemper's Division passed south of Chinn Ridge, Colonel Hunton attempted to turn his brigade to the left and attack McLean's left (south) flank. He was initially unsuccessful, but, following him, Colonel Corse was able to wheel his brigade left and attack toward McLean's flank.[20]

In response to this threat, McLean repositioned his brigade so that it faced southwest. Hunton was eventually able to turn his brigade, and he joined Corse in the attack. Jenkins then turned his brigade to the north and reinforced Corse and Hunton. In the meantime, McLean had been reinforced with Brig. Gen. Zealous B. Tower's Second Brigade from Ricketts's division. Ricketts's Third Brigade, commanded by Col. John W. Stiles, reinforced the Chinn Ridge defense shortly thereafter.[21]

The attack was then reinforced by Col. Henry L. Benning's brigade from Jones's Division. As the defenders were being driven back, Col. John A. Koltes's brigade and then Col. Wladimir Krzyzanowski's brigade arrived and joined the fight. Eventually, the Confederates flanked these last defenders, and the Union force retreated from Chinn Ridge. However, these Union brigades had bought valuable time for Pope to dispatch units to Henry Hill. The defenses on that hill increased from one brigade to six.[22]

Including his own troops, McLean's critical decision brought five Union brigades, five Confederate brigades and part of another Confederate brigade

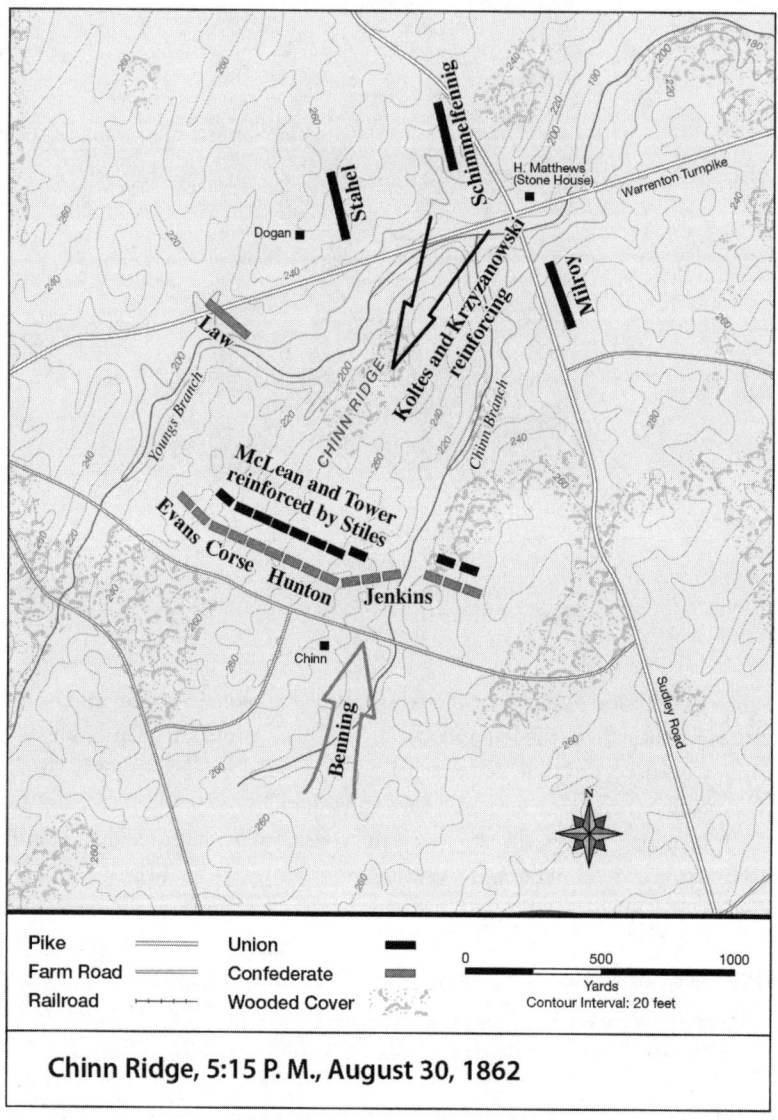

Chinn Ridge, 5:15 P. M., August 30, 1862

into the fight for Chinn Ridge. Four Confederate brigades and part of a fifth would take so many casualties, become so disorganized, and expend so much ammunition that they could not continue on and attack the Henry Hill position. Of the Confederate brigades attacking the Chinn Ridge position, only Benning's Brigade would have the strength and cohesiveness to continue the offensive.

Saturday, August 30, 1862

Colonel Henry L. Benning, CSA, Commanding Toombs's (Benning's) Brigade, Jones's Division, Longstreet's Right Wing, Army of Northern Virginia. Library of Congress.

In the normal course of events, Evans's Brigade and part of Hood's, as the ridge was across their avenue of approach, should have attacked McLean's position. Even the left turn by Corse's brigade to hit the flank was a justified commitment of forces. However, the commitment of Hunton's, Jenkins's, and Benning's Brigades to this attack was a misuse of available combat power. Henry Hill, not Chinn Ridge, was the true objective of Longstreet's attack. These brigades should have continued on east, crossed the Sudley Road, and enveloped and attacked the defenses on Henry Hill. Their failure to do so gave Pope time to reinforce Henry Hill and reduced the combat power of the attacks there. It also allowed valuable time to slip away.

Alternate Decision and Scenario

The importance of McLean's critical decision is emphasized if we explore what might have transpired had he chosen differently. If McLean had followed Reynolds's division or fallen back to the better position at Henry Hill and joined Milroy, the sequence of events from that point on would have been completely different.

In this alternate scenario, assume that McLean redeployed his brigade to Henry Hill after Reynolds had marched to the north side of the Warrenton Turnpike. This decision would have been better than following Porter, and it would have positioned McLean's brigade with Milroy's on good, defensible terrain. Also assume that McDowell redirected Hardin's brigade and returned it south of the turnpike. At this point there would have only been

Nineteenth-century view of the Sudley Road as it passes along west edge of Henry Hill. View is to the north. Sudley Road intersection with the Warrenton Turnpike is in left background; Stone House is to the right. Library of Congress.

two brigades—Warren's and Harden's—south of the turnpike and west of the Sudley Road (and Henry Hill) to confront Longstreet's attack.

Reinforced by Evans's Brigade, Hood's Texas Brigade would have initially swept aside Warren's small brigade and then proceeded on and overrun Hardin's position. This action would have left no Union defenders west of Henry Hill. Hood and Evans would have then maneuvered unopposed, except for Union artillery in the vicinity of the Dogan House, on to Chinn Ridge. Once Chinn Ridge was occupied, the Confederate force there could have served in a multifunctional role. It could have protected the left flank of the remainder of Longstreet's attack, served as a pivot for those units to envelop the Union defenders on Henry Hill, and conducted a supporting attack toward Henry Hill at the appropriate time.

In the meantime, Kemper's and Jones's Divisions could have maneuvered unopposed to the Sudley Road and crossed it, then wheeled left (north) and flanked or enveloped the Henry Hill defenders. Maj. Gen. Richard H. Anderson's three-brigade division entered the attack late in the afternoon. This unit could have joined in the action on the western side of the hill, reinforced the envelopment, or maneuvered farther east and deeper into Pope's rear area.

Had McLean chosen this alternate option, the sequence of the fighting south of the turnpike and on Henry Hill would have been totally different. Henry Hill's capture would have been highly probable. As a result, a major portion of Pope's army would have been cut off and destroyed or captured.

Saturday, August 30, 1862

Col. Nathaniel C. McLean's critical decision to remain on Chinn Ridge prevented this alternate scenario from happening. His choice played a prominent role in saving Pope's army and began the sequence of events that would define the battle for the rest of the day—from about 4:30 p.m. to 6:45 p.m. The actions resulting from McLean's decision bought Pope time to reinforce Henry Hill, prevented the hill's capture, and kept open Pope's route of retreat across Bull Run.

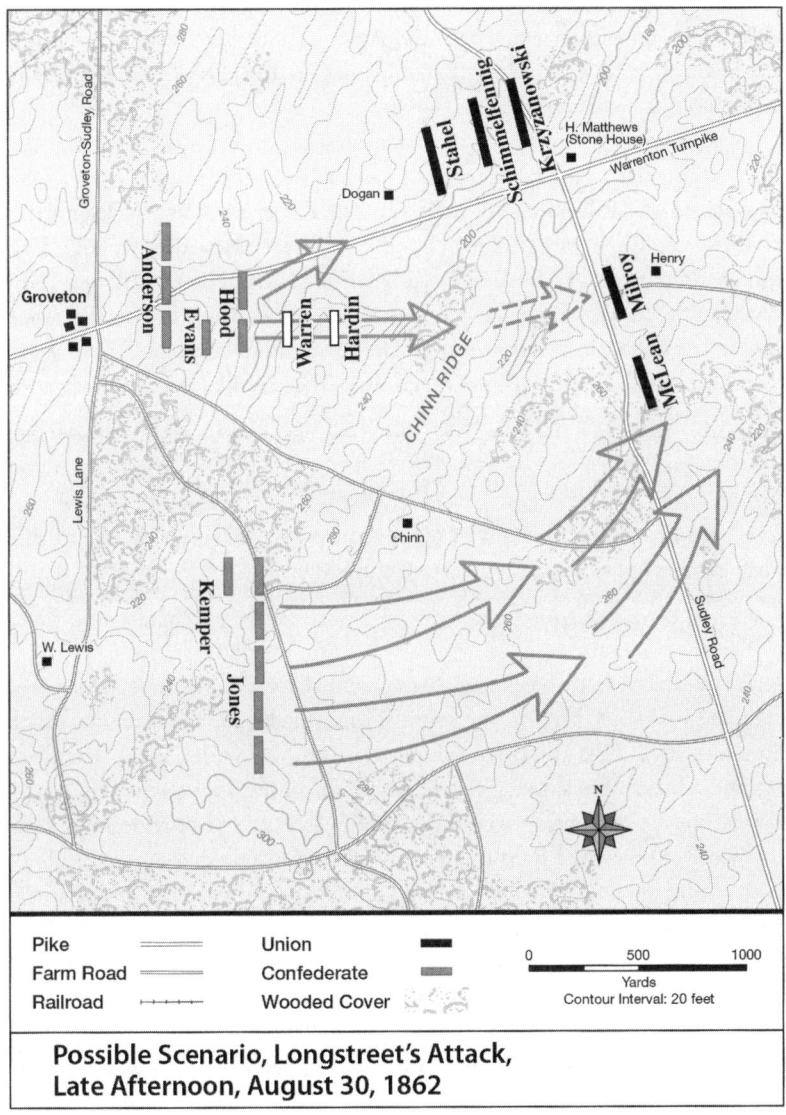

Possible Scenario, Longstreet's Attack, Late Afternoon, August 30, 1862

Pope Decides to Retreat

Situation

Pope's Army of Virginia and the reinforcements from the Army of the Potomac had been engaged with the Army of Northern Virginia since late Thursday afternoon (August 28). On Friday (August 29), Pope concentrated his forces and conducted a series of day-long piecemeal attacks against Jackson's position on the "Stony Ridge." On his south flank he attempted to have Porter maneuver toward Gainesville, envelop Jackson's position, and cut him off. Meanwhile, unbeknown to Pope, the Army of Northern Virginia reunited when Longstreet's Right Wing, accompanied by Lee, arrived and went into position on Jackson's right.

On Saturday (August 30) Pope renewed the fight. Still believing, despite intelligence to the contrary, that Jackson was attempting to retreat and Longstreet was still en route, Pope ordered Porter to attack Jackson. This attack was repulsed, and McDowell incorrectly repositioned Reynolds's division. A desperate fight for Chinn Ridge ensued, and Henry Hill was reinforced. At 6:00 p.m. Pope's and Lee's armies were engaged generally along the Sudley Road, north and south of the Warrenton Turnpike. There was a little over one hour of daylight remaining. The day had pretty much gone against Pope; he now had to make another decision.

Options

Pope's options were to remain in his current position, withdraw a short distance to a new position, or retreat to Centreville.

Option 1

Pope could choose to remain in his current defensive position, which was anchored by Henry Hill on the south. From this location it extended north along a series of hills and small ridges parallel to the Sudley Road. The Confederate attacks were slowing down, and it was only a short time until night. The darkness would bring a cessation of the attacks and provide Pope time to prepare to renew the fight the next morning. He would occupy a good defensive location along the Sudley Road, and he would have the advantage of fighting from it if Lee continued to attack. However, additional troops would have to be sent to Henry Hill.

Two other corps from the Army of the Potomac were marching to reinforce Pope. As time went by, they closed their distance from Pope's army. The Sixth Corps was already at Centreville, and the Second Corps was expected to arrive there the next day. Both corps could be expected to reach Pope on Sunday (August 31).

This disadvantage of this option was that Lee might decide to maneuver against one or both of Pope's flanks the next day. This move could drive the Union defenders up against Bull Run, trap part of the Union army, and increase casualties.

Option 2

Pope could decide to withdraw a short distance and establish a new position on the ground just east of Bull Run. The low hills that ran parallel to Bull Run would provide a good defensive position. Bull Run would also provide a natural obstacle in front of the defenses. Withdrawing a short distance would provide Pope's troops with a short standoff distance and gain them time to organize a good position. In addition, supplies and ammunition could also be brought forward from Centreville.

A defensive position along Bull Run would be even closer to the corps marching to reinforce Pope. The Sixth Corps at Centreville could march and reach his position in about three hours. When it reached Centreville the next day, the Second Corps could continue marching and join Pope. He would gain two additional divisions initially and another two soon afterward. Sizeable reinforcements were marching to join Lee, but they would not begin to arrive until after the battle was over. If Lee was going to resume attacking or maneuvering against Pope, he would have to do it with the forces at hand.[22]

Maj. Gen. Nathaniel Banks's two-division Second Corps was still at Bristoe Station—eleven miles away. A night march of five or six hours could bring units from that corps to a supporting and reinforcing distance if either the first or second option was chosen.

Option 3

Pope could concede the battle to Lee and retreat six miles to Centreville, where substantial defensive positions were available. A retreat would put some space between Pope's army and Lee's. The time and distance gained could be profitably used to regroup and resupply. At Centreville Pope would find the Army of the Potomac's Sixth Corps, with the Second Corps soon arriving.

One of the disadvantages was that Pope would concede victory to Lee, an action with a variety of negative ramifications. By breaking contact with the Confederate forces, Pope was also placing Lee in a position where he could take the initiative and again conduct a turning movement or envelopment.

Union troops used the Stone Bridge to cross Bull Run during the retreat to Centreville. Library of Congress.

Decision

Pope decided to break contact with Lee and retreat to Centreville. Not all of Pope's subordinate commanders, among them corps commander Maj. Gen. Franz Sigel, division commander Brig. Gen. George W. Sykes, and brigade commander Brig. Gen. Robert H. Milroy, agreed with this choice. Between 5:30 and 6:00 p.m. Pope ordered his subordinates to withdraw a short distance and be prepared to depart. At 8:00 p.m. the order for the army to retreat to Centreville was sent out.[23]

Results/Impact

As soon as they received Pope's order to retreat, units broke contact with the Confederate forces in their vicinity and proceeded east. Many crossed Bull Run at the Stone Bridge, while others used available fords. A number of units reached Centreville that night, and the remainder arrived the next day (August 31).

Maj. Gen. John Pope's critical decision to retreat to Centreville brought the Second Battle of Manassas to a close. That night Lee sent a telegram to President Jefferson Davis, declaring, "This army achieved today on the plains of Manassas a signal victory over the combined forces of Genls. McClellan and Pope." The battle was over, but the campaign was not. Lee had other plans.[24]

CHAPTER 5

THE CAMPAIGN CONTINUES—
SUNDAY, AUGUST 31
TO TUESDAY, SEPTEMBER 2, 1862

The last day of August and the beginning of September saw the final days of the campaign. Since the Battle of Cedar Mountain on August 9, Lee had moved the center of the war in Virginia from the vicinity of Richmond and the central part of the state to within thirty miles of Washington. He would move it even closer. These three days would see Lee order another turning movement against Pope as his army retreated toward Washington. On the last of these days, Lee would make a decision that would end the campaign but position his army to capitalize on its successes.

Lee Decides on Another Turning Movement

Situation

In the late afternoon and early evening of August 30, Pope's army had defended positions along the line of the Sudley Road, north and south of the Warrenton Turnpike. After dark, Maj. Gen. John Pope ordered a retreat to Centreville, where there were prepared defensive positions. Pope's army arrived at Centreville that night and the following day and was reinforced by the Second and Sixth Corps of the Army of the Potomac.[1]

Pope's retreat left Gen. Robert E. Lee in possession of the battlefield and a tactical victory. This victory had moved the war in Virginia from Richmond and central Virginia to near Washington, DC. However, Lee had not accomplished all that he intended. He was now faced with another decision.

Options

Lee had four choices as to his next actions. First, he could directly pursue Pope, regain contact, and attack him near Centreville. Second, he could remain where he was on or in the vicinity of the battlefield and await developments. Third, after recovering as much abandoned Union equipment and supplies as possible, he could move his army away from the battlefield in either a north, west, or south direction. Fourth, Lee could again resort to maneuver (a turning movement) and attempt to cut Pope off from Washington and bring him to battle away from the Centreville defenses.

Option 1

If Lee decided to pursue Pope he would essentially continue the battle into another day. With his lead units and perhaps his cavalry maintaining contact with the Union rear guard, a continuous advancing and delaying action would continue throughout the day until the Centreville defensive position was reached. This option would keep Lee's army in contact with Pope's, which would reduce Pope's ability to maneuver or rapidly retreat. Once Centreville was reached, Lee would have to attack Pope's defenses. The relative size of the two forces would not be in Lee's favor in an attack. He also lacked the necessary time and troops to conduct a siege operation.

Option 2

Lee could also remain where he was on the battlefield. In doing so, he would end the campaign and give his troops a short period of time to rest and resupply. Additionally, he could collect the weapons, ammunition, and equipment Pope had left behind when he retreated. While at this location Lee would be reinforced. The lead brigades of the "reinforcing column" from Richmond had already arrived, and the rest would arrive on September 2 and immediately thereafter. These forces included an additional three infantry divisions (ten brigades plus artillery), four artillery battalions, and one cavalry brigade—a total of about twenty-four thousand troops to offset the Army of Northern Virginia's approximately nine thousand casualties.[2]

By remaining in position, Lee would lose the momentum that he had developed since Jackson's turning movement began on August 25. In addition, he would be giving up one of the campaign's major objectives, destruction of Pope's army. If he continued to await developments, he would also surrender the advantage of the initiative.

Lincoln could not allow a Confederate army to remain so close to Washington. Political pressure would demand that action be initiated against this force. A reorganization of Union forces with Maj. Gen. George B. McClellan in command, as was actually ordered on September 2, would probably take place. McClellan and the reorganized Army of the Potomac would be expected to maneuver against Lee's army and drive it away from the capital.

Option 3

Lee could move away from the battlefield in a south, west, or north direction. Though it would end the campaign, this choice would also allow Lee to retain the initiative to some degree. Union forces would still have to respond to Lee's movements. Lee might choose this option and move north and cross into Maryland. As a result, he might have the opportunity to reengage in combat on the terrain and at the time of his choosing. Lee had successfully moved the fighting from Richmond to just outside of Washington. He and his army could take credit for this achievement and for a tactical victory on the plains of Manassas. But Lee would have to give up his objective of destroying Pope's army.

Option 4

Lee's fourth option was to continue the campaign and use another turning movement to sever Pope's route of retreat. Selecting this option kept the initiative with Lee. If successful, a large part of Pope's force might be cut off and destroyed or captured, and the political ramifications of such events happening just outside of Washington would be enormous. Lee did not have the strength to place Washington under siege. Yet he could continue to maneuver to block or destroy routes into and out of the Union capital. With the loss of a large part of Pope's army, the ability to counter Lee's maneuvering would be greatly reduced. Additional time would be needed to bring the Union army back up to strength. Lee would thus have additional time to capitalize on his success.

Decision

Lee chose to continue the campaign and conduct another turning movement. Jackson was again selected for the maneuver. Longstreet was to remain on the battlefield to keep Pope's attention focused on his wing, then follow Jackson.[3]

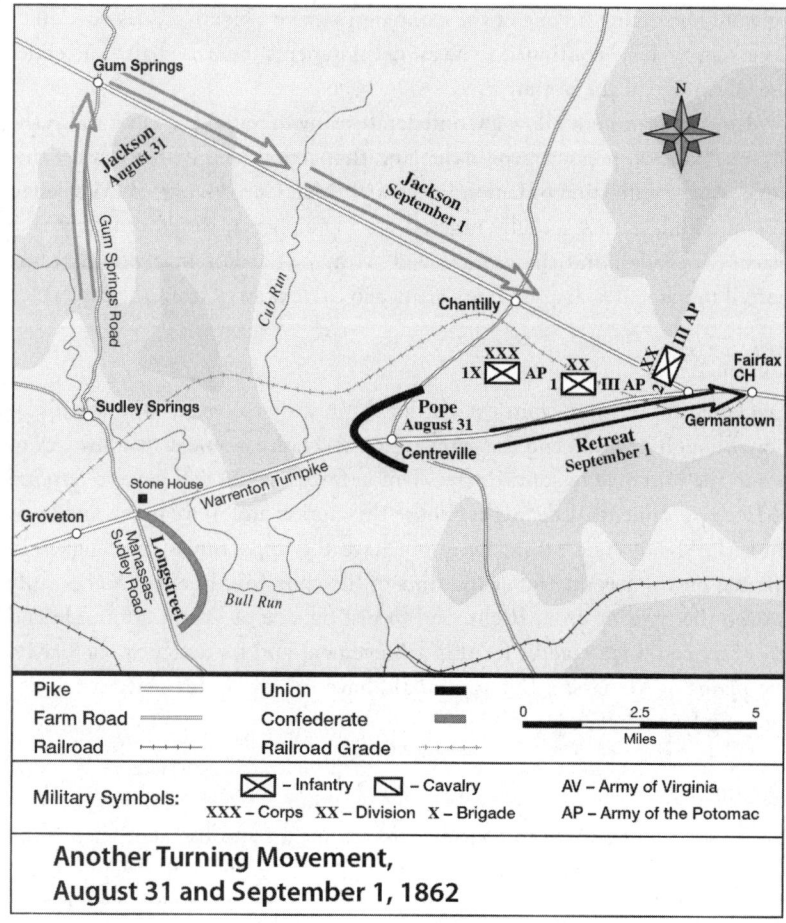

Another Turning Movement, August 31 and September 1, 1862

Result/Impact

On August 31 Jackson's Left Wing crossed Bull Run at Sudley Ford and marched eight miles north on the Gum Springs Road to the Little River Turnpike. Once on this turnpike, a thirteen-mile march southeast through Chantilly would bring Jackson to Germantown. At Germantown, one and one-half miles west of Fairfax Court House, the Little River Turnpike intersected the Warrenton Turnpike. This intersection was seven miles east of Pope's position at Centreville. Once Jackson arrived at Germantown, Pope's route of retreat to Washington would have been blocked. Longstreet followed Jackson the next day (September 1). Lee intended for Longstreet to join Jackson and for the reunited army to interpose itself between Pope's forces and Washington, where they would again decisively engage.[4]

Sunday, August 31 to Tuesday, September 2, 1862

Major General Philip Kearny, USA, Commanding First Division, Third Corps, Army of the Potomac. Killed during the Battle of Ox Hill on September 1, 1862. Library of Congress.

Brigadier General Isaac I. Stevens, Commanding First Division, Ninth Corps, Army of the Potomac. Killed during battle of Ox Hill on September 1, 1862. Library of Congress.

Things did not go as Lee planned. Rain, muddy roads, and tired troops slowed Jackson's march on the first day. After a late start, Jackson's troops covered ten miles and camped beside the Little River Turnpike. The next morning (September 1) Jackson continued to march southeast on the turnpike. However, Pope had received information that Confederate forces were marching around his right flank. In response he ordered an eight-and-one-half mile retreat to Fairfax Court House. To prevent his route from being severed, Pope sent the two divisions of the Ninth Corps (Stevens's and Reno's) supported by Kearny's division toward the Little River Turnpike. This force engaged Jackson's troops near Chantilly. With rain falling in torrents, the Battle of Chantilly (also called Ox Hill) was fought, Jackson was brought to a halt, and darkness again ended the fighting. Pope's main body of troops completed its retreat to Germantown and Fairfax Court House. The troops at Chantilly broke contact with Jackson and marched to rejoin the main body. Two Union generals, Maj. Gen. Philip Kearny and Brig. Gen. Isaac I. Stevens, were both killed during the fighting on September 1.[5]

Lee's decision to attempt a turning movement extended the campaign and fighting for another two days. Although unsuccessful, this opportunity was his last to regain contact with, fight, and damage Pope's army. If Lee had chosen any of the other options, he would have surrendered the opportunity to maneuver and strike Pope again.

Lee was now faced with one more critical decision, the last of the campaign.

Lee Decides to Redeploy His Army

Situation

When Lee assumed command of the Army of Northern Virginia on June 1, the center of the war in Virginia was just outside of Richmond. In the last week of June, Lee commenced a series of offensive operations that turned this situation upside down. The first operation, the Seven Days, drove McClellan's Army of the Potomac to the James River and eventually caused its evacuation from the Peninsula. After reorganizing his army, Lee deployed Jackson's Left Wing to central Virginia. There, on August 9, Jackson fought and halted Pope's advanced guard at Cedar Mountain. Lee then moved Longstreet's Right Wing to join Jackson.[6]

The next several weeks saw several unsuccessful attempts by Lee to envelop, trap, and decisively engage Pope's Army of Virginia. Concerned that Pope was being reinforced by units of the Army of the Potomac, on August 25 Lee sent Jackson on a turning movement around Pope's right. Jackson successfully cut Pope's supply line when he captured Bristoe Station and then the Union supply depot at Manassas Junction. These successes forced Pope to move his army back north. Lee followed Jackson's triumph by sending Longstreet along the same route to join him. Lee's maneuvering and Pope's counter-maneuvering brought on the Second Battle of Manassas, a clear victory for Lee. Lee then unsuccessfully attempted another turning movement.[7]

On September 2 Lee's army was at Chantilly. Pope's army continued to retreat, arriving at the fortified lines at Alexandria's and Washington's defensive works. Lee was now faced with the decision as to what he would do next.

Options

Lee had four options: threaten Washington by remaining in the vicinity of Fairfax and Manassas, move his army to the northwest in preparation for another campaign, move his army westward into the northern area of the Shenandoah Valley, or march back into central Virginia.

Option 1

When Pope retreated into the Washington defenses, he surrendered control of the territory west, southwest, and northwest of the Union capital to Lee.

Sunday, August 31 to Tuesday, September 2, 1862

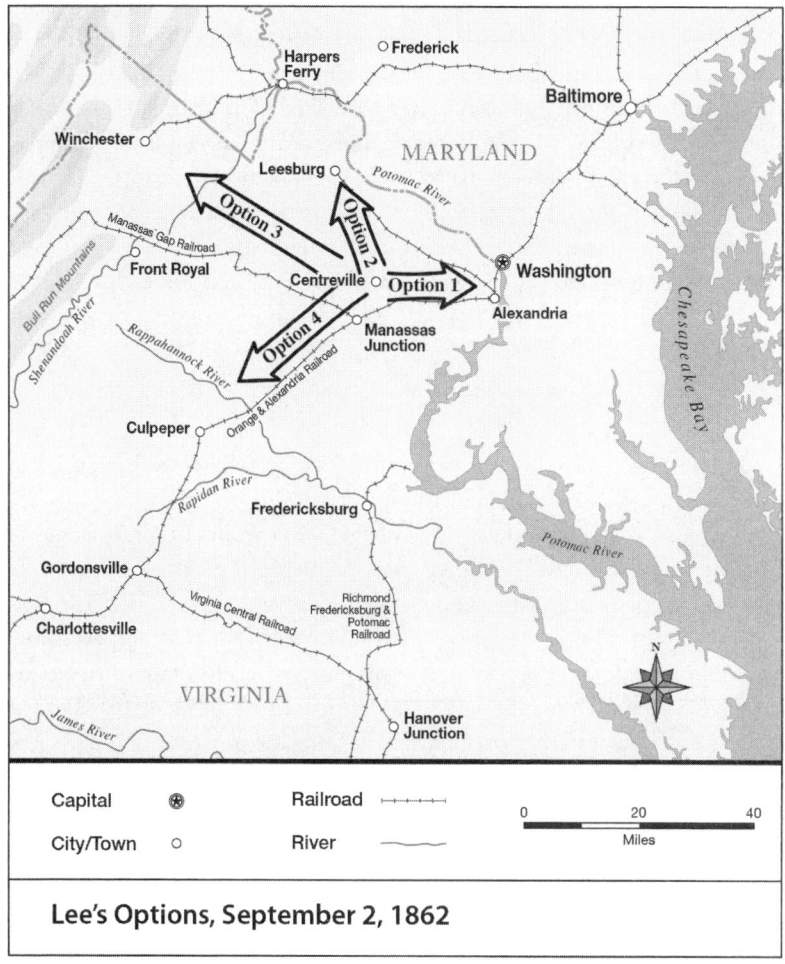

Lee's Options, September 2, 1862

Lee then had the option of remaining where he was or moving even closer to Washington. A Confederate army in close proximity to Washington and threatening it would have adverse political consequences for Lincoln's administration. The Union high command would be under enormous pressure to respond to such a threat. Accordingly, the Union army would move out from Washington and provide Lee with another opportunity to maneuver and engage them in the open.

However, this option had several disadvantages. Lee could only threaten Washington as he did not have sufficient strength to actually attack the defenses or conduct a siege. If he remained in place for very long, he would lose the initiative and operational momentum he had developed since the Seven Days.

Fairfax County, where Lee's army was, had been occupied by one army or another since 1861 and had been completely stripped of food and forage. Lee's supply line from Richmond to his army was 110 miles long. The Virginia Central Railroad and the Orange and Alexandria Railroad could move supplies for sixty miles to the Rapidan River. The bridges over the Rapidan River and the Rappahannock River to the north had been destroyed during the campaign. From this point supplies, food, forage, and ammunition would have to be transported the remaining fifty miles by wagon train. However, Lee did not have sufficient wagons to sustain such a supply line.[8]

Option 2

Additionally, Lee could move his army to the northwest. This measure would place him in a position to begin another campaign. Moreover, such a move would take Lee's army to an area that had not been extensively foraged by either Union or Confederate forces.

A position somewhere near the Potomac River would continue to pose a threat to Washington and perhaps even Baltimore. Political considerations would bring pressure on the Union high command to move against Lee. When the enemy did strike, having distance between his army and Washington would provide Lee the necessary time and space to receive a warning and formulate a plan of maneuver. Lee could also use a position along the Potomac River to continue his offensive momentum, keep the initiative, and cross into Maryland. Such a maneuver would bring the Union army after him and give him the opportunity to fight it on ground of his choosing.

The disadvantage of this plan was that Lee could not remain in his new position long. He would have to maneuver or risk having his supply line (minimal as it was) severed. The longer he remained static, the better the chances that one Union force would block the Potomac River fords from the Maryland side, while another force attacked Lee from the Virginia side. In addition, even with the arrival of the "reinforcing column" from Richmond, Lee's combat strength was considerably less than the potential strength of the Union forces around Washington.

Option 3

Another alternative was for Lee to move his army sixty-six miles west to Winchester, at the northern end of the Shenandoah Valley. Redeploying to Winchester would result in breaking contact with the Union forces around Washington. It would provide a relatively secure area in which to forage and resupply. While marching west, part of the army could also be diverted to capturing Harper's Ferry and the supplies and weapons there.

A Union army approaching this area from the east would have to travel through passes in the Bull Run and Blue Ridge Mountains. These passes could be watched by Stuart's cavalry to provide early warning of an enemy approach.

Winchester could provide a staging area for Lee to move north, cross the Potomac River, and operate in Maryland and perhaps Pennsylvania. If Union forces around Washington had not commenced moving to regain contact with Lee, crossing the river would surely bring them after him. Another Army of Northern Virginia victory while in Maryland or Pennsylvania would have tremendous negative repercussions for Lincoln's administration. This option was favored by Maj. Gen. Thomas J. Jackson.[9]

Lee would have to be careful not to remain at Winchester for too long. The absence of a threat into Maryland might result in a Union force moving south toward Richmond while another force kept a watch on Lee. Such a move would force Lee back into central Virginia and forfeit much of the campaign's gains.

Option 4

Lee's final option was to redeploy his army southwest into central Virginia. This choice would allow him to break contact with the Union forces around Washington and move into a location where he could be more efficiently supplied by railroad. Lee would also be situated to effectively block another Union overland move against Richmond. From this area he could resume offensive operation in several directions.

However, such redeployment would give up much of the gains from the campaign and would reduce the threat to Washington and Union territory north of the Potomac River. Essentially, it would place Lee back where he was when he sent Jackson on the turning movement that started the Second Manassas Campaign.

Decision

Lee decided to redeploy his army seventeen miles northwest to Leesburg (Option 2). The troops began moving on September 3. The next day Lee's Army of Northern Virginia was positioned at Leesburg and along the Potomac River. There, it was joined by the "reinforcing column" from Richmond.

Results/Impact

This critical decision terminated the Second Manassas Campaign. The choice of any of the other options except remaining in position (Option 1) would have also ended the campaign. In making this decision Lee situated his army where he could capitalize on his successes, retain the initiative, and maintain the operational momentum he had created since taking command. Although he had ended the campaign, Lee was now in a position to cross the Potomac River and commence a different operation. This new campaign could potentially see the Confederate army maneuvering in Maryland and Pennsylvania. Such maneuvering with a tactical victory on Union territory could provide a tremendous political gain for the Confederacy.

CHAPTER 6

CONCLUSIONS

On June 1, 1862, Gen. Robert E. Lee assumed command of the Confederate army that had retreated up the Peninsula to the outskirts of Richmond. Lee renamed his new command the Army of Northern Virginia. Within thirty-two days Lee had partially reorganized his forces, reinforced them, and during the Seven Days Battles led them in driving Maj. Gen. George B. McClellan's Army of the Potomac away from Richmond, across the Peninsula, and to a defensive enclave on the James River.

Eleven days later Lee sent Maj. Gen. Thomas J. Jackson and part of the army to central Virginia. Jackson and these troops would confront the advance guard of Maj. Gen. John Pope's newly organized Army of Virginia. Thirty-two days later (August 14), under orders, McClellan began to evacuate the Peninsula. Simultaneously Lee, Major General Longstreet, and the remainder of the army joined Jackson.

On August 25, ten days after his army was reunited, Lee sent Jackson on a turning movement that carried him into Pope's rear area and commenced the Second Manassas Campaign. Three days later the armies fought the Battle of Second Manassas (August 28–30), a defeat for Pope. Lee attempted another turning movement that Pope escaped. On September 2 Pope was retreating into the defensive works at Washington and Alexandria, and Lee was poised just twenty miles from the Union capital.

Ninety-four days passed between Lee's assumption of command of the Army of Northern Virginia and his arrival at the approaches to Washington. In that time, he had transferred the center of the war in Virginia from the Confederate capital ninety-eight miles north to an area just outside the Union capital. The Seven Days Battles and the Second Manassas Campaign completely destroyed the Union's high hopes for victory that summer as McClellan approached Richmond.

The Second Manassas Campaign had cost the Army of Virginia and that part of the Army of the Potomac that was attached 17,354 casualties (soldiers killed, wounded, and captured). It had cost the Army of Northern Virginia 9,197 men. In the Army of Northern Virginia, senior leadership casualties had been severe. The casualties (those killed, mortally wounded, and wounded) included two division commanders, nine brigade commanders, and forty-one regimental commanders. This was almost the leadership equivalent for three infantry divisions. Senior leadership casualties in the Army of Virginia and the attached corps from the Army of the Potomac were just as severe, comprising two division commanders, nine brigade commanders, and forty-six regimental commanders. These officers, too, were the leadership equivalent for three infantry divisions.[1]

Although many important decisions were made prior to, during, and just after the Second Battle of Manassas, only a select number were critical decisions. These fourteen decisons shaped the combat's historical course and gave us the battle as we know it today. Of the fourteen critical decisions one was an organizational decision, five were operational decisions, and eight were tactical decisions. Viewing the decisions from the levels of command, there are two national-level decisions, six army-level decisions, five wing- or corps-level decisions, and one brigade-level decision. Nine were made by a Union commander, and five were made by a Confederate commander.

Lincoln Decides to Create an Army:
National-Level Organizational Decision

President Abraham Lincoln's decision to combine the three separate Union commands in central and western Virginia created the Army of Virginia. It also brought these three distinct organizations (reorganized as corps) under a single commander, Maj. Gen. John Pope. The result was a combat force with sufficient strength to have an effect on operations in central Virginia. Without the creation of this army, nothing that eventually followed would have occurred.

Halleck Decides to Evacuate the Peninsula: National-Level Operational Decision

During the Seven Days Battles, McClellan's Army of the Potomac had retreated across the Peninsula to an enclave on the James River. While not the threat to Richmond it had been, the Union army was still a hazard and could not be ignored. McClellan had lost all creditability with Maj. Gen. Henry W. Halleck, the newly appointed general-in-chief. Halleck, therefore, made the critical decision to bring McClellan's army back to the Washington area by ships. Doing so removed one of the threats to Richmond and allowed Lee to concentrate on Pope's army. This Lee did, and he swiftly moved his army to central Virginia.

Lee Decides on a Turning Movement: Army-Level Operational Decision

In mid- to late August, Lee had made several unsuccessful attempts to maneuver and engage Pope's army. A stalemate resulted, with both armies facing each other along the line of the Rappahannock River. Lee realized that time was not on his side as McClellan's army was being transferred to Washington, from which it could march to join Pope's troops. To break this impasse, Lee sent Jackson on a successful turning movement around Pope's right and deep into his rear area. This critical decision broke the stalemate, began a period of maneuver, and ultimately led to the Second Battle of Manassas. Without it, some form of operation would probably have brought the two armies to battle, but not at Manassas.

Jackson Moves to the "Stony Ridge": Corps/Wing-Level Operational Decision

After executing his successful turning movement, cutting Pope's supply line, and capturing and destroying Pope's main supply depot, Jackson needed to move away from the Union forces closing on him. He needed a new location where he could wait for the arrival of Longstreet's Wing. Jackson decided to move to a section of high ground in close proximity to the old First Manassas battlefield. This critical decision by Jackson determined where the Battle of Second Manassas would be fought. Had he gone to some other location, the sequence of events and fighting would have been entirely different.

Ricketts's Division Fights Alone: Corps-Level Tactical Decision

After Jackson had completed the turning movement and while Longstreet was marching to join him, their wings were briefly separated by the Bull Run Mountains. Only a few gaps in the mountains allowed troops to pass through them. McDowell's critical decision not to position a strong force to block Thoroughfare Gap cost him and Pope the best opportunity to keep Jackson and Longstreet separated and to defeat each in detail.

Jackson Decides to Attack: Corps/Wing-Level Tactical Decision

From his position on the "Stony Ridge" on August 28, Jackson observed a Union division marching east on the Warrenton Turnpike in the late afternoon. Knowing Lee's intentions to engage Pope before McClellan could join his army with Pope's, Jackson decided to attack. This critical decision commenced the Battle of Second Manassas and drew the other units from both armies into the fight.

Pope Decides to Attack: Army-Level Tactical Decision

On August 29 Pope incorrectly believed that Jackson was attempting to retreat from the "Stony Ridge" position. To hold him in place so he could be enveloped and destroyed, Pope ordered a series of attacks against the Confederate position. This critical decision set the pattern and sequence of fighting for that day.

Porter Decides Not to Attack: Corps/Wing-Level Tactical Decision

Positioned on the south flank of the Union army, Porter was ordered to use his corps and McDowell's to conduct an attack to Gainesville. This maneuver would cut off Jackson's supposed route of retreat. Porter, faced with an unknown enemy force, made the critical decision not to carry out this attack. This choice removed any opportunity for Union forces to engage the right of Longstreet's Wing. Such an attack would have provided solid intelligence that Longstreet had arrived and the Army of Northern Virginia was reunited. The next day, the lack of this information had consequences that almost destroyed Pope's army.

Conclusions

Pope Decides to Attack Again:
Army-Level Tactical Decision

On August 30 Pope ordered a major attack against Jackson's right-center position along the unfinished railroad. Pope acted against all advice—he still believed Jackson was attempting to retreat, and he ignored evidence of Longstreet's presence. This attack sent Porter's reinforced corps into a kill zone of cross fire from artillery and protected infantry. Ultimately, the assault was repulsed with heavy casualties in the forward units. This critical decision set the stage for Longstreet to attack Pope's left flank with overwhelming force. It also established and drove the character and sequence of the battle on this day.

McDowell Decides to Reposition Troops:
Corps/Wing-Level Tactical Decision

As Porter's troops fell back from their unsuccessful attack, they were followed for a short distance by a Confederate counterattack. Maj. Gen. Irvin McDowell saw this retreat and limited pursuit. Concerned that it would break the center of the Union line (which was very substantial and on good terrain), McDowell ordered Brig. Gen. John F. Reynolds to move his division from the south side of the Warrenton Turnpike to the north side. This shift left only a minimal force to face the attack of Longstreet's five divisions. McDowell's critical decision exposed Pope's left south of the turnpike to destruction. Additionally, it opened the way for the capture of Henry Hill, the interdiction of the army's main route of retreat, and the destruction or capture of many of Pope's units.

McLean Decides to Defend Chinn Ridge:
Brigade-Level Tactical Decision

When Reynolds's division crossed to the north side of the Warrenton Turnpike, only three separately positioned brigades that were not mutually supporting constituted Pope's left flank south of the turnpike. (One of Reynolds's brigades would return prior to the attack.) The brigade commanded by Col. Nathaniel McLean was positioned on the tactically important Chinn Ridge. On his own initiative, McLean decided to remain on Chinn Ridge and confront Longstreet's attack. This critical decision bought time for Chinn Ridge to be reinforced, which in turn bought additional time for the defenses of Henry Hill to be strengthened. Had McLean chosen otherwise, Henry Hill would probably have been quickly captured. The consequences for Pope's army would have been devastating.

Pope Decides to Retreat: Army-Level Tactical Decision

The successful delay on Chinn Ridge allowed the defenses on Henry Hill and on the terrain to the north to be organized into effective defensive positions. These defenses were able to hold until dark. Pope thus had the options of continuing to defend, either where he was or slightly east, or of retreating. He chose to retreat. This critical decision ended the Second Battle of Manassas as a Confederate victory. However, it did not end the campaign.

Lee Decides on Another Turning Movement:
Army-Level Operational Decision

Lee decided he would try to cut Pope's line of retreat and again bring him to battle. Lee once more sent Jackson on a turning movement around Pope's right. Because of Union reconnaissance and the shifting of forces, this maneuver resulted in the Battle of Chantilly (Ox Hill), which was not a Confederate success. However, this critical decision extended the campaign for another two days and forced Pope to continue the retreat to the defenses of Washington and Alexandria.

Lee Decides to Redeploy His Army:
Army-Level Operational Decision

With Pope's continued retreat, Lee controlled most of the territory west of Washington. His next decision was where to go and what to do. Lee opted to move his army northwest to Leesburg and cross the Potomac River there, invade northern territory, and commence the Maryland Campaign. This critical decision ended the Second Manassas Campaign and also gave Lee the capability to capitalize upon his successes.

Afterward

On September 3 Lee marched his army to Leesburg, where he was joined by the "reinforcing column" from Richmond. This column of three infantry divisions (with their artillery), four artillery battalions (of the Artillery Reserve), and one cavalry brigade had a strength of twenty-four thousand troops and more than made up for Lee's campaign losses.[2]

Conclusions

Pope was relieved of his command on September 5. On September 6 he was reassigned to command the Department of the Northwest, and three days later he departed for Minnesota.[3]

McClellan was given command of the defenses of Washington and all troops in the vicinity. Shortly thereafter the Army of Virginia passed into history when it was absorbed into the Army of the Potomac, the First, Second, and Third Corps becoming respectively the Eleventh, Twelfth, and First Corps (Army of the Potomac).[4]

But Lee was not finished. He fully understood that military operations have to support a political objective—in this case the acceptance and recognition of the Confederate States of America. Lee also realized that his army could not afford to remain static; he had a short period of time in which to exploit his recent successes. To further the political objective and maintain the operational initiative, Lee's army crossed the Potomac River into Maryland on September 4 and commenced another campaign.

Shortly thereafter, McClellan's reorganized Army of the Potomac followed Lee's troops in order to engage the Confederates and drive them from Union soil. The two armies, many of them units that had fought at Second Manassas, engaged in the bloodiest day in American military history on September 17 along Antietam Creek.

McClellan's failed tactics and lack of aggressiveness let an opportunity to do irreparable damage to Lee's army slip away. The next night Lee retreated back into Virginia. Though fought to a standstill, McClellan was still able to claim a strategic victory. Lincoln therefore had all he required to issue the Emancipation Proclamation.

In December the maneuvering came full circle. Both armies faced each other across the Rappahannock River at Fredericksburg, just thirty-five miles downriver from where the Second Manassas Campaign had begun.

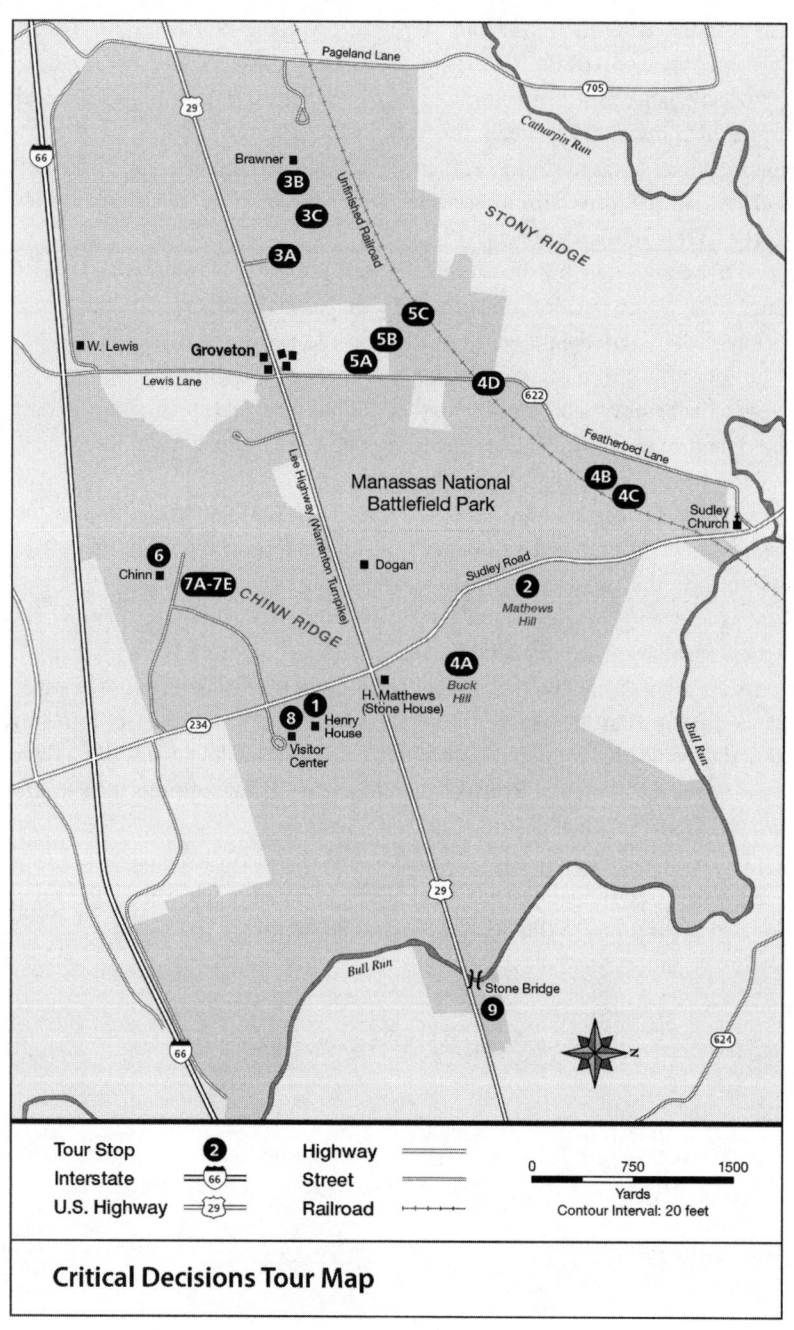

Critical Decisions Tour Map

APPENDIX I

BATTLEFIELD GUIDE TO THE CRITICAL DECISIONS AT SECOND MANASSAS

Begin your battlefield tour of the critical decisions at the National Park Visitor Center. Before you depart on the tour, you may wish to visit the museum and bookstore.

There is value in being in close proximity to the place where a critical decision was made or carried out. Seeing the terrain as those who reached and implemented the decisions once did provides a perspective that can't be gained through reading or studying maps. This appendix provides a battlefield tour that will place you on the ground where critical decisions were made and/or carried out, or as close to them as possible.

The tour is designed to follow the battle's events in chronological order. Driving and walking instructions will move you around, the Manassas National Battlefield Park, an adjacent area that was part of the 1862 battlefield, and two other areas that were part of the campaign. Driving, walking, and positioning directions are provided. Orientation information is provided for each stop, including which direction to face, what units were in your vicinity, the critical decision that was made, and the resulting action and consequences of that decision. Wherever possible, primary source material has been used to allow the participants to tell you about the critical decisions. If you need more information, read the decision discussion in the appropriate chapter. Words in the primary material may be spelled differently than they are today, but they have been left as they were written by the participants. For example, the present-day spelling of *re-enforced* is *reinforced*.

Second Manassas was a fluid battle. Therefore, when looking at the maps in this appendix the reader must remember they represent a brief snapshot in time of many unit movements. The maps are designed to be a frame of reference that will assist a reader in visualizing events.

When placing maps in a book, it is normal practice to orient them so that the top of the page corresponds to the direction of north. Some maps in this appendix depart from that practice. One of the basic rules of map reading is that you orient the map with the terrain. As you stand at a particular location, you will read instructions informing you where to walk, where to position yourself, and which direction to face. When you then look at the map for that stop, it will be oriented correctly with the terrain. It will not be necessary for you to rotate the book, even when you page back and forth between the text and the maps. Additionally, the maps contain a compass indicating north.

Six of the fourteen critical decisions were made or carried out within the confines of the Manassas National Battlefield Park. Four other critical decisions were made in proximity to the park. Three of these decisions are included as optional excursion stops.

Four of the critical decisions that shaped the battle were not made on or near the battlefield. It is not practical for the tour to include these decisions as stops. Prior to beginning the tour, it would be beneficial for you to review these four critical decisions.

President Abraham Lincoln made the first critical decision when he formed the Army of Virginia. In addition to Maj. Gen. George B. McClellan's Army of the Potomac, three other commands were operating in Virginia: Maj. Gen. Irvin McDowell's corps of thirty thousand men (detached from McClellan's army) near Fredericksburg, Maj. Gen John C. Fremont's Mountain Department with fifteen thousand troops, and Maj. Gen. Nathaniel P. Banks's twenty-three thousand troops in the Shenandoah Valley. The total strength of these three commands represented considerable combat power. However, because their operations were not coordinated with or supporting each other, that power was fragmented. Lincoln's decision brought these three commands into one organization, the Army of Virginia. Under the command of Maj. Gen. John Pope, these troops were positioned in central Virginia. The creation and location of this army would lead directly to the Second Manassas campaign and battle.

The next critical decision was made by the newly appointed Union general-in-chief, Maj. Gen. Henry W. Halleck. McClellan had transported his army from Washington and Alexandria to the tip of the Peninsula in March. In

April he began a campaign that brought him to the outskirts of Richmond. This success was reversed in late June and early July by Gen. Robert E. Lee's continuous offensive operation in the Seven Days Battles. McClellan's army retreated across the Peninsula to Harrison's Landing on the James River. McClellan then presented several plans to renew offensive operations, but Halleck decided to return the Army of the Potomac to northern Virginia by water transport. This decision freed Lee from having to simultaneously watch two Union armies and allowed him to concentrate on Pope.

The third critical decision was made by Lee. Lee had transferred Maj. Gen. Thomas J. "Stonewall" Jackson's Left Wing to central Virginia to block Pope's movement south toward Richmond. When the threat from McClellan's army was removed, Lee dispatched Maj. Gen. James Longstreet's Right Wing to join Jackson's. With the Army of Northern Virginia reunited, Lee began a series of maneuvers to decisively engage Pope's Army of Virginia. Poor staff work, insufficient coordination, bad weather, and a rising river caused unsuccessful results.

Concerned that the Army of the Potomac would complete its redeployment then reinforce Pope, Lee boldly sent Jackson on a turning movement into Pope's rear area. This decision broke the stalemate, forced Pope to reposition his army, and commenced the maneuver phase that resulted in the Second Battle of Manassas.

Jackson made the final critical decision away from the battlefield. He commenced the turning movement on August 25, marching around Pope's right and through Thoroughfare Gap in the Bull Run Mountains. Jackson then captured Bristoe Station on the Orange and Alexandria Railroad. This seizure severed Pope's supply line and brought his army after Jackson. From Bristoe Station, Jackson marched to Manassas Junction, captured Pope's main supply depot, and destroyed it. From Manassas Junction, Jackson moved his wing to the vicinity of the old First Manassas battlefield. On August 28 Jackson's three divisions took up position along the "Stony Ridge" and unfinished railroad to await developments and the arrival of Longstreet's wing. Although he might not have realized it at the time, Jackson had selected where the battle would be fought when he occupied this position.

Stop 1: Terrain Orientation

When you are finished in the Visitor Center, walk out the back exit on the west side of the building. Follow the wide path northwest for two hundred yards to the Henry House. Stand on the west side of the house so that you have a view to the west, northwest, and north.

Appendix I

You are standing on Henry Hill. This hill is one of the most important pieces of key terrain on the battlefield, if not the most important one. Two hundred yards directly in front of you, at the base of the hill, is the south-to-north (your left to right) Sudley Road. Five hundred yards farther on is the northern section of Chinn Ridge. The woods between you and Chinn Ridge today were smaller in 1862, and much of the ridge could be seen from where you are.

Five hundred thirty yards to your right is the west-to-east Warrenton Turnpike (present-day Lee Highway/US 29). On the other side of the turnpike is the Matthews House (Stone House). Six hundred yards to your right front is the intersection of the Sudley Road and the Warrenton Turnpike (where the stoplight is). These are the two most important roads on the battlefield. The Warrenton Turnpike provides entry onto and away from the battlefield from the east and the west. The Sudley Road provides entry to or away from the battlefield from the south and north. Depending on unit orientation, both roads provide lateral routes of movement across the battlefield.

For Pope, control of these roads in the vicinity of the intersection was vital. The Sudley Road allowed a rapid movement of his corps south of the battlefield to a central position. The Warrenton Turnpike provided a direct route for reinforcement and supplies coming from the east. It also provided the major route of retreat, if that became necessary.

The intersection, the Sudley Road south of the intersection, and the Warrenton Turnpike east of the intersection were controlled by whatever force occupied Henry Hill. Four hundred yards north of the turnpike and the Stone House is the crest of Buck Hill. A force on this hill would control part of the Sudley Road north of the intersection. These troops could also assist in controlling the intersection if there was a friendly force on Henry Hill. If enemy soldiers occupied Henry Hill, then direct fire and maneuver would make Buck Hill untenable.

Five hundred yards farther north from Buck Hill (1,430 yards from your location) is Matthews Hill. This high ground provides additional control of the Sudley Road north of the intersection. Henry Hill, Buck Hill, and Matthews Hill form a good south-to-north defensive position.

Return to your car for the drive to Matthews Hill. Depart the parking lot and drive west on the park road to the Sudley Road. At the Sudley Road turn right. Drive north on the Sudley Road for one mile, straight through the intersection where the stoplight is, to a parking area for Matthews Hill. The parking area will be on your right. Turn right into the parking area, park, and leave your car. Find the walking path on the southeast edge of the parking area (the trail is marked "Matthews Hill Loop Trail"). Walk southeast on this path for three hundred yards to the location of the artillery pieces. Stop, turn around, and face back northwest. Disregard the guns; they are part of the First Battle of Manassas.

Stop 2: Jackson Moves to the "Stony Ridge"

You are standing on Matthews Hill. The Sudley Road is in front of you, at the bottom of the hill. In front of you at a distance of 850 yards (0.46 mile), there is a large wood that extends to your right and left. Another 500 yards (0.3 mile) into that wood is the unfinished railroad, and just beyond that lies the "Stony Ridge."

Jackson completed the turning movement by capturing Bristoe Station and severing Pope's supply line on August 26. He then seized a major supply depot at Manassas Junction. Learning that Union forces were closing on his location, Jackson departed Manassas Junction on the night of August 27. The next day he occupied the positions on the "Stony Ridge" and along the unfinished railroad.

Report of Maj. Gen. Thomas J. Jackson, CSA, Commanding Left Wing, Army of Northern Virginia

Orders were given to supply the troops with rations and other articles which they could properly make subservient to their use from the captured property [at Manassas Junction]. It was vast in quantity and of great value, comprising 50,000 pounds of bacon, 1,000 barrels of corned beef, 2,000 barrels of salt pork, 2,000 barrels of flour, quartermaster's, ordnance, and sutler's stores deposited in buildings and filling two trains of cars. Having appropriated all that we could use, and unwilling that the residue should again fall into the hands of the enemy, who took possession of the place next day, orders were given to destroy all that remained after supplying the immediate wants of the army. This was done during the night. General Taliaferro moved his division that night across to the Warrenton and Alexandria turnpike, pursuing the road to Sudley's Mill, and crossing the turnpike in the vicinity of Groveton, halted near the battle-field of July 21, 1861. Ewell's and Hill's divisions joined Jackson's [Taliaferro's Division] on the 28th.[1]

After Jackson departed Manassas Junction, part of his Left Wing marched to the area described above on the morning of August 28. This was Maj. Gen.

Appendix I

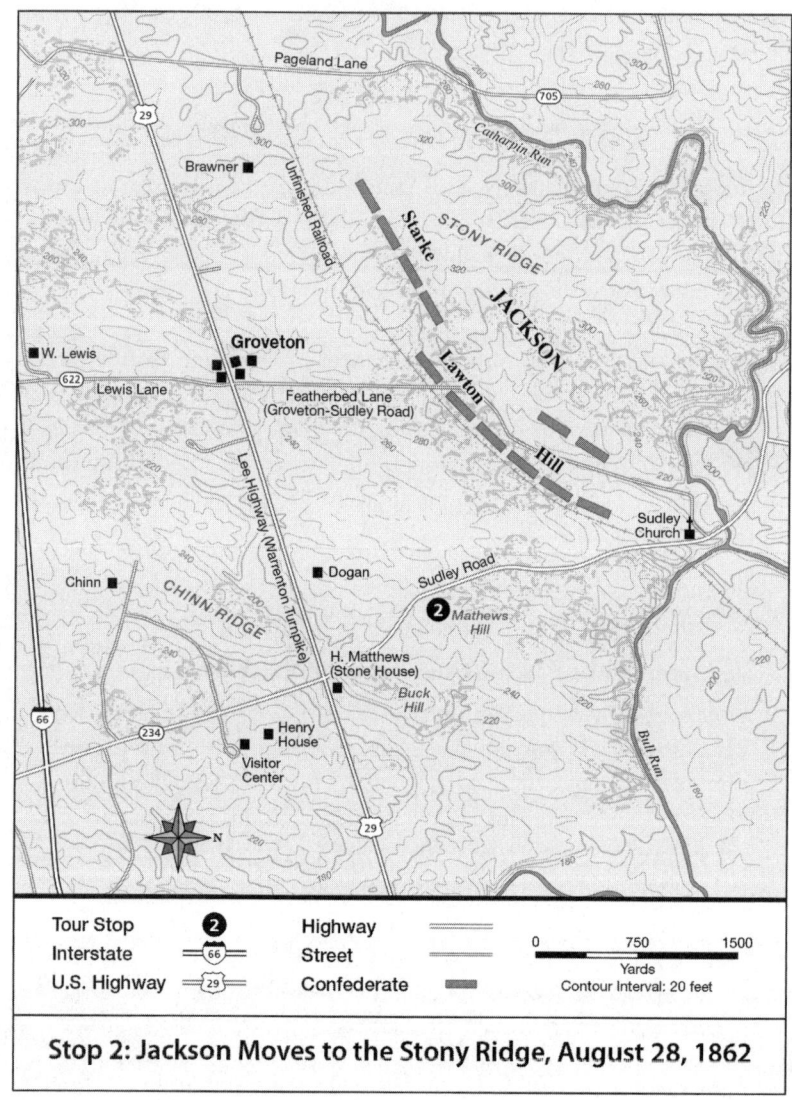

Stop 2: Jackson Moves to the Stony Ridge, August 28, 1862

Ambrose P. Hill's division. A. P. Hill's Division then marched north from the intersection on the Sudley Road, passed by your current location, traveled farther north, and then turned left onto the "Stony Ridge" and the unfinished railroad. Jackson's two other divisions probably used other roads that went off of the Warrenton Turnpike to reach the "Stony Ridge."

Hill's Division was on Jackson's left. Its left flank was 1,800 yards (1.0 mile) to your right front. Jackson's right flank was 3,000 yards (1.7 miles) to your left (west southwest). Brig. Gen. William B. Taliaferro's division (later commanded by Brig. Gen. William E. Starke) was the right flank division. Between these two divisions was Maj. Gen. Richard S. Ewell's division (later commanded by Brig. Gen. Alexander R. Lawton). These units formed a defensive position with a frontage of 3,000 yards (1.7 miles).

Jackson's position provided him with several tactical advantages. It was a covered and concealed position on dominant terrain from which he could either conduct a defense or attack any Union force marching along the Warrenton Turnpike or the Sudley Road. Jackson was only eleven miles from Thoroughfare Gap, which Longstreet's Wing captured that evening. If necessary, Jackson could march to join Longstreet as his Right Wing marched east. If this plan was not feasible, Jackson could march north a short distance, then travel northwest to Aldie through a gap in the Bull Run Mountains, then turn south to reunite with Longstreet.

This critical decision by Jackson placed him in a position to initiate offensive action and commence the battle.

Return to your car for the drive to Stop 3.

Drive from the parking area. At the Sudley Road turn left and drive south for 0.7 mile to its intersection with the Warrenton Turnpike (where the stoplight is). Turn right and drive southwest on the Warrenton Turnpike for 1.7 miles until you reach the park road on your right. Turn right on to this park road, and drive a short distance to a parking area. Park, leave your car, walk 30 yards to the artillery and look in the direction the guns are pointed, which is north and northeast.

Stop 3: Jackson Decides to Attack

Position A—Initial Contact

In 1862 the road you turned off of was named the Warrenton Turnpike. It was a major feature that traversed the entire battlefield generally from west to east. East of the battlefield the turnpike went to Centreville, Fairfax, and Alexandria. West of the battlefield it reached to Gainesville and then on to Warrenton. At Gainesville it connected with a road that extended to and through Thoroughfare Gap. The Warrenton Turnpike provided a key route for both armies to concentrate from the east or the west.

The terrain where you are located looks very much as it did in 1862. To your left (west) was a wood. On the other side of the wood was the Brawner

Appendix I

farmhouse. Seven hundred yards to your right was the crossroads hamlet of Groveton. In front of you on the higher ground, a wood stretched to the northeast. An unfinished railroad was also located on this higher ground. In many places cuts and berms had been constructed to level the bed for the rail tracks. The unfinished railroad provided a strong defensive position for whoever occupied it.

Late in the afternoon of August 28, the three divisions of Jackson's Left Wing were situated on the "Stony Ridge," the higher ground north and northeast of your location. Directly in front of you were the four brigades of Jackson's Division, commanded by Brig. Gen. William B. Taliaferro. To Taliaferro's left (your right front) was Maj. Gen. Richard S. Ewell's four-brigade division. Farther to Ewell's left and reaching to the Sudley Road were the six brigades of Maj. Gen. Ambrose P. Hill's division. Longstreet's Right Wing was located eleven miles west of you (to your left) at Thoroughfare Gap.

Pope's forces were spread out from Gainesville, four miles west of you, to Manassas Junction, seven miles southeast of you. Many of Pope's units were marching toward Manassas Junction under the false belief that Jackson was still there.

Late in the afternoon Brig. Gen. Rufus King's First Division of Maj. Gen. Irvin McDowell's Third Corps was marching east on the Warrenton Turnpike. The order of march for King's division was the brigades of Brig. Gens. John P. Hatch, John Gibbon, Abner Doubleday, and Marsena R. Patrick. The four batteries of the division's artillery were interspersed with the infantry. Hatch's brigade marched past this location without interruption. What occurred as the head of Gibbon's brigade reached this location showed the Union commanders exactly where Jackson was located.

Jackson knew that Lee intended to engage and defeat Pope's Army of Virginia before it could be significantly reinforced or combined with McClellan's Army of the Potomac. He also knew that Lee, Longstreet, and the remainder of the Army of Northern Virginia were just a short distance away at Thoroughfare Gap. Accordingly, Jackson decided to engage the Union forces crossing his front to draw the remainder of Pope's army to this location.

The first Confederate unit into action was Lieut. Asher W. Garber's Staunton Battery from Ewell's Division. Garber's Battery went into a firing position on the high ground nine hundred yards to your right front. Garber's target was Hatch's brigade as it marched along that section of the Warrenton Turnpike to your right rear. Hatch's infantrymen took cover, and Capt. John A. Reynolds's Battery L, First New York Artillery deployed into a position five hundred yards to your right and opened fire. The time was approximately 5:00 p.m. Sunset was at 6:45 p.m., with darkness coming at 7:12 p.m. There was a little over two hours in which to fight a decisive engagement.

Battlefield Guide to the Critical Decisions at Second Manassas

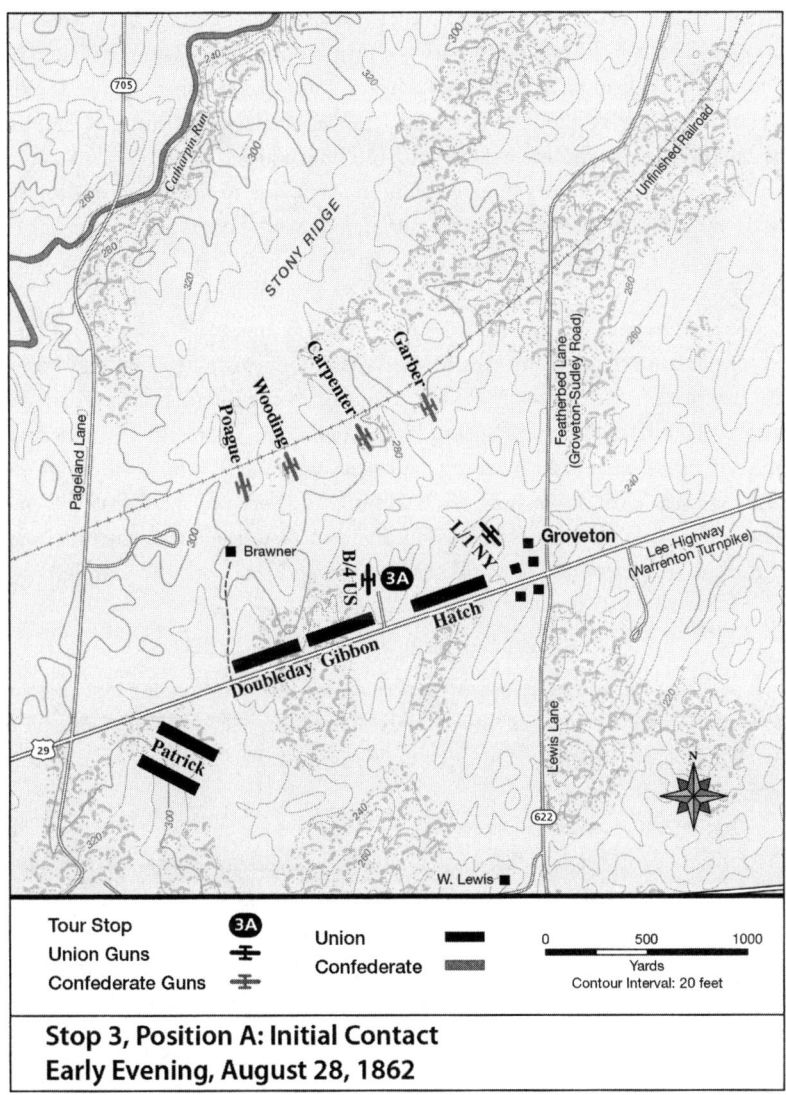

**Stop 3, Position A: Initial Contact
Early Evening, August 28, 1862**

Next, Capt. George Wooding's Danville Battery from Jackson's (Taliaferro's) Division, located nine hundred yards to your left front, commenced firing upon Gibbon's brigade, which had been following Hatch's. Gibbon ordered Capt. Joseph B. Campbell's Battery B, Fourth US Artillery in to action. Campbell's battery went into position where you stand, and it commenced firing.

Appendix I

Soon after Wooding's and Garber's Batteries opened fire, they were reinforced by Capt. Joseph Carpenter's Virginia Battery and Capt. William T. Poague's Rockbridge Battery. Sixteen guns were now firing on the Union troops along the Warrenton Turnpike. As the artillery continued to fire, infantry from both sides moved forward and opened fire.

The center of the fully deployed Union battle line stood 450 yards directly in front of you. The first Union units to deploy were positioned on the left of this line. You will now go to that position.

Return to your car for the drive to Position B.

Drive from the parking area to the Warrenton Turnpike. Turn right onto the turnpike, and drive southwest for 0.9 mile to the intersection with Pageland Lane. Turn right onto Pageland Lane, and drive 0.4 mile to the park road on your right. Turn right onto the park road, and follow it for 0.3 mile to the parking area. Park, leave your car, and walk 300 yards to the restored farmhouse. Continue past the farmhouse for 240 yards to the top of the hill. Stop at the end of a fence line 60 yards to your left, and face north (to your left).[2]

Position B—Left of the Union Line

You are between the positions of the Second Wisconsin to your left and the Seventh Wisconsin to your right. To the left of the Second Wisconsin stood the Nineteenth Indiana. The Second Wisconsin was the first of Gibbon's regiments to deploy.

One hundred seventy-five yards in front of you are cannons that represent the artillery position of Jackson's (Taliaferro's) Division, commanded by Maj. Lindsay M. Shumaker on August 29, and then Col. Stephen D. Lee's artillery battalion on August 30. To your right front at a distance of 550 yards are cannon that represent Shumaker's position on August 30. On August 28 no artillery was present at either of these positions.

Report of Maj. Gen. Thomas J. Jackson, CSA, Commanding Left Wing, Army of Northern Virginia

My command had hardly concentrated north of the turnpike before the enemy's advance reached the vicinity of Groveton from the direction of Warrenton. General Stuart kept me advised of the general movements of the enemy. Dispositions were promptly made to attack the enemy, based upon the idea that he would continue to press forward upon the turnpike toward Alexandria; but as he did

> not appear to advance in force, and there was reason to believe that his main body was leaving the road and inclining toward Manassas Junction, my command was advanced through the woods, leaving Groveton on the left, until it reached a commanding position near Brawner's house. By this time it was sunset; but as his column appeared to be moving by, with its flank exposed, I determined to attack at once, which was vigorously done by the divisions of Taliaferro and Ewell. The batteries of Wooding, Poague, [Garber's,] and Carpenter were placed in position in front of Starke's brigade and above the village of Groveton, and, firing over the heads of our skirmishers, poured a heavy fire of shot and shell upon the enemy. This was responded to by a very heavy fire from the enemy, forcing our batteries to select another position. By this time Taliaferro's command, with Lawton's and Trimble's brigades on his left, was advanced from the woods to the open field, and was now moving in gallant style until it reached an orchard on the right of our line and was less than 100 yards from a large force of the enemy. The conflict here was fierce and sanguinary.[3]

Going into position directly in front of the Second Wisconsin was Col. William S. H. Baylor's Stonewall Brigade. At a range of approximately one hundred yards both units opened fire. The Second Wisconsin's left flank was threatened by the extended line of the Stonewall Brigade. To prevent the position from being flanked, Gibbon deployed Col. Solomon Meredith's Nineteenth Indiana to the left of the Second Wisconsin. Gibbon next deployed Col. William Robinson's Seventh Wisconsin to the right of the Second Wisconsin.

> ### Report of Brig. Gen. John Gibbon, USA, Commanding Fourth Brigade, First Division, Third Corps, Army of Virginia
>
> The division was marching on Centreville from Gainesville, my brigade following General Hatch's, on the Warrenton turnpike.... Hatch's artillery was engaging the enemy in front, when from a point to his left and rear one of the enemy's batteries opened on my column. I directed the men to lie down in the road, and ordered up Captain Campbell with the battery. It came up at a gallop, formed

Appendix I

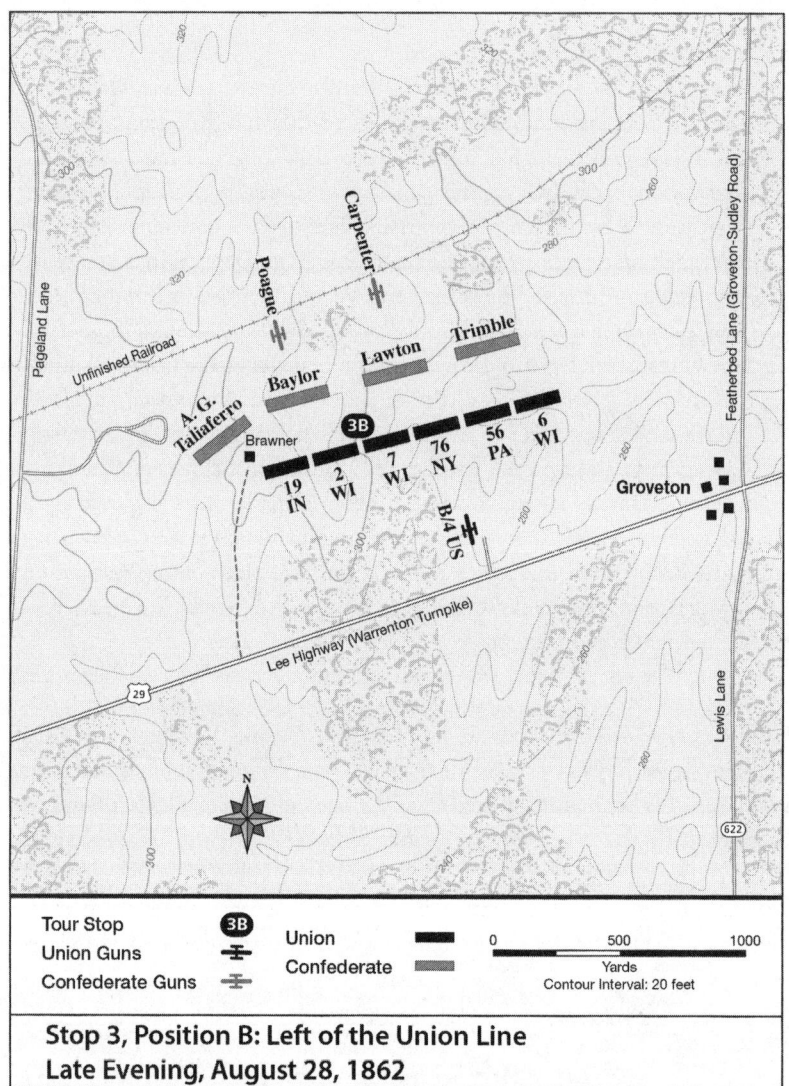

**Stop 3, Position B: Left of the Union Line
Late Evening, August 28, 1862**

in battery under a heavy fire, and opened with such vigor that the enemy's battery was soon silenced and made to retire. In the mean time I found that two of the enemy's pieces had been planted to our left and rear and were firing on Doubleday's brigade, which was behind us. I had no information of the presence of an [enemy] infantry force in that position. I therefore supposed that this was one of the

Brigadier General John Gibbon, USA, Commanding Fourth Brigade, First Division, Third Corps, Army of Virginia. Library of Congress.

> enemy's cavalry batteries, and ordered the Second Wisconsin to face to the left and march obliquely to the rear against these pieces to take them in flank. As it rose an intervening hill it was opened upon by some infantry on its right flank. The left wing was thrown forward to bring the regiment facing the enemy, and the musket firing became very warm. The Nineteenth Indiana was now ordered up in support and formed on the left of the Second Wisconsin, whilst the Seventh Wisconsin was directed to hold itself in reserve. As the enemy appeared to be now heavily re-enforced, the Sixth and Seventh Wisconsin were both ordered into line.[4]

Almost simultaneously, Brig. Gen. Alexander R. Lawton's brigade of Ewell's Division moved up on Baylor's left and joined the fight. As Lawton's line extended past the right of the Seventh Wisconsin, Gibbon deployed his last regiment, Col. Lysander Cutler's Sixth Wisconsin, three hundred yards to the right of that regiment to engage the left of Lawton's Brigade.

Jackson attempted to strike Gibbon's left flank (the Nineteenth Indiana) as the fighting progressed. The first threat to the Nineteenth Indiana's left came in the form of Capt. John Pelham's Virginia Battery. As darkness approached, Pelham was able to position two of his guns one hundred yards from the Nineteenth Indiana and open a devastating fire. This point-blank fire was maintained until two companies of the Nineteenth Indiana crept forward, opened a close-range fire on Pelham's gunners, and forced the battery to fall back to a new firing position.

The artillery was soon replaced by an even greater threat to Gibbon's flank. Three regiments of Col. Alexander G. Taliaferro's brigade approached Gibbon's left. To counter this threat, Col. Solomon Meredith ordered his Nineteenth Indiana to fall back a short distance to a better position and open fire on Taliaferro's approaching troops.

With all of these units deployed, the close-range firefight assumed horrific proportions. This fighting continued without pause until it became dark.

Face right, and walk northeast 525 yards on the trail (partially through the wood) to the marker for the Seventy-sixth New York. You will walk past the Seventh Wisconsin marker (do not take a left or right off of the trail). Stop at the Seventy-sixth New York marker, and face left so you can look through the thin wood line in front of you.

Position C—Center of the Union Line

You are at the center of the Union battle line after it deployed. The firing position of Battery B, Fourth US Artillery (Position A) was on the higher ground 450 yards behind you.

The Seventy-sixth New York was deployed where you are standing. To the regiment's right were the Fifty-sixth Pennsylvania and the Sixth Wisconsin. To its left were the Seventh Wisconsin, Second Wisconsin, and Nineteenth Indiana.

Lawton's Brigade was positioned in front of this location on the higher ground. Baylor's Brigade stood to their right (your left), and Trimble's Brigade stood to their left (your right).

The far right of Gibbon's line was held by the Sixth Wisconsin. The regimental commander was wounded during the action, and the regimental lieutenant colonel assumed command. His report gives a good example of the fighting at the regimental level.

> ### Report of Lieut. Col. Edward S. Bragg, USA, Commanding Sixth Wisconsin Infantry, Fourth Brigade, First Division, Third Corps, Army of Virginia
>
> Colonel Cutler having received a severe wound in the engagement of the 28th ultimo, the command of the regiment devolved upon

Lieutenant Colonel Edward S. Bragg, USA, Commanding Sixth Wisconsin, Fourth Brigade, First Division, Third Corps, Army of Virginia. Library of Congress.

me. When he left the field I found my right wing engaging the enemy in front at short range, and receiving not only his fire, but also suffering from an oblique fire of an enemy lying upon the crest of the hill, extending beyond our right. I immediately changed position, moving my line to the left so far as was necessary to protect the right flank from this second fire by cover of a point of wood extending down to my front, and from which we had dislodged the enemy.

Having changed position, I caused the fire to be resumed until the enemy withdrew from our front and ceased to reply. I then caused details to be made to remove the dead and wounded, which having been done, I withdrew the regiment about 500 yards and placed it under cover of wood and facing the field, and advanced a line of pickets upon the field of battle to protect me from surprises should the enemy desire to renew the contest.

Our list of casualties is as follows: Colonel [Lysander] Cutler severely wounded; Lieut. [Jerome] B. Johnson, Company E, wounded and a prisoner; Capt. [John] F. Marsh slightly wounded. Enlisted men—wounded, 61; killed 8; missing 3; total 75. Total engaged, 504.[5]

Appendix I

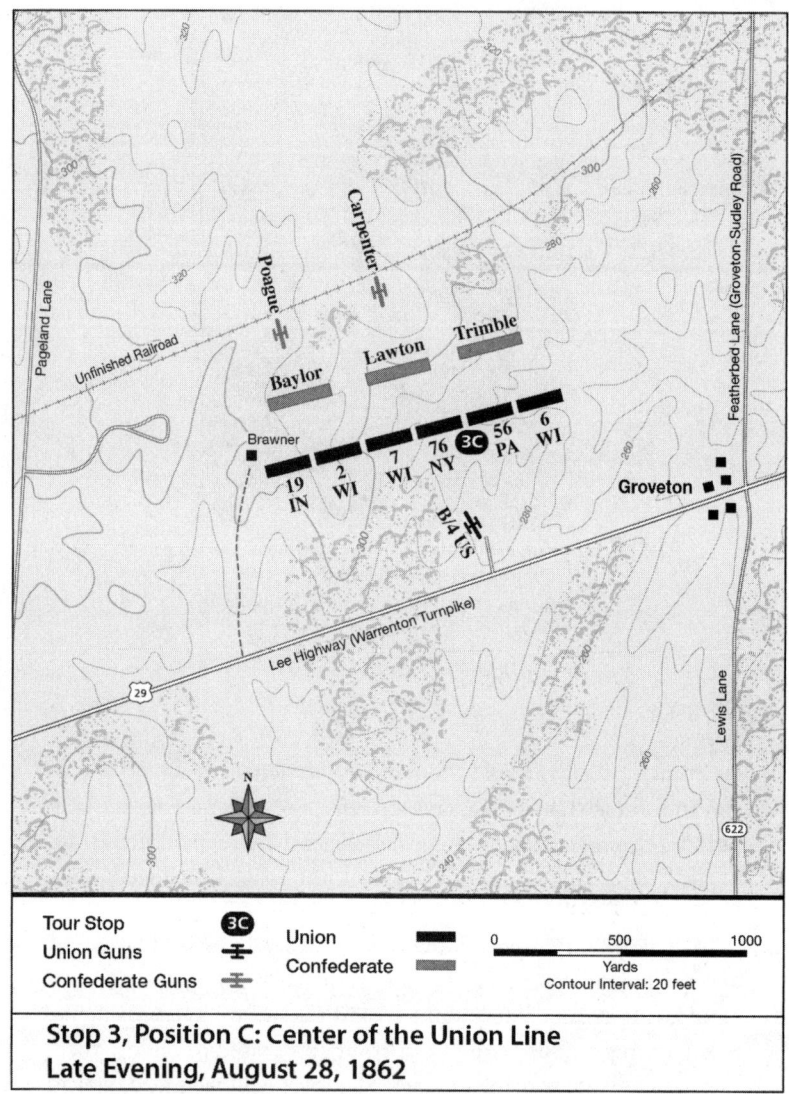

**Stop 3, Position C: Center of the Union Line
Late Evening, August 28, 1862**

At your current location, Brig. Gen. Abner Doubleday deployed two of his regiments, the Seventy-sixth New York and the Fifty-sixth Pennsylvania, to fill the gap in Gibbon's line. As these units deployed, Brig. Gen. Isaac Trimble's brigade from Ewell's Division went into position on Lawton's left.

Report of Brig. Gen. Abner Doubleday, USA, Commanding Second Brigade, First Division, Third Corps, Army of Virginia

On Thursday, August 28, about 5.30 p.m., while my brigade was marching in rear of Gibbon's brigade, on the road from Gainesville to Centreville, a well directed and heavy fire opened upon us at very short range from a battery on a hill to the north of us. Sheltering my men as much as possible behind a small rise of ground in the road, I directed them to halt and await orders. Receiving none, and unable to obtain them, I almost immediately sent two regiments of my brigade—the Fifty-sixth Pennsylvania, under Col. Sullivan A. Meredith, and the Seventy-sixth New York, under Col. William P. Wainwright—to aid General Gibbon, who had pushed his whole brigade forward through a piece of woods to attack the battery, under the impression that it was merely supported by cavalry. General Gibbon was received with a tremendous fire from a large [force] in position, under Jackson, Ewell, and Taliaferro. Knowing he would be overpowered if not succored, I immediately complied with his

Brigadier General Abner Doubleday, USA, Commanding Second Brigade, First Division, Third Corps, Army of Virginia. Library of Congress.

> earnest request and sent him the two regiments referred to, leaving myself but one regiment in reserve.
>
> Campbell's battery [B, Fourth US Artillery], attached to Gibbon's brigade, was posted on the right, but, [had] no infantry support. I was thus compelled to send my only remaining regiment, the Ninety-fifth New York, under Lieutenant-Colonel [James B.] Post, as a support to the battery. The battle lasted until the approach of night, when the enemy ceased to fire, and the contest ended.[6]

When Doubleday's two regiments deployed, the Seventy-sixth New York was positioned where you are standing. To your immediate right was the Fifty-sixth Pennsylvania, and farther to the right was the Sixth Wisconsin.

> ### Report of Lieut. Col. J. William Hoffman, USA, Commanding Fifty-sixth Pennsylvania, Second Brigade, First Division, Third Corps, Army of Virginia
>
> This regiment was ordered into the field to attack the battery and its support. The regiment was led by its colonel [Sullivan A. Meredith], but he was early severely wounded and obliged to leave the field, leaving the regiment under my command. The regiment sustained a withering fire from the enemy for about thirty minutes, maintaining its ground until the firing of the enemy ceased. Half an hour after the regiment was drawn off, [it] subsequently marched to Manassas.
>
> During the action the regiment sustained the following loss: Wounded, 1 colonel, 4 captains (one, Captain [George] Corman, since died), 2 lieutenants, and 55 enlisted men.
>
> The regiment took into the action about 180 men; a large number had dropped out exhausted on the road.[7]

Lieutenant Colonel J. William Hoffman, USA, Commanding Fifty-sixth Pennsylvania, Second Brigade, First Division, Third Corps, Army of Virginia. USAMHI.

Report of Brig. Gen. John Gibbon, USA—continued

I ordered the line to fall back, which was done in good order. We, however, occupied the ground with our pickets and collected the wounded.

Of the conduct of my brigade it is only necessary for me to state that it nobly maintained its position against heavy odds. The fearful list of killed and wounded tells the rest. The troops fought most of the time not more than 75 yards apart.

The total loss of the brigade is, killed, 133; wounded, 539; missing, 79. Total, 751, or considerably over one-third of the command.

The gallant Colonel O'Connor, Second Wisconsin, fell mortally wounded whilst placing his regiment in position. His major [Thomas S. Allen] was wounded in two places, but kept the field. Colonel Cutler, Sixth Wisconsin, whilst bravely moving up to the assistance of his comrades, was badly wounded in the leg. Every field officer of the Seventh Wisconsin (Colonel [William W.] Robinson, Lieutenant-Colonel [Charles A.] Hamilton, and Major [George] Bill) was wounded, the lieutenant-colonel remaining on the field

> and bringing off his regiment in the best possible manner. The major of the Nineteenth [Isaac M. May] fell mortally wounded whilst his regiment was sustaining a most destructive fire on the left of the line.[8]

Face left, retrace your steps, and walk southwest for 525 yards to the top of the hill. You will walk past the Seventh Wisconsin marker (do not take a left or right off of the trail). When you arrive at the top of the hill, stop. You have returned to Position B.

All along the positions you have walked, the Union and Confederate infantry exchanged short-range deadly fire until dark brought an end to the fighting.

Although Jackson had the preponderance of combat power, he was unable to bring sufficient brigades into the fight to successfully conclude it before nightfall. After dark, Jackson's forces regrouped on the higher ground to await the coming of daylight.

Jackson's critical decision to attack had revealed his exact location and set the stage for where the battle would be fought. During the hours of darkness, King's division withdrew from the battlefield and marched southeast toward Manassas Junction. Also during the night, Pope issued a series of orders that moved the spread-out elements of his army to the Manassas Battlefield. The battle both army commanders had been seeking would commence in earnest the next day.

Retrace your previous path to the farmhouse. Time permitting, this would be a good opportunity to visit the restored dwelling. Then continue on to the parking area for the drive to Stop 4.

Leave the parking lot, and drive back to Pageland Lane. Turn left onto Pageland Lane, and drive south for 0.4 mile to the intersection with the Warrenton Turnpike (Lee Highway–US 29). Turn left on the Warrenton Turnpike, and drive east for 2.6 miles to the intersection with the Sudley Road (where the stoplight is). Continue through the intersection for 0.1 mile to a parking area on your left. Turn left into the parking area, park, leave your car, and follow the walking path west (toward the Stone House) for 70 yards to the intersection with another trail on your right. Turn right, and walk north on this trail for 250 yards to a position on the top of Buck Hill where you have a good view west and northwest. When you stop, look to the northwest.

Stop 4: Pope Decides to Attack
Position A—Overview

You are in the center of a north-to-south section of high ground formed by Henry Hill (930 yards to your left), Buck Hill (where you are), and Matthews Hill (500 yards to your right). This 1,430-yard-long terrain feature is parallel to the Sudley Road, and it was a good position, if properly organized, against any enemy attack from the southwest, west, or northwest. It also protected the Warrenton Turnpike as it went east from its junction with the Sudley Road. The turnpike was the major route of communication, supply, and movement of reinforcements forward. If necessary, it could also be a route of retreat for Pope's army.

Directly in front of you at a distance of 1,400 yards (0.8 mile) is the edge of a wood; another 500 yards (0.3 mile) into this wood is the unfinished railroad. The unfinished railroad runs from the northeast to the southwest. That portion of the unfinished railroad 1,900 yards (1.1 mile) to your front was the left center of Jackson's Left Wing. This was also the center of A. P. Hill's Division. Hill's left flank (and Jackson's) was 2,100 yards (1.2 miles) to your right front. Your view of this area is blocked by an intervening wood and hill. The center of Jackson's position was located 2,100 yards (1.2 miles) to your left front. This area was defended by Ewell's Division, now commanded by Brig. Gen. Alexander R. Lawton since Ewell's wounding the previous evening. To Lawton's right (your left), Jackson's (Taliaferro's) Division, commanded by Brig. Gen. William E. Starke since Taliaferro was also wounded the previous evening, extended the position so that Jackson's right flank was 3,000 yards (1.7 miles) to your left.

Groveton was situated 2,300 yards (1.3 miles) southwest of your current location. There, the Warrenton Turnpike was intersected by the Groveton-Sudley Road (today Featherbed Lane). The Groveton-Sudley Road goes south from the intersection as Lewis Lane. From the intersection it also extends north for 0.9 mile, where it crosses the unfinished railroad. From the railroad, the Groveton-Sudley road continues northeast for 1.3 miles to Sudley Springs. This 1.3-mile section is behind and parallel to the unfinished railroad position defended by Lawton and A. P. Hill. As such it, provided the capability to laterally move reinforcing troops.

The area defended by Lawton and A. P. Hill was subjected to eight separate, mostly uncoordinated attacks throughout the day.

When Jackson revealed his position, Pope ordered his army to terrain near your current location. On August 29 Pope deployed the majority of his troops in the area west, northwest, and north of the Warrenton Turnpike–Sudley Road intersection.

Appendix I

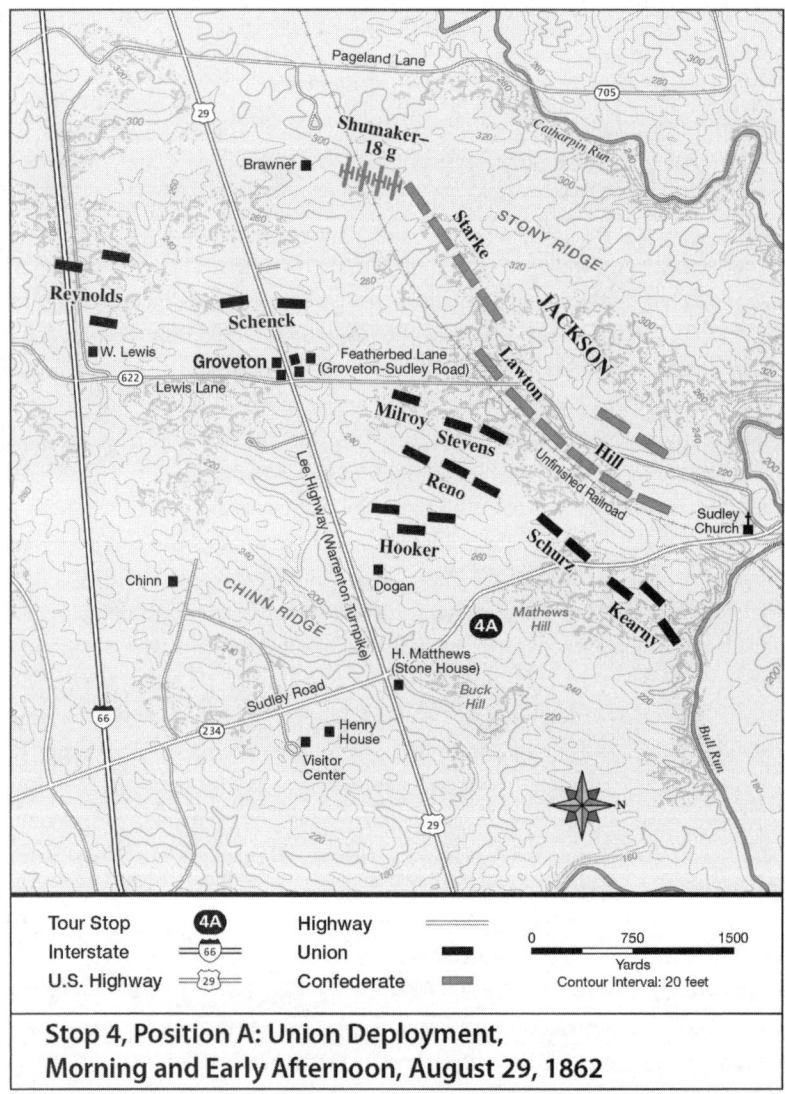

Stop 4, Position A: Union Deployment, Morning and Early Afternoon, August 29, 1862

Maj. Gen. Franz Sigel's First Corps (Army of Virginia) spent the night in this vicinity. In the morning the troops deployed into the area between the Warrenton Turnpike and the Sudley Road. Brig. Gen. Robert C. Schenck's First Division deployed near Groveton, and Brig. Gen. Robert H. Milroy's Independent Brigade deployed to Schenck's right along the Groveton-Sudley Road. Brig. Gen. Carl Schurz's Third Division established itself in the open area in front of you and to your right front. Brig. Gen. John Reynolds's Pennsylvania Reserves Division went into position along Lewis Lane to the left of Schenck.

The divisions of Maj. Gen. Samuel P. Heintzelman's Third Corps (Army of the Potomac) arrived next. Maj. Gen. Philip Kearny's First Division marched west on the turnpike from Centreville, arrived at 9:00 a.m., and deployed to your right front. At 11:00 a.m. Maj. Gen. Joseph Hooker's Second Division, following Kearny's, deployed in the area in front of you.

The Ninth Corps was also marching west on the turnpike, and it began to arrive at 11:30 a.m. Brig. Gen. Isaac I. Stevens's First Division deployed farther in front of you to the west. Stevens was followed by Maj. Gen. Jesse L. Reno's Second Division. Reno's men went into position in close proximity to Stevens's division. The early morning Union strength in the area was nine brigades. By early afternoon, the number of brigades had increased to twenty.

Pope incorrectly believed that Jackson was attempting to retreat to the west. He ordered the Fifth Corps (Army of the Potomac) and the Third Corps (Army of Virginia), which were 3.7 miles south (left) of you, to advance northwest to Gainesville and block Jackson's supposed route of retreat. The Union brigades in this area would conduct attacks to develop the situation and prevent Jackson from retreating. But Jackson's troops were not retreating.

Pope's misunderstanding of the tactical situation and the orders that followed resulted in a series of piecemeal attacks against A. P. Hill's and Lawton's Divisions. Some of these attacks had limited success in penetrating or forcing back part of the defenders. However, Pope did not coordinate these assaults or use the full combat strength available in just one or two coordinated attacks. As a result, Confederate units were shifted laterally to stop penetrations, reinforce the defenses, and counterattack.

Pope's decision to attack in this manner was a misapplication of his combat power. His choice produced no favorable results, but it defined the combat in this area throughout the day.

You will now proceed to two separate Confederate defensive positions along the unfinished railroad. There, you will explore some of these piecemeal attacks.

Return to your car for the drive to Position B (Stop 4).

Drive out of the parking lot, and turn right (west). At the stoplight turn right onto the Sudley Road, and drive north for 1.5 miles to a parking area on your left. Turn left into the parking area, park, and get out of your car. Leave the parking area and walk southwest along the unfinished railroad grade for 650 yards to the marker for Gregg's Brigade. Stop at this marker, and face left (southeast).

Appendix I

Position B—Krzyzanowski's Attack / Gregg's Defense

Maj. Gen. A. P. Hill deployed his division with four brigades in the first line and two brigades in a supporting and reserve line. You are standing in the left center of A. P. Hill's defensive position. Gregg's Brigade was at this location. To Gregg's left was Branch's Brigade. Thomas's Brigade was to Gregg's right, and Fields's Brigade was stationed farther to the right. Pender's and Archer's Brigades formed the second line and were across the Groveton-Sudley Road that is behind you. Ewell's Division, commanded by Brig. Gen. Alexander R. Lawton, was to Hill's right.

The first attack against the Confederate defenses was made by Col. Wladimir Krzyzanowski's Second Brigade of Schurz's division. Shortly after this attack commenced, Brig. Gen. Milroy led his brigade forward against the defenses 1,500 yards to your right.

This is the position where Krzyzanowski's brigade made contact with Brig. Gen. Maxcy Gregg's brigade of Hill's Division. Passing through the open area, Krzyzanowski's troops entered the edge of the wood and proceeded toward your location. The regiments of Gregg's Brigade were deployed behind you. As the skirmishers from both brigades made contact in this vicinity, the brigade commanders began moving regiments forward to engage each other. Colonel Krzyzanowski initially deployed two of his three regiments. The Fifty-fourth New York was on the right (your left) of his line, and the Fifty-eighth New York was on the left (your right). He kept the Seventy-fifth Pennsylvania in reserve.

Report of Col. Wladimir Krzyzanowski, USA, Commanding Second Brigade, Third Division, First Corps, Army of Virginia

Scarcely had the skirmishers passed over 200 yards when they became engaged with the enemy. For some time the firing was kept up, but our skirmishers had to yield at last to the enemy's advancing column. At this time I ordered my regiments up, and a general engagement ensued. However, I soon noticed that the Fifty-fourth and Fifty-eighth Regiments had to fall back, owing to the furious fire of the enemy, who had evidently thrown his forces exclusively upon those two regiments. The Seventy-fifth Regiment Pennsylvania Volunteers, which up to this time had not taken part in this engagement, was (at the time the Fifty-eighth and Fifty-fourth retired)

Colonel Wladimir Krzyzanowski, USA, Commanding Second Brigade, Third Division, First Corps, Army of Virginia. USAMHI.

now nobly led on by Lieutenant-Colonel Mahler upon the right flank of the enemy, and kept him busy until I had brought the Fifty-eighth at a double-quick up to its previous position, when those two regiments successfully drove the enemy before them, thereby gaining the position of the [Independent Line of the] Manassas Gap Railroad. [This is the unfinished railroad.][9]

Behind you, the five regiments of Gregg's Brigade were deployed in a five-hundred-yard-long double line. As the Union and Confederate skirmishers made contact, Gregg moved the First South Carolina forward to this location. The troops then engaged the advancing Union line.

Report of Lieut. Col. Edward McCrady, CSA, Commanding First South Carolina, Gregg's Brigade, A. P. Hill's Division, Jackson's Left Wing, Army of Northern Virginia

I was directed to detail a company to act, with others from other regiments of the brigade, as skirmishers to cover our front and flank.

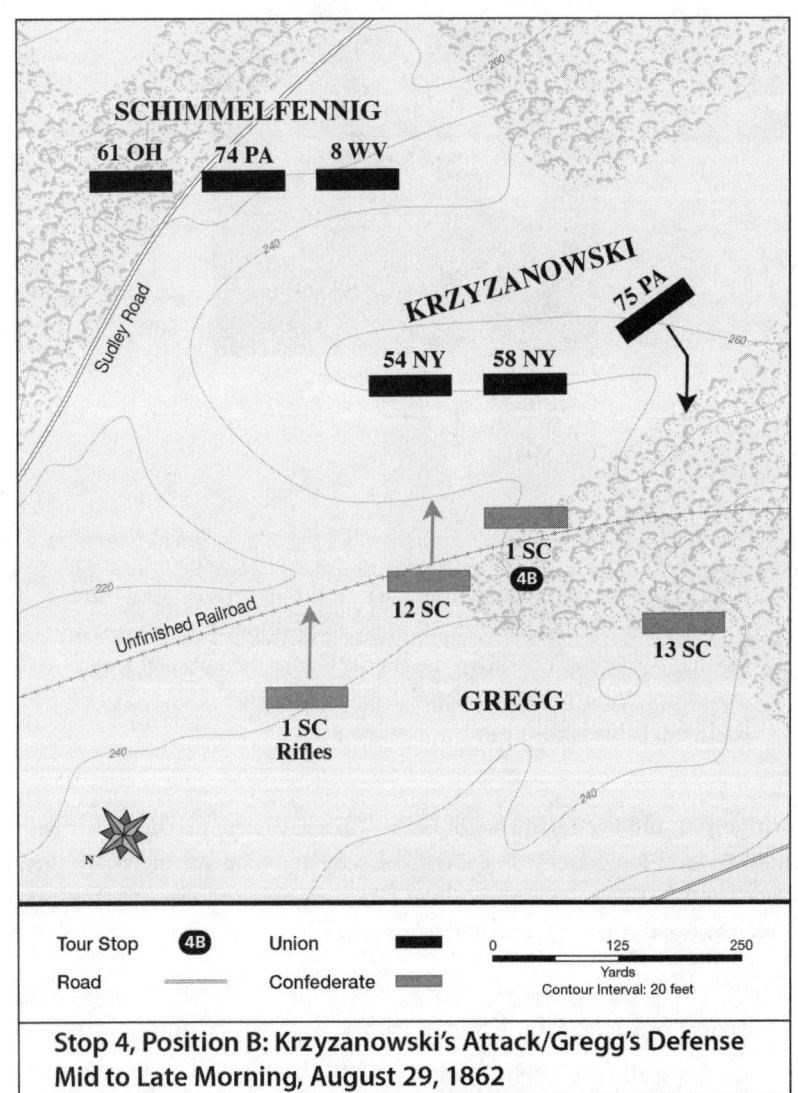

Stop 4, Position B: Krzyzanowski's Attack/Gregg's Defense
Mid to Late Morning, August 29, 1862

Shortly after the skirmishers had been deployed, by General Gregg's order I marched the regiment to the front, and was placed in position by General Gregg 60 yards behind and parallel with the cut of the projected Independent Railroad from Gainesville to Alexandria. At this point, the ground rising to some extent, the grade of the road immediately in our front rendered the depth of the cut about 6 feet; but the ground sloping to our right and left, reduced this depth to about 1 or 2 feet upon our flanks. The ground upon our side of the cut, upon which our line was formed, was almost entirely bare, while that on the other side was covered with quite a thick growth of brush. On our right, too, this growth of brush extended to about 50 yards of our flank, while on our left, at about the same distance, was a field inclosed by a worm fence. The portion of this field nearest our position was open, but the other side was covered with a thick growth of corn. Soon after assuming this position, by General Gregg's directions I moved the regiment across the cut, crossing by one rank at a time, and gaining the other side, met Lieutenant [J. B.] Fellers, of the [Thirteenth South Carolina], who was to direct us to the ground in which General Gregg informed me the enemy had taken position. General Gregg's instructions to me were, upon coming up with them, to give them two or three volleys and then to charge them with the bayonet. Our advance soon drew upon us the fire of the enemy, who were posted in a hollow. The ground through which we were advancing was quite thickly wooded and covered with underbrush, rendering it difficult to see more than a very few yards in our front. Here, too, it sloped both to our front and flanks, and in the hollow at the bottom of the slope lay the enemy awaiting our approach. From this hollow they opened fire upon us as soon as we were in range. This fire was returned, as directed; but endeavoring to move forward to the charge I found the enemy were in force upon our left, from which they opened on our left and rear. Finding, therefore, that it would be impossible to dislodge them by ourselves, I sent a messenger telling General Gregg of their position upon our left. This messenger had scarcely gone when a fire was opened upon us also from our right and rear. We thus were exposed to fires from our front and both flanks, and so completely were we flanked that the rear of our wings was also exposed. Finding the enemy in such force, I then sent Captain [William P.] Shooter to explain our position to General Gregg and ask for re-enforcements, saying at the

> same time that we would endeavor to hold our position until they should arrive. Soon after Captain Shooter had gone, however, the fire became so heavy that I determined to fall back some distance in order to withdraw from the exposure of my flanks and rear. My order to this effect, I regret to say, was executed with considerable confusion; but Captain [Michael P.] Parker and Lieutenant [James] Armstrong soon succeeded in rallying Company K (the color company) around the colors. Company F, too (Lieutenant [George R.] Congdon in command), rallied almost at the same time, and upon these two companies the regiment was soon reformed.[10]

As Lieutenant Colonel McCrady's regiment was driven back and then reformed, the Twelfth South Carolina reinforced it, coming forward and deploying on its left flank. The regimental commander was mortally wounded at Antietam, and the battle report was written by his next in command.

> **Report of Lieut. Col. Cadwalader Jones, CSA, Commanding Twelfth South Carolina, Gregg's Brigade, A. P. Hill's Division, Jackson's Left Wing, Army of Northern Virginia**
>
> Colonel [Dixon] Barnes, accompanied by Major [William H.] McCorkle and myself, advanced across the road with eight companies, under orders to drive back the enemy, who were then coming up. We crossed the road with and on the left of the First South Carolina Regiment. Very soon the enemy, in numbers considerably exceeding our own, were seen advancing through the woods on our left. It became necessary immediately to change front, which being done we exchanged several rounds with the enemy, when the Twelfth advanced and the enemy retreated. They soon reformed with the assistance of fresh troops, who endeavored to flank us on the left.[11]

Joining the First and Twelfth South Carolina Regiments was the Thirteenth South Carolina, which moved forward and attempted to connect with the First South Carolina's right. This connection was not made, and a gap existed between these two regiments. Meanwhile, on the left of the position, the First South Carolina Rifles moved forward to reinforce the First and Twelfth South Carolina.

Report of Lieut.Col. Edward McCrady, CSA—Continued

Just at this time Colonel Barnes, with the Twelfth Regiment, came up on our left, and joining him, we charged and drove the enemy some distance beyond the point from which we had retired; but finding the enemy still strong upon our right, and again receiving his fire from that flank and in our rear, I halted the regiment, and throwing back the right wing, endeavored thus to hold our position, which now became necessary for the safety of Colonel Barnes, who had pressed forward upon our left. General Gregg had sent Colonel [Oliver E.] Edwards, with the Thirteenth, to our support on the right, but the denseness of the undergrowth rendering it impossible to see him, I sent Sergt. L. A. Smith, Company C, who volunteered to go to communicate with Colonel Edwards and to guide him to our position. Colonel Edwards, in moving to our support, had met the enemy in such force as to compel him to engage them there and to prevent his effecting a junction with us. About this time I received a message from Lieutenant-Colonel [Cadwalader] Jones, of the Twelfth, requesting me to move forward to the support of Colonel Barnes, who, having pushed the enemy to some distance in advance, was then being pressed by them in superior numbers. The enemy, however, upon our right rendered it impossible for me to advance—indeed, it was all we could do to hold our own position, and had we moved forward Colonel Barnes and ourselves would both have been attacked in our rear and cut off.

Just at this time Colonel [J. Foster] Marshall, with the [First South Carolina] Rifles, came up and advanced to Colonel Barnes' support. I remained, holding the position protecting their rear and flank. After some time, learning that Colonel Edwards [Thirteenth South Carolina] was retiring, and seeing Colonel Marshall moving his regiment from our left and passing us by a flank in our rear, I supposed an order to fall back had missed me, which I accordingly did, joining the rear of Colonel Marshall's regiment.[12]

Face to your left and walk on or beside the railroad bed for 100 yards, stop, face to your right so that you are again looking south.

Appendix I

Position C—Schimmelfennig's Attack / Barnes's Counterattack

Approximately one hour after Krzyzanowski's Second Brigade made contact with elements of Gregg's Brigade, Schurz sent his First Brigade under the command of Col. Alexander Schimmelfennig forward on Krzyzanowski's right (your left). Schimmelfennig deployed his three regiments with the Eighth West Virginia on his left (your right), the Seventy-fourth Pennsylvania in the center, and the Sixty-first Ohio on his right (your left). Moving across the open ground south of this location, they entered the wood and made contact with the First South Carolina Rifles and the Twelfth South Carolina just forward of where you are.

The commander of the Seventy-fourth Pennsylvania provides a description of Schimmelfennig's attack as seen from the regimental level.

Report of Maj. Franz Blessing, USA, Commanding Seventy-fourth Pennsylvania, First Brigade, Third Division, First Corps, Army of Virginia

Under cover of skirmishers in the front and right flank we advanced in quick-time over an open field until we arrived at the center of the woods, where in an opening we halted. The skirmishers met the skirmishing line of the enemy, opened fire, and drove them from the woods. Forced by the heavy artillery fire of the enemy we changed several

Major Franz Blessing, USA, Commanding Seventy-forth Pennsylvania, First Brigade, Third Division, First Corps, Army of Virginia. USAMHI.

times our positions. From the right flank came the report that a strong column was advancing, but it was impossible to recognize whether friend or foe. It was afterward ascertained to be General Kearny's [division] for our relief. The regiment was then ordered to the left, where it took its position in the general battle line, after advancing about 400 yards under the heavy fire of the enemy, driving the latter back and out of his positions; but by the withdrawing of a regiment stationed on the left of the Seventy-fourth the enemy took advantage, and, outflanking us, we were forced back about 100 yards.[13]

The enemy Major Blessing referred to was Col. Dixon Barnes's Twelfth South Carolina Infantry Regiment. Barnes attacked into the gap between Schimmelfennig's left flank and Krzyzanowski's right flank. This attack helped to halt Schurz's two brigades.

Report of Lieut. Col. Cadwalader Jones, CSA, Commanding Twelfth South Carolina, Gregg's Brigade, A. P. Hill's Division, Jackson's Left Wing, Army of Northern Virginia

Here one or two of our companies on the left were caused to change front and fire on the flanking column. A single well-directed volley put them to flight. Wheeling these companies again into line, the Twelfth charged in the most gallant manner, firing as it advanced, and putting the enemy completely to rout, pursued them with heavy slaughter through the woods and until they crossed the field beyond and ran out of sight. Being now about half a mile from our starting point, we fell back into the woods a short distance. Very soon a fresh column of the enemy, probably three regiments, were seen advancing. Just at this time the First Rifles, most opportunely, were also seen advancing through the woods to our support. Forming a line with and on the left of [the Twelfth South Carolina] regiment, together we gave them battle, and without much difficulty or loss again drove back the enemy. Soon thereafter, under orders from Brigadier-General Gregg, we returned to our first position.

These engagements lasted nearly three hours, during which time the regiment was almost constantly under fire. We carried into

Appendix I

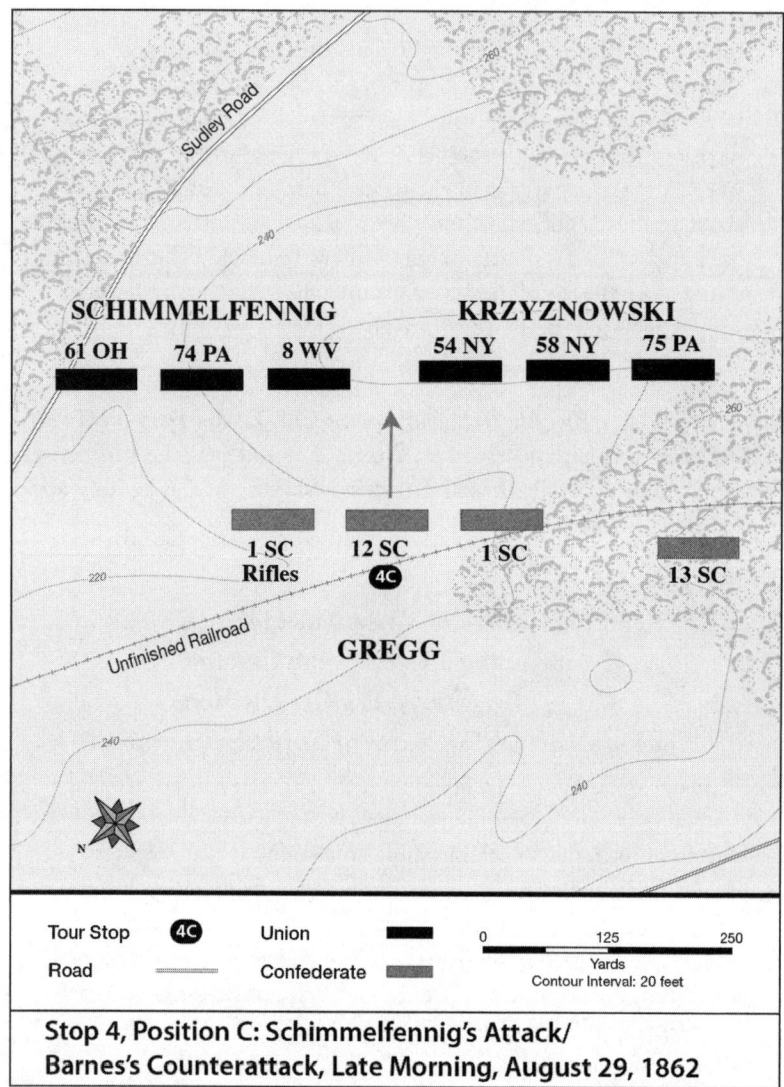

Stop 4, Position C: Schimmelfennig's Attack/
Barnes's Counterattack, Late Morning, August 29, 1862

action 320 men, less the two first-mentioned companies [assigned as skirmishers], numbering together not more than 50 men, leaving 270 men actually engaged. The loss was 23 killed, 121 wounded, and 2 missing, being a loss of more than a half.[14]

Having stopped Schurz's attack, Gregg withdrew his regiments back north from the unfinished railroad bed to the higher ground they had occupied earlier. However, Schurz was not ready to quit. He recommenced his attack, and it reached the railroad bed. On Schurz's right the Seventy-fourth Pennsylvania and Sixty-first Ohio pushed beyond the railroad for about eighty yards.

> ### Report of Maj. Franz Blessing, USA—Continued
> Forming again in column for attack the regiment advanced in quick-time toward the enemy, who gave way until he arrived at the other side of the railroad [bed]. Here again flanked by the enemy, and under a galling fire of grape-shot and canister, the regiment had to leave its position, which it did by making a flank movement to the left, forcing the enemy to withdraw from the woods. We advanced over our former position, capturing an ambulance with two wounded officers, to the seam of the woods. At this point a heavy shower of grape-shot and canister pouring into us, we withdrew to the railroad [bed].[15]

The Seventy-fourth Pennsylvania and Sixty-first Ohio retreated when they were hit in the right flank by two regiments of Brig. Gen. Lawrence Branch's brigade, supported by Capt. William G. Crenshaw's Virginia Battery.

The attacks by these two brigades illustrate the events of the day and the wasting of combat power as a result of Pope's critical decision. Both brigades had some success in penetrating the Confederate defenses. Because the attacks were uncoordinated and Union reserves were unavailable to reinforce their success, Confederate reserves were able to drive them out of the penetrations.

Face left, follow the unfinished railroad and walking path northeast and north, and return to the parking area and your car for the drive to Position D (Stop 4).

Drive from the parking area, turn left (north) onto the Sudley Road (Highway 234), and drive 0.1 mile to the intersection with the Groveton-Sudley Road on your left. Today this road is named Featherbed Lane or Road 622. Turn left, and drive for 0.5 mile. Pull over to the right and stop.

From this point forward for 0.5 mile, several of the separate Union attacks penetrated the defenses and reached the road before being repulsed.

Appendix I

Continue driving on the Groveton-Sudley Road for 0.8 mile to the parking area on the left. Turn into the parking area, and park. Leave your car, walk back to the Groveton-Sudley Road, and stand in a safe location where you can look south down the road. For a different view, you can cross the road and follow the trail for 30 yards to higher ground. BE EXTREMELY CAREFUL OF TRAFFIC.

Position D—Nagle's Attack

You now stand in the center of Ewell's Division, commanded by Brig. Gen. Alexander R. Lawton. To your right was Trimble's Brigade, commanded by Capt. W. F. Brown after Trimble was wounded. The brigade was deployed in two lines. In the first line, the Twelfth Georgia occupied the left, and the Fifteenth Alabama formed the right. Two other regiments, the Twenty-first Georgia and Twenty-first North Carolina, were deployed in the second, supporting, line. Their relative position to each other is unknown. The position of a fifth unit, the First North Carolina Battalion, is unknown, but the troops were probably deployed as a skirmish line to the front.

To your left was Lawton's Brigade, commanded by Col. Marcellus Douglass. This brigade had six regiments, three of which were deployed in the first line. The right flank regiment was astride the road, and the other two units were positioned to its left. Two regiments were in the second supporting line. The location of the sixth regiment is not known, though it may have provided a skirmish line in front of the brigade. Additionally, the relative position of each regiment by unit designation is unknown. To Douglass's left flank was Field's Brigade of A. P. Hill's Division.

This attack was not the first in this area. That morning Brigadier General Milroy's Independent Brigade attacked and ruptured the defenses to your right. As there were no following and supporting units, the penetration was stopped and driven back by Confederate reserves.

Separate attacks occurred 1,300 yards to the left of your location, which is where Krzyzanowski then Schimmelfenning attacked Gregg. These attacks were followed with attacks by Kearny's division (two brigades), Grover's brigade, and Leasure's brigade. These Union assaults were uncoordinated, and after some initial success they were repulsed.

Late in the afternoon Col. James Nagle's First Brigade of Reno's Second Division, Ninth Corps (Army of the Potomac) attacked this part of the defensive position. Nagle deployed two of his regiments in his front line, the Second Maryland on the right (your left as you view it) and the Sixth New Hampshire on the left (your right). The Forty-eighth Pennsylvania was held in reserve, and it followed the first line. The attack reached the wood, and the

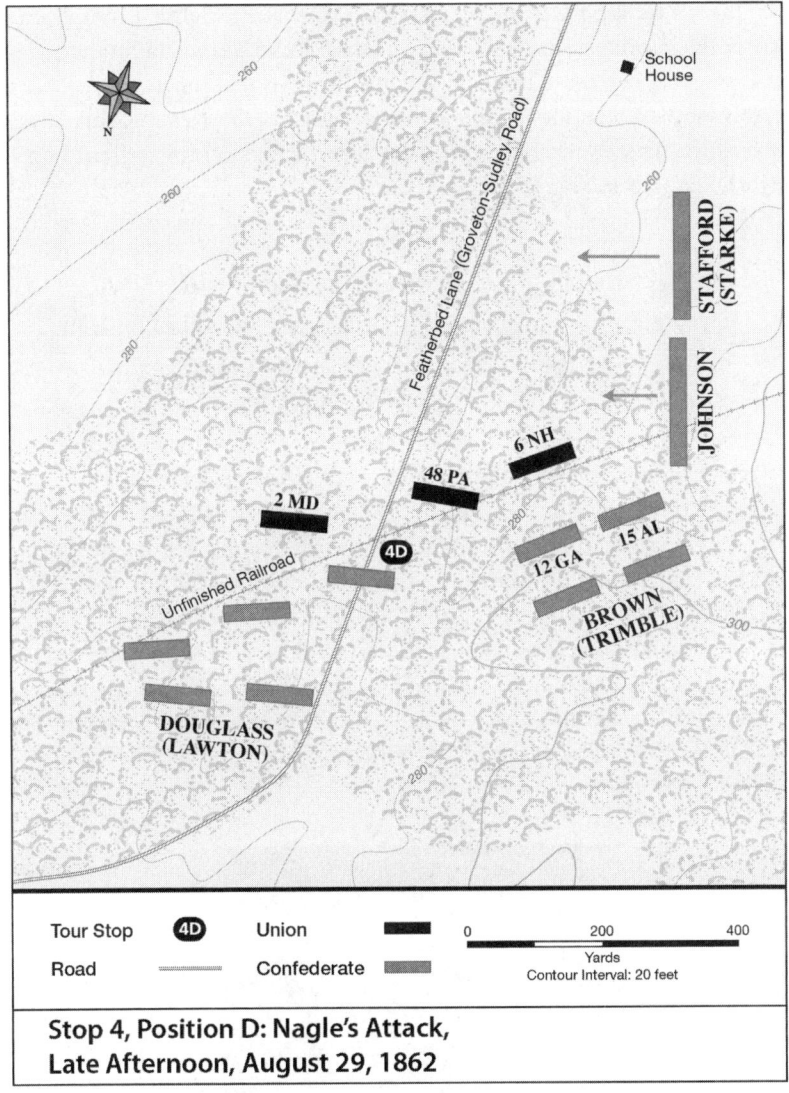

Stop 4, Position D: Nagle's Attack, Late Afternoon, August 29, 1862

Second Maryland oblique to the right, the Sixth New Hampshire oblique to the left, and the Forty-eighth Pennsylvania moved forward into the opening in the center of the line. In this configuration the attack hit the Confederate defenses in this vicinity. Nagle's regiments drove the defenders back one hundred yards. The right of Douglass's line and the left of Brown's line fell back before the attack, creating a salient in the defenses. It was almost a breakthrough, but not quite.

Appendix I

The center regiment of Nagle's attack, the Forty-eighth Pennsylvania, struck this position. Farther to your left the Second Maryland hit the center of Douglass's defenses. The Forty-eighth Pennsylvania drove the defenders at this location back for about one hundred yards. However, a counterattack against the Sixth New Hampshire's left flank eventually impacted the Forty-eighth Pennsylvania.

Narrative of Quartermaster Sgt. Joseph Gould, USA, Forty-eighth Pennsylvania, First Brigade, Second Division, Ninth Corps, Army of the Potomac

The Forty-eighth was formed with the Sixth New Hampshire and the Second Maryland, in line of battle, marched through an open field into the woods, and through a very heavy infantry fire. We gained an old abandon railroad cut, and were busily engaging in our front with the enemy, when a heavy firing took place on our left and rear. A first it was thought that it came from some of our own troops, but upon displaying the colors more conspicuously, the firing became hotter and hotter, and the orders to fall back were given. At first the line moved slowly and in perfect order, but it soon became evident the brigade was flanked. The men began dropping in the ranks, dead or wounded, the rebels appeared and the line broke

Quartermaster Sergeant Joseph Gould, USA, Forty-eight Pennsylvania, First Brigade, Second Division, Ninth Corps, Army of the Potomac. USAMHI.

> and fled in confusion to the edge of the woods, where it was again formed. The loss of the regiment, for the day, was one hundred and fifty killed, wounded and missing.[16]

Pope's mistaken belief that Jackson was retreating, even after there was sufficient intelligence to the contrary, led him to order a total of eight separate, uncoordinated, unsupported attacks against the 1,900-yard position held by Hill's and Ewell's (Lawton's) Divisions. This decision established the sequence of the fighting between the Warrenton Turnpike and the Sudley Road. In the early evening Pope ordered Hatch's division to attack west on the Warrenton Turnpike; the operation was unsuccessful. While focused on Jackson, Pope completely missed the indicators that Longstreet's powerful Right Wing had arrived on Jackson's right.

Return to your car for the drive to Stop 5.

Drive from the parking area, turn left onto the Groveton-Sudley Road, and drive south for 0.3 mile to a parking area on your right. Turn into the parking area, park, leave your car, and walk back to the Groveton-Sudley Road. Just before reaching the road, turn right. Walk south beside the road for 175 yards to the place where a walking trail goes off to the west (your right). Follow this trail for at least 10 yards so that you are away from the road. Stand so that you can look 525 yards across the open ground to the berm, where a monument is located. The monument is 25 yards in front of the unfinished railroad bed that forms a cut (the "Deep Cut") in the vicinity.

Stop 5: Pope Decides to Attack Again

Position A—Porter's Attack Position

You are just forward of and centered on the position of Maj. Gen. Fitz John Porter's force when it formed for an attack on the afternoon of August 30.

That morning began with Pope still believing that Jackson was planning to retreat or had begun to do so. Pope also believed that Longstreet had yet to arrive. This thought process had been further influenced by the earlier movement of two Confederate divisions. After the evening and night engagement along the Warrenton Turnpike between the divisions of Brig. Gen. John P. Hatch and Brig. Gen. John B. Hood, the Confederate forces had withdrawn west to defensive positions. During the night, Longstreet's last arriving division, Maj. Gen. Richard H. Anderson's, marched east on the Warrenton

Turnpike and joined the Army of Northern Virginia. Not knowing the exact location of the Confederate and Union lines, Anderson's Division had marched too far east and was in close proximity to Pope's position. When this mistake was discovered, Anderson's Division marched back west and moved into position as a reserve. Anderson's westward movement reinforced Pope's earlier belief that the Confederates were retreating and had to be pursued.

In the early morning hours Pope's army was deployed with its left flank unit, Maj. Gen. John F. Reynolds's three-brigade division, to your left rear and south of the Warrenton Turnpike. Maj. Gen. Fitz John Porter's two-division Fifth Corps, positioned to Reynolds's left (south) the previous day, had been ordered to march north and join the army in the vicinity of the Warrenton Turnpike. Arriving early that morning, Porter had placed his corps in a position 1,400 yards (0.8 mile) behind you on Dogan's Ridge. Porter then moved forward to an attack position along the Groveton-Sudley Road. His force was situated just behind you on the other side of the road. The remainder of Pope's army was in a position from Dogan's Ridge that went northeast to and across the Sudley Road. In several locations the position was two divisions deep, on good defensible terrain, and supported by artillery.

Lee's army was deployed in defensive positions with Jackson on the left and Longstreet on the right. Jackson continued to occupy the now 3,600-yard-long position (2.1 miles) along the unfinished railroad that extended southwest from the vicinity of Sudley Church to an area just north of the Brawner Farm. A. P. Hill's Division was on the left, Ewell's Division (commanded by Brig. Gen. Alexander R. Lawton—hereafter Lawton's Division) was in the center, and Jackson's Division (commanded by Brig. Gen. William E. Starke—hereafter Starke's Division) was on the right. To the right of Starke's Division were the massed guns of his divisional artillery under the command of Maj. Lindsay M. Shumaker.

Longstreet's position went south from Jackson's right for 4,250 yards (2.4 miles). Jackson's and Longstreet's positions formed an approximately 115-degree angle, which looked like a wide V. Eighteen guns from Col. Stephen D. Lee's artillery battalion anchored Longstreet's left. Lee's guns were positioned so as to place enfilading fire on any force attacking Jackson's center and right. To the right (south) of Lee's Battalion was Wilcox's Division. Hood's Division, with Evans's Brigade in support, was located in front of Wilcox's right and astride the turnpike. To Hood's right was Kemper's Division, and farther right was Jones's Division. No Union force stood in front of Jones's Division. Anderson's Division was in army reserve behind Longstreet's left center in the vicinity of the Warrenton Turnpike and Pageland Lane intersection. Cavalry was deployed to Longstreet's right and Jackson's left.

Lee's plan for August 30 was to remain on the defense, thereby giving Pope the opportunity to attack him again and perhaps cause major damage to Pope's army. However, Lee could not afford to remain in this position for very long. Units from Maj. Gen. George B. McClellan's Army of the Potomac were continuing to arrive from the Peninsula. Maj. Gen. Samuel P. Heintzelman's Third Corps, Maj. Gen. Fitz John Porter's Fifth Corps, and Brig. Gen. John F. Reynolds's division were already on the battlefield and attached to Pope's army. Others were en route. Time would provide Pope with additional reinforcements. If both Union armies were to completely unite, then Lee would be faced with an overwhelming enemy force. Fully aware that time favored Pope, Lee had decided to resume the offense if he wasn't attacked on August 30. Longstreet's Right Wing would hold Pope in position while Jackson's Left Wing would disengage and conduct a turning movement around Pope's right flank. The objective of this maneuver would be cutting Pope off from Washington and reinforcements. With Pope's army between two major Confederate forces, Lee could initiate a battle of annihilation.

Saturday began with Pope's critical decision to attack again. The day would be one of indecision, misunderstanding, and finally disaster. Pope initially ordered Porter, supported by Reynolds's and Hatch's divisions, to pursue what he thought were retreating Confederates west along the Warrenton Turnpike. At the same time, Brig. Gen. James B. Ricketts was ordered to move part of his division forward and strike Jackson's left. Ricketts gave this mission to Brig. Gen. Abram Duryea. At midmorning Duryea maneuvered his brigade against A. P. Hill's (Jackson's) left, but a strong defense immediately stopped him. Duryea's repulse was reported to Pope.

Before Porter could get into position to move down the Warrenton Turnpike, he was ordered to attack Jackson's right and right center. This directive caused Porter to move his force into the Groveton Woods, which began six hundred yards to your left (south) and extended north along the east side of the Groveton-Sudley Road to the unfinished railroad. However, before Porter could launch his attack, he received another order telling him to again "pursue the retreating Confederates" west along the turnpike. Porter could not move his force directly to the turnpike without dangerously exposing its right flank. He decided to attack forward from Groveton Woods, strike what was thought to be the end of Jackson's line, maneuver left, attack the Confederate flank, move south and southwest, gain the turnpike, and conduct a pursuit to the west.

Pope still believed that Jackson was in the process of retreating. He had developed this concept the previous day, and after misinterpreting bits and pieces of information that were coming to him, he continued with this belief on Saturday. Pope also discounted reports indicating that Longstreet was deployed on Jackson's right and therefore overlapping his army's left flank.

Throughout the morning, Pope had received four separate warnings that Jackson was holding a strong defensive position rather than retreating. The first caution was from Porter, who told Pope of a strong Confederate force (this was Longstreet's Right Wing) in front of his corps when it was south of the Warrenton Turnpike the previous day. Reynolds later reported that when he had moved forward to the vicinity of Groveton and the area west, he had encountered strong enemy skirmish lines. Behind this covering force he believed Confederate units were maneuvering and deploying to the south, movements that would outflank Pope's army. Earlier in the morning, Duryea had reported that his brigade encountered a strong defense when it moved forward on the right of the Union line. Brig. Gen. Isaac I. Stevens, also in the right half of Pope's position, sent a strong reconnaissance-in-force forward from his division in the late morning. This reconnaissance immediately ran into strong Confederate defenses along the unfinished railroad and was driven back with losses. Stevens reported that the Confederates to his front were not retreating but holding strong defensive positions.

Disregarding any information that did not support his preconceptions about Jackson's retreat, Pope made the critical decision to attack again and ordered Porter forward. Pope's decision would set in motion a sequence of events that was almost catastrophic for his army.

You are just forward of the center of Porter's attack formation. Porter's force was composed of three divisions: Hatch's, Morell's, and Sykes's. To your right rear, across the road, was Brig. Gen. John P. Hatch's First Division of McDowell's Third Corps. Hatch had deployed his four brigades one behind the other, with the brigades having multiple lines. All total, Hatch's division was seven battle lines deep. The formation of his division indicates that he planned to hit the Confederate position with a narrow frontal assault column that was seven lines deep. This plan would allow Hatch to reinforce each attacking line, and it would provide him a sufficiently strong follow-on force to exploit any success. From the road, Hatch's formation stretched back east (behind you) for 325 yards.

Part of Maj. Gen. George W. Morell's First Division of Porter's Fifth Corps was deployed to your left rear, across the road. During the early-morning march north from the Gainesville-Manassas Road, Morell and his five-regiment Second Brigade, commanded by Brig. Gen. Charles Griffin, had mistakenly assumed Porter's corps was marching to Centreville and had marched east and off the battlefield. The other two brigades of this division were present with the corps, and they were commanded by Brig. Gen. Daniel

Battlefield Guide to the Critical Decisions at Second Manassas

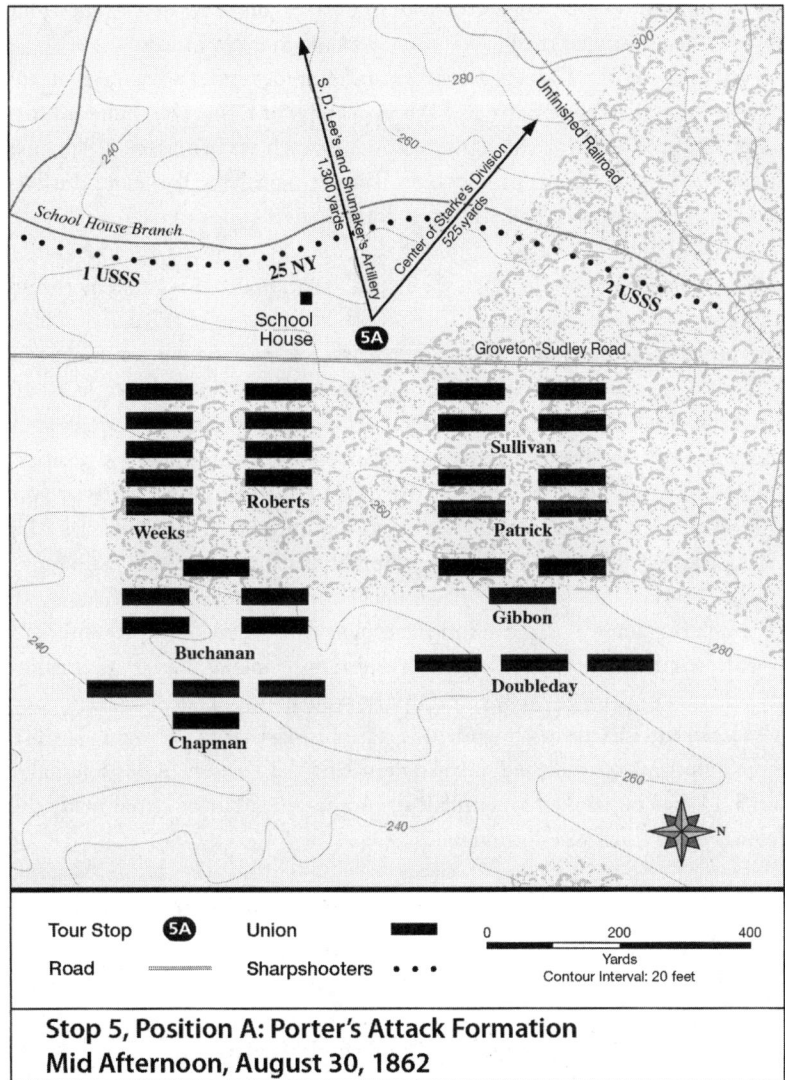

Stop 5, Position A: Porter's Attack Formation
Mid Afternoon, August 30, 1862

Butterfield. Butterfield deployed both brigades abreast with their regiments in column. Col. Charles W. Roberts's First Brigade was on the right. Butterfield's Third Brigade, commanded by Col. Henry A. Weeks, was on the left.

Behind Butterfield's formation were the two US Regular brigades of Brig. Gen. George Sykes's Second Division of Porter's Fifth Corps. Butterfield's and Sykes's divisions had a depth of 750 yards. Both of Butterfield's brigades were deployed so that they could jointly attack on a two-regiment front. Sykes's units would be used as reinforcements or to exploit success.

All total, Porter's attack formation initially occupied a frontage of 460 yards—210 yards to your left and 250 yards to your right. One hundred fifty yards to your front was the School House Branch watercourse. A skirmish line of the First US Sharpshooters, the Twenty-fifth New York, and the Second US Sharpshooters used its depression for cover.

Col. Stephen D. Lee's artillery battalion was stationed 1,300 hundred yards southwest of your location. The guns' position is represented by the artillery you could see from Stop 3, Position B. You can't see Lee's position from here because of the woods to your left front, which were not there in 1862. To Lee's left, your right, and in front of you stood the batteries of Jackson's (Starke's) Division under the command of Major Shumaker. The trees seven hundred yards in front of you keep you from seeing Shumaker's position. These trees were not there in 1862. Five hundred twenty-five yards to your right front, where the ground rises up to the unfinished railroad, was Maj. Gen. Jackson's right flank division, commanded by Brig. Gen. William E. Starke. Starke's (Jackson's) Division had four brigades. Col. Bradley T. Johnson's brigade was deployed in the center. Col. Leroy Stafford's (Starke's) brigade was deployed to Johnson's left (your right). Col. William S. H. Baylor's brigade was positioned to Johnson's right (your left) and slightly back. Col. Alexander G. Taliaferro's brigade was stationed farther to the right. The brigades behind the unfinished railroad berm and the artillery under Shumaker and S. D. Lee positioned for enfilade fire across the infantry's front made this defensive position quite formidable.

Follow the walking trail west for 150 yards to a small stream, which may be dry part of the year. Today, this intermittent stream is called School House Branch.

Position B—The Attack Begins

School House Branch extends to your left and right. The small depression created by the water flow marks the position of the Union skirmish line. Your current location is the position of the Twenty-fifth New York. The Second United States Sharpshooters were positioned to this unit's right and bending slightly back so as to touch the road. The First United States Sharpshooters occupied terrain to the left of the Twenty-fifth New York. From these positions the Union skirmishers exchanged fire with Confederate skirmishers who were approximately two hundred yards in front of you.

While the skirmish line was engaged, the attack formation began to move out of the woods and crossed the road behind you. Crossing the road to your right was Sullivan's first assault line (the Thirtieth New York and Twenty-fourth New York). As these troops crossed the road and entered the field to your right, they commenced a right wheel, came under fire from the Confederate defenders, and attacked toward the unfinished railroad. They were followed by Sullivan's second line (the Twenty-second New York and Eighty-fourth New York).

On Sullivan's left and directly behind you, Roberts's brigade moved forward, deploying into a battle line as it crossed the road. As the brigade passed through your location, it had the Thirteenth New York in the center, the First Michigan on the right, and the Eighteenth Massachusetts on the left. The Second Maine followed in the second, supporting line. Just prior to or upon reaching School House Branch, Roberts's brigade executed a half right wheel and attacked the Confederate defenders. The center of the brigade moved to where you see the monument on the higher ground to your right front. This terrain, which was the scene of intense fighting, is called Deep Cut.

To Roberts's left, Weeks's brigade moved from the woods and crossed the road, entering into what was then an open field on your left—the trees were not there in 1862. Weeks did not deploy his brigade from its column-of-regiments formation until it entered the open field and came under Confederate artillery fire. Leading the brigade, the Seventeenth New York moved up on Roberts's left and engaged the Confederates.

After much confusion, casualties, and loss of time, the remainder of the brigade was finally deployed. The Twelfth New York and Forty-fourth New York moved forward and joined the attack on the Seventeenth New York's left. The Eighty-third Pennsylvania and Sixteenth Michigan moved forward as a second, supporting line.

At this location you can gain an appreciation for the musket and artillery projectiles that were fired into the attack. Numbers on the strength of Confederate regiments are not available, but we know the strength of some brigades. Average regimental size can be assumed through extrapolation. Numbers of Starke's Division were categorized as follows: Johnson's Brigade had 800 troops in 4 regiments for an average of 200 troops per regiment, and Stafford's Brigade had 1,000 troops in 5 regiments for an average of 200 troops per regiment.

Johnson deployed 2 regiments in his first line and 2 in his second line. Stafford placed 3 regiments in the first line and 2 in the second line. This arrangement initially placed 5 regiments in the first line and 4 regiments in a second or a reserve line. These 5 regiments totaled 1,000 troops (muskets). In

Appendix I

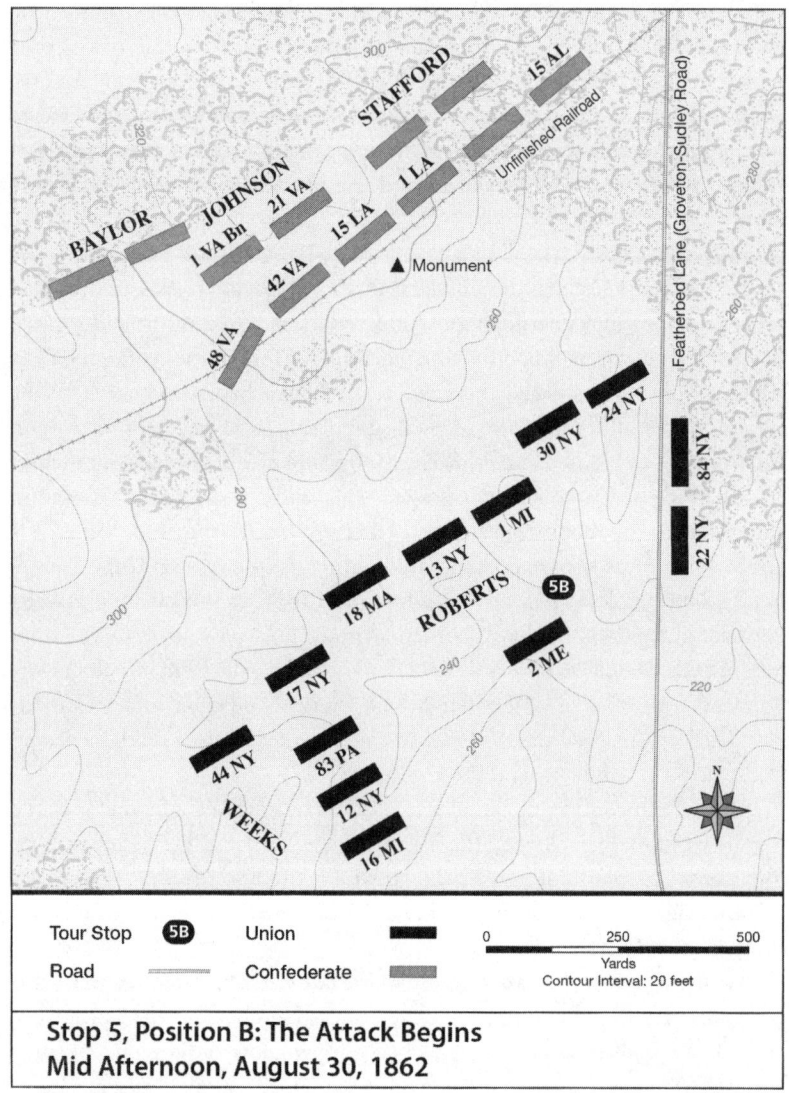

**Stop 5, Position B: The Attack Begins
Mid Afternoon, August 30, 1862**

addition, the Fifteenth Alabama (the right regiment of Trimble's Brigade) on Stafford's left would also have had 200 troops. All total, 1,200 troops were in position to fire on the attacking Union regiments.

Although the rifled musket had a longer effective range, new research indicates that engagements were done at shorter ranges. For illustrative purposes, assume the defenders opened fire when the attacking force reached a point 300 yards from the defenses. In an attack, infantry normally moved at "Quick Time" until close to the enemy position, then changed to "Double-Quick Time." "Quick Time" required 1 minute and 10 seconds for every 100 yards of forward movement. "Double-Quick Time" required 40 seconds for every 100 yards of forward movement.[17]

If the attacking troops came under musket fire beginning at 300 yards from the defenders, moved at "Quick Time" for 200 yards, then moved at "Double-Quick Time" for the last 100 yards, they would require 3 minutes to reach the defensive position. A trained infantryman could fire up to 3 rounds a minute for a short period of time. Volume of fire from 1,200 infantrymen (at 3 rounds per minute) for 3 minutes would be 10,800 rounds.

In addition to the frontal infantry fire, Porter's attack was also subjected to enfilade (flanking) fire. Col. Steven D. Lee reported that he had 18 guns in action. These guns were in position to deliver enfilading fire against the attack's left flank. In addition, Maj. Lindsay M. Shumaker may have had up to 20 guns from Starke's Division available to deliver enfilade and oblique fire into the attack. These 38 guns, each firing 2 rounds a minute, would fire 76 rounds in one minute. In the 3 minutes it took the attacking infantry to cross 300 yards, the artillery fired 228 rounds. This number was probably higher, as the artillery could have engaged the attack before the defending infantry.

In summary, the leading and immediately following regiments of Porter's attack probably had 10,800 musket rounds and 228 artillery rounds fired at them in the space of 3 minutes!

Report of Col. Charles W. Roberts, USA, Commanding First Brigade, First Division, Fifth Corps, Army of the Potomac

My skirmishers advancing through the skirt of woods, the command following them closely. We had passed nearly through the belt of timber to our front, when upon the opposite edge beyond the wood my skirmishers, receiving an exceedingly hot musketry fire from the railroad cut, were obliged to halt. Colonels Johnson and Berdan immediately notified me that unless they could have better support from the skirmishers on their right it would be Impossible to advance farther. Upon going to the front I found that their report was correct. Fearing that our skirmishers did not properly connect with those of General [Hatch's] on the right I deployed two

Colonel Charles Roberts, USA, Commanding First Brigade, First Division, Fifth Corps, Army of the Potomac. Library of Congress.

companies of the Eighteenth Massachusetts to correct the error, if possible, which they succeeded in doing satisfactorily. I then sent Captain [Charles J.] Powers to General Porter, reporting our true position; requested a more decided support on the right, or else, on account of an enfilading fire from the enemy, it would be futile to commence the attack. By an orderly I sent a similar dispatch to General Butterfield. From General Porter I received the following reply: I will at once send infantry upon your right. Wait until they arrive, then push vigorously forward.

From General Butterfield, through his aide, Lieutenant [Henry W.] Perkins, I was directed to be sure and make the connection with General Hatch, allowing no mishap to occur in so doing. I then requested Captain Powers to confer with the officer in command of General Hatch's advanced regiment, requesting him to speedily move on, as we had no time to lose. General Hatch came forward very slowly and in a confused manner, and I was obliged to move my entire command slightly to the left, in order more speedily to get into position the advancing brigade.

I then notified General Butterfield that the desired connection was at last accomplished. We then, by General Butterfield's order, simultaneously with the Third Brigade, together with three deafening cheers from the respective regiments, charged across the open field hoping to be enabled to sweep around to the left and take the guns of the enemy, but the musketry fire, both from the right and front, was so galling that the troops were obliged to halt and in line of battle resist it, an incessant artillery cross-fire at the same time being poured into them from the left. In this position we remained upward of thirty minutes.[18]

While Weeks's, Roberts's, and Sullivan's brigades moved across the open field, they were subjected to a deadly flanking fire from S. D. Lee's and Shumaker's artillery.

You will now follow the center of the attack to the unfinished railroad.
Continue to walk northwest along the trail for 325 yards to the lone monument on the higher ground. Stop when you have almost reached the monument.

Position C—Assault to the Unfinished Railroad

You are standing in the center of the farthest advance of Porter's attack. The brigade here was Col. Roberts's First Brigade, First Division, Fifth Corps (Army of the Potomac). Situated to your left were the Thirteenth New York, then the Eighteenth Massachusetts. To your right stood the First Michigan, then the Thirtieth and Twenty-fourth New York Regiments from Colonel Sullivan's First Brigade, First Division, Third Corps (Army of Virginia). The Seventeenth, Twelfth, and Forty-fourth New York Regiments from Colonel Weeks's Third Brigade, First Division, Fifth Corps (Army of the Potomac) were positioned to Roberts's left.

The commander of the Thirteenth New York provided a brief description of the fighting to your left.

Report of Col. Elisha G. Marshall, USA, Commanding Thirteenth New York, First Brigade, First Division, Fifth Corps, Army of the Potomac

When we arrived at the edge of the skirt of timber our skirmishers were held by the enemy. After about two hours we were ordered to push on to the enemy in connection with the troops on our right,

Appendix I

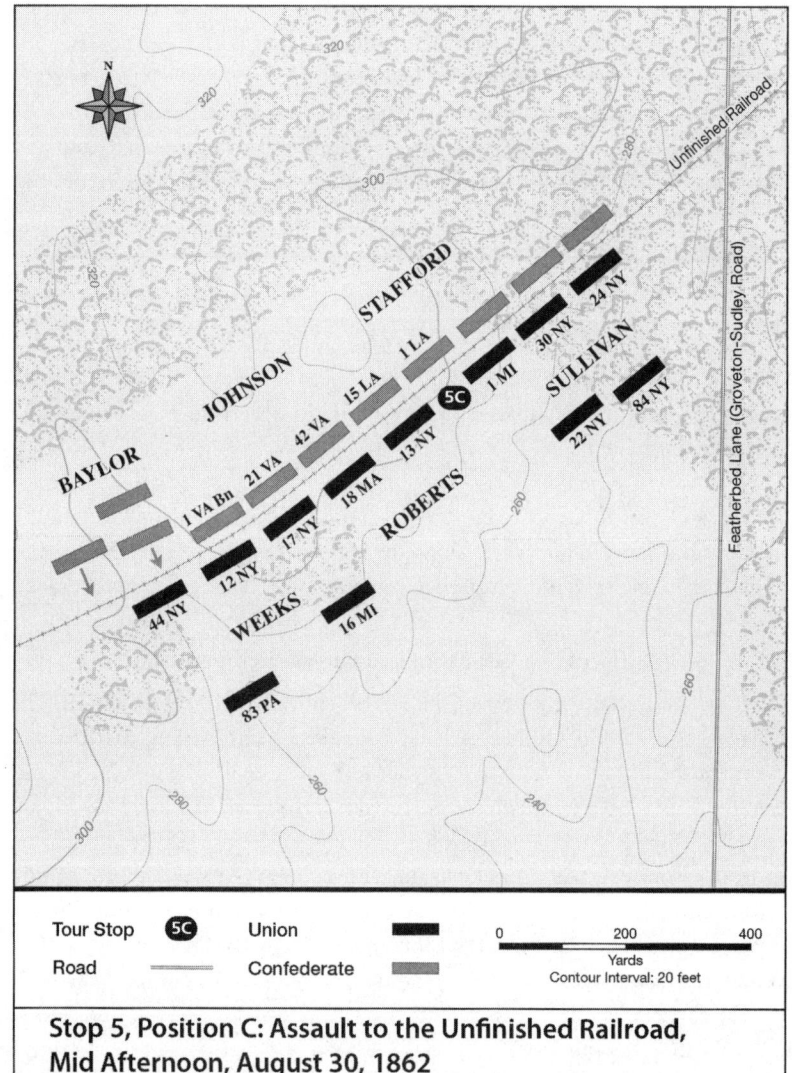

Stop 5, Position C: Assault to the Unfinished Railroad, Mid Afternoon, August 30, 1862

take the railroad, and push around our right and hold the railroad. I reported this to you [Roberts] and General Butterfield. The Eighteenth Massachusetts, sustained by myself, then pushed on across this field under a severe fire and held for a long time our ground under a cross-fire of the enemy. Re-enforcements were started to us

Colonel Elisha G. Marshall, USA, Commanding Thirteenth New York, First Brigade, First Division, Fifth Corps, Army of the Potomac. Library of Congress.

> but did not arrive. Our right in the timber gave way; still we held our ground, hoping that re-enforcements would arrive. Owing to the continuous cross-fire to which we were exposed we were finally forced to retreat.[19]

To the Thirteenth New York's right was the First Michigan. After the war, the commander of Company C wrote of the fighting that afternoon.

> **Narrative of Capt. George C. Hopper, USA, Commanding Company C, First Michigan, First Brigade, First Division, Fifth Corps, Army of the Potomac**
>
> At the dry watercourse [today's School House Branch] we received our first check; the line tumbled into it, in more or less confusion; the guns of Longstreet, away on our left, dropped their shells into it with a quickness and precision which gave me a new experience.
>
> The line was new formed; and the advance continued; but hardly had we started when the musketry fire from the railroad cut began to tell upon us. It was so severe that the regiment to our right swerved away to the right, leaving a large gap between us. Our commands to our men were merely, "Steady, men—steady, and touch to the left." The line was doing well, and it seemed as if we would soon

be upon the foe, but at fifty yards from the cut it stopped, and here the slaughter commenced.

The enemy in the curved line of the railroad, on our right, was almost on a line with us, and began an oblique fire on our right flank; the enemy in front and well protected and only fifty yards away and Longstreet's guns were still as active as ever.

Just as we came to a halt Lieut. [John G.] Hatch, in command of Company F, came up to me with a mangled arm and said, "Captain, will you take care of my company; I am hit," and went to the rear. The men were standing up and loading and firing, but they were so exposed that I ordered them to lie down. Just then a bullet paid its respects to my right thigh. A moment after Capt. [Charles E.] Wendell came to me and said: "The colonel is killed and I am in command. There are troops in the woods in the rear of us, and I think they are going to charge. We must hang on here, keep down the enemy's fire, and go in with them when they reach us."

I said; "I am wounded, but will hang on as long as I can;" I looked back at the woods and saw a Zouave regiment in line of battle. In doing so, I took a step or two away from the Captain, a shell burst over our heads, so near that I felt the flash on my face. I turned to him, and saw him holding one broken arm in the other hand and going to the rear. Before he had got two rods [one rod = 5 ½ yards] away a ball from the enemy in the cut pierced and instantly killed him.

The men were falling so fast that several of the officers picked up the muskets which [had been] dropped and used them. Among the number was Lieut. [Henry C.] Arnold, who in his earnestness got back a little too far from cover, and an oblique shot struck him in the forehead, and he too, instantly died.

Capt. [Eben T.] Whittlesey received his death wound at the same time that Col. [Horace] Roberts did, when the charge was made; and Lieut. [Irwin L.] Garrison was killed farther to the left of the line, while fighting by the side of Capt. [Clinton] Spencer.

The numbness from my wounded limb passed away, and the pain that followed admonished me that I had better bandage it. While doing so Capt. [Russell H.] Alcott, who was then in command, came to me and said; "Captain, to save our colors, and our men, I must order a retreat; the Thirteenth New York are going back and we are doing no good here." I said, "All right, I will be with you soon," and, with head bent down, continued to fix my bandage.

> All at once I heard the Captain say: "Don't fire; we surrender," and looking up I saw a half score of men in gray uniforms, with muskets cocked and leveled at us who replied, "If you surrender, give up your arms," and looking beyond them I saw a hundred men or more of the old regiment massed around the colors, moving swiftly, but in good form, nearly to the woods. I suppose that the same thought had come to Capt. [Edward] Pomeroy, that was in the mind of Capt. Alcott, as to the uselessness of keeping up the contest; and he, therefore, ordered a retreat. If so, it was the last order he ever gave, for a shot from the foe then and there ended his earthly career.[20]

To see the terrain and the attack from the Confederate view; walk 20 yards past the monument, be careful, walk down into the unfinished railroad cut for a few feet, turn around, and look back across the field. Caution: there may be ticks and snakes in the railroad cut.

You are in a position between the Fifteenth Louisiana and First Louisiana of Stafford's (Starke's) Brigade. These were Stafford's right regiments. His other three regiments were initially arranged to the left. On Stafford's left was Brown's (Trimble's) Brigade, the right brigade of Lawton's (Ewell's) Division. Brown's right regiment was the Fifteenth Alabama, which fired oblique into the regiments in the right of Porter's attack. Johnson's Brigade was stationed to Stafford's right. Baylor's Brigade occupied a position to Johnson's right and slightly back.

> ### Report of Col. Leroy A. Stafford, CSA, Commanding Starke's Brigade, Jackson's Division, Jackson's Left Wing, Army of Northern Virginia
>
> The enemy commenced throwing forward large bodies of skirmishers in the woods on our left, who quickly formed themselves into regiments and moved forward by brigades to the attack, massing a large body of troops at this point with the evident design of forcing us from our position. They made repeated charges upon us while in this position, but were compelled to retire in confusion, sustaining heavy loss and gaining nothing. It was at this point that the ammunition of the brigade gave out. The men procured some from the dead bodies of their comrades, but the supply was not sufficient, and

Appendix I

Colonel Leroy Stafford, CSA, Commanding Starke's (Stafford's) Brigade, Jackson's Division, Jackson's Left Wing, Army of Northern Virginia. USAMHI.

> in the absence of ammunition the men fought with rocks and held their position. The enemy retreated. We pressed forward to the road, and there halted.[21]

Porter's plan was for all eight brigades to go forward in the attack. Those units should have had sufficient strength to break through the defenses and exploit their success. However, because of the volume of artillery fire from S. D. Lee's and Shumaker's guns, only four brigades (Week's, Roberts's, Sullivan's, and Patrick's) advanced to the unfinished railroad. The other four were halted before they had left the woods east of the road.

Report of Col. Stephen D. Lee, CSA, Commanding Lee's Artillery Battalion, Longstreet's Right Wing, Army of Northern Virginia

> I placed my batteries on a commanding ridge immediately to [Hood's] left and rear. On the general line of battle this ridge was about the center, Jackson's [wing] being immediately on my left and Longstreet's on my right. It was an admirable ridge of over a quarter of a mile, generally overlooking the ground in front of it for some 2,000 yards. This ground was occupied by several farms, with corn fields, orchards, fences, &c., making it much desired by the enemy for their skirmishers, being quite undulating. Opposite the top of the ridge and distant about 1,300 yards was a strip of timber with quite a fall of ground behind it. Between this strip and General Jackson's right, along an old railroad excavation, was an open field.

During the morning the enemy had massed his infantry behind the timber before mentioned . . . and about 4 p.m. moved from out these woods in heavy lines of attack on General Jackson's position. The left of the ridge was held by [Capt. John L.] Eubank's battery of four smooth-bores, who opened on the enemy as soon as he discovered their advance. At the same time I shifted to his assistance with two howitzers of [Capt. William W.] Parker's battery, two of Rhett's battery [commanded by Lt. William Elliot], and one of [Capt. Tyler C.] Jordan's battery, at the same time directing nine other pieces (mostly rifles) on the right of the ridge, under Captains Jordan and [James S.] Taylor, to change their position, so as to fire on the enemy in flank and on the woods containing their reserves. With these eighteen guns a continuous fire was kept up on the enemy during his attack, which lasted about half an hour. His reserves moved twice out of the woods to the support of the attacking columns and twice were they repulsed by the artillery and driven back to the woods. After the reserves failed to reach the front or attacking columns they were repulsed and endeavored to rally in the open field, but the range of every part of the field was obtained, and a few

S. D. Lee's Artillery Battalion firing into the left of Porter's attack; afternoon August 30, 1862. Library of Congress.

Appendix I

Colonel Stephen D. Lee, CSA, Commanding Lee's Artillery Battalion, Longstreet's Right Wing, Army of Northern Virginia. Library of Congress.

> discharges broke them in confusion and sent them back to the woods. While firing on the infantry two batteries of the enemy were firing on us, but generally overshot us. Our position was an admirable one and the guns were well served.[22]

Unable to penetrate the defense and taking a high rate of casualties, the attackers fell back across the open ground. For many, going back was just as dangerous as moving forward had been. Many Union troops did not stop at the Groveton-Sudley Road, but continued on east through the woods and across the open fields. Followed for a short distance by a limited Confederate counterattack, the retreat had all the appearances of a rout. Troops in the rear eventually stopped the retreat. The retreat of Porter's attack force brought on a situation and a critical decision that could potentially destroy Pope's forces. You will explore this situation at the next two stops.

Return to your car for the drive to Stop 6 by following the trail back to the road and then the parking area. Do not walk on the road.

Depart the parking area, turn right on the Groveton-Sudley Road, and drive south for 0.5 mile to the Warrenton Turnpike. Turn left on the Warrenton Turnpike, and drive east for 1.2 miles to the intersection with the Sudley Road (where the stoplight is). Turn right onto the Sudley Road, and drive south for 0.4 mile to the first park road on your right. Turn right onto this park road, and drive 0.6 mile to a T intersection. At the T intersection turn right, and drive west for 0.2 mile to the parking area for Chinn Ridge. Park, leave your car, walk to the other side of the Chinn House foundation, and face so you can look southwest at the terrain sloping gently downhill.

Stop 6—McDowell Decides to Reposition Troops

On the afternoon of August 29, Reynolds's three-brigade, four–artillery battery Pennsylvania Reserves Division was positioned on the open terrain in front of you. That morning Reynolds's position had been along Lewis Lane, 1,400 yards (0.8 mile) to the west. After making contact with a strong Confederate skirmish line, because of its exposed position, Reynolds had withdrawn his division to this location. Here, Reynolds's troops formed the left flank of Pope's army. A gap existed between Reynolds and the remainder of the army north of the Warrenton Turnpike. Col. Nathaniel C. McLean's Second Brigade, First Division, First Corps (Army of Virginia) was deployed to fill this gap. McLean's brigade was behind you and along the top of the ridge.

Porter's attack was repulsed, and many of his troops retreated toward the Sudley Road. McDowell saw this situation develop, and he worried that the confusion of the retreat and the following Confederates might pose a significant threat to the center of Pope's position. As a result, McDowell made the critical decision to reposition troops. He ordered Reynolds to move his division to the north side of the Warrenton Turnpike.

> **Report of Brig. Gen. John F. Reynolds, USA, Commanding Pennsylvania Reserves Division, Attached to Third Corps, Army of Virginia**
>
> When the commanding general [McDowell], observing the attack of Porter to have been repulsed, [he] ordered me with my division across the field to the rear of Porter, to form a line behind which the troops might be rallied. I immediately started my division in the direction indicated, but before the rear of my column had left the position the threatened attack by the enemy's right began to be felt, and the rear brigade, under Colonel [Hardin, with Kerns's battery], were obliged to form on the ground on which they found themselves to oppose it. Passing across the field to the right, with Meade's and Seymour's brigades, my course was diverted by the difficult nature of the ground, and the retreating masses of [Porter's] broken columns among the troops of Heintzelman's corps, already formed, by which much time was lost and confusion created, which allowed the enemy to sweep up with his right so far as almost to cut us off from the pike, leaving nothing but the rear brigade of my division and scattered troops of other commands to resist the advance of the enemy upon our left.[23]

Appendix I

McDowell's critical decision reduced the Union defenses south of the turnpike to almost nothing. With an overwhelming force, Longstreet now commenced his attack to capture Henry Hill and control and sever the Warrenton Turnpike in Pope's rear area.

You will now walk to Stop 7. Walk back to the parking area, then walk west to the point at which the parking area intersects with a path that extends to your left and right. Turn right, follow the walking path north for twenty-five yards, stop, and face left. You are now looking west.

Stop 7: McLean Decides to Defend Chinn Ridge

Position A—McLean's Initial Position

You are on the main part of Chinn Ridge. This piece of ground was a critical position for delaying Longstreet's attack while other Union forces established defensive positions on Henry Hill, the crest of which is 2,000 yards (1.1 mile) to your right rear (northeast). The Chinn house was located to your left rear. Directly behind you at a distance of 400 yards, in the low ground, is Chinn Branch. The high ground another 450 yards east is the Bald Hill. The woods in front of you looked different in 1862. There was a wood directly in front of you. However, in 1862 the woods you see to your right front did not exist; the ground was an open field. The terrain descends west off of Chinn Ridge to low ground, with an intermittent stream bordered by vegetation located at a distance of 325 yards. From this point the terrain rises to the high ground, where Hardin's brigade was overrun by Hood's Brigade. The terrain descends again to Young's Branch, then rises up the ground where Warren's brigade was located. Warren's position was 900 yards from where you are. In 1862, unlike today, Hardin's and Warren's position could be seen from this location.

This place marks the initial position of Col. Nathaniel C. McLean's four-regiment brigade (Second Brigade, First Division, First Corps, Army of Virginia), which was accompanied by Battery I, First New York Artillery (four guns). McLean was ordered into this location in the early afternoon to provide a connection with Reynolds's division on the left and Porter's Corps on the right. Shortly after occupying this ridge, McLean was surprised to see Reynolds's division leave its position and march north to the other side of the Warrenton Turnpike. Shortly thereafter he saw the commencement of Longstreet's attack. McLean realized the disaster that would result if Pope's left flank was enveloped by the assault. On his own initiative, he decided to remain on Chinn Ridge to delay Longstreet's attack long enough for a strong defensive line to be established on Henry Hill.[24]

McLean's position initially faced west and northwest. You stand where his left regiment, the Seventy-third Ohio, was located. To that regiment's right were the Twenty-fifth Ohio, then Battery I, First New York Artillery, and then the Seventy-fifth Ohio, with the Fifty-fifth Ohio as the right flank regiment.

After overrunning Warren's position, Hood's Brigade attacked and drove away the Third Brigade of the Pennsylvania Reserves Division. Commanded by Col. Martin D. Hardin. This brigade was on the small ridge 450 yards in front of you. Today, you can't see the ridge because of the trees, which were not there in 1862. Closely followed by Brig. Gen. Nathan G. Evans's brigade, Hood's Brigade began to maneuver toward this position. As it moved from the ground Hardin's men had occupied, the brigade came under enfilading artillery fire from Union batteries on Dogan Ridge 1,300 yards to your right, just across the Warrenton Turnpike. This artillery prevented the left of Hood's Brigade from advancing farther. Hood's three right regiments (Fifth Texas, Hampton Legion, and Eighteenth Georgia) reached the low ground in front of you because the wood provided some degree of concealment from the batteries on Dogan Ridge.

At this point in time, McLean's brigade was the only Union force standing between Longstreet's attacking divisions and Henry Hill. Although other brigades were being sent to this position, the fight would now be up to McLean's four regiments.

The first attack was made by two regiments of Hood's Brigade, the Hampton Legion and the Eighteenth Georgia. These soldiers came out of the woods in front of you and attacked toward the center of McLean's position. Rifle and cannon fire drove them back in a very short time.

Report of Col. Nathaniel C. McLean, USA, Commanding Second Brigade, First Division, First Corps, Army of Virginia

Soon after I had taken this position, much to my surprise General Reynolds put his troops in motion and marched entirely past and across my front to the right, to what point I am not informed. Finding that this movement had entirely exposed my left flank I immediately changed the position of my troops, and deployed in line of battle ... with the battery in the center and two regiments on each side. I could by this time see the enemy advancing on my front and a little to the right, driving before them a regiment of Zouaves

> [from Warren's brigade]. They came on rapidly, when some troops [Hardin's brigade] advanced to meet them from behind a hill on my right. These troops were also driven back in confusion, and as soon as they got out of the way I opened upon the enemy with the four pieces of artillery, throwing first shell, and as they approached nearer, canister. I also commenced a heavy fire with infantry, and in a short time the enemy retreated in great confusion.[25]

Four regiments of Evans's Brigade followed closely behind Hood's Brigade. Three regiments used the woods to approach closer to the defenders and were thus protected from the Union artillery on Dogan Ridge. The brigade's left regiment, the Twenty-third South Carolina, advanced over the open ground toward McLean's right regiments and was driven back. The artillery on Dogan Ridge and the rifle fire of the Seventy-fifth Ohio and Fifty-fifth Ohio inflicted heavy losses on the Twenty-third South Carolina. The right three regiments of Evans's Brigade emerged from the trees in front of you and advanced toward this position. As you view the attack the regiments were arranged as follows from left to right: Holcombe Legion, Eighteenth South Carolina, and Seventeenth South Carolina. The Fifth Texas took position on the right flank of Evans's Brigade, and all four regiments attacked toward your present location. This attack was also repulsed.

The next attack was conducted by the Eighteenth South Carolina and the Seventeenth South Carolina, who again emerged from the woods. These units moved directly toward McLean's left two regiments, the Seventy-third Ohio and Twenty-fifth Ohio. In this assault, however, the Fifth Texas to the right of the Eighteenth South Carolina maneuvered farther to its right and hit the Seventy-third Ohio in its left flank. The combination of flank and frontal fire caused the Seventy-third to collapse and retreat. In turn, this development allowed flanking fire to be aimed into the flank of the Twenty-fifth Ohio. These troops also retreated, and Battery I, First New York Artillery followed them. As the next regiment (the Seventy-third Ohio) to the right was attempting to face left to counter the Confederate threat, the artillery withdrew through their lines. This shift threw the regiment into confusion. Two companies completed the change in direction, but the remaining ones joined the retreat. All three of these regiments retreated over the crest to the east side of the ridge. Suddenly, McLean only had two companies from one regiment and one intact regiment to defend an area previously occupied by four regiments and an artillery battery.

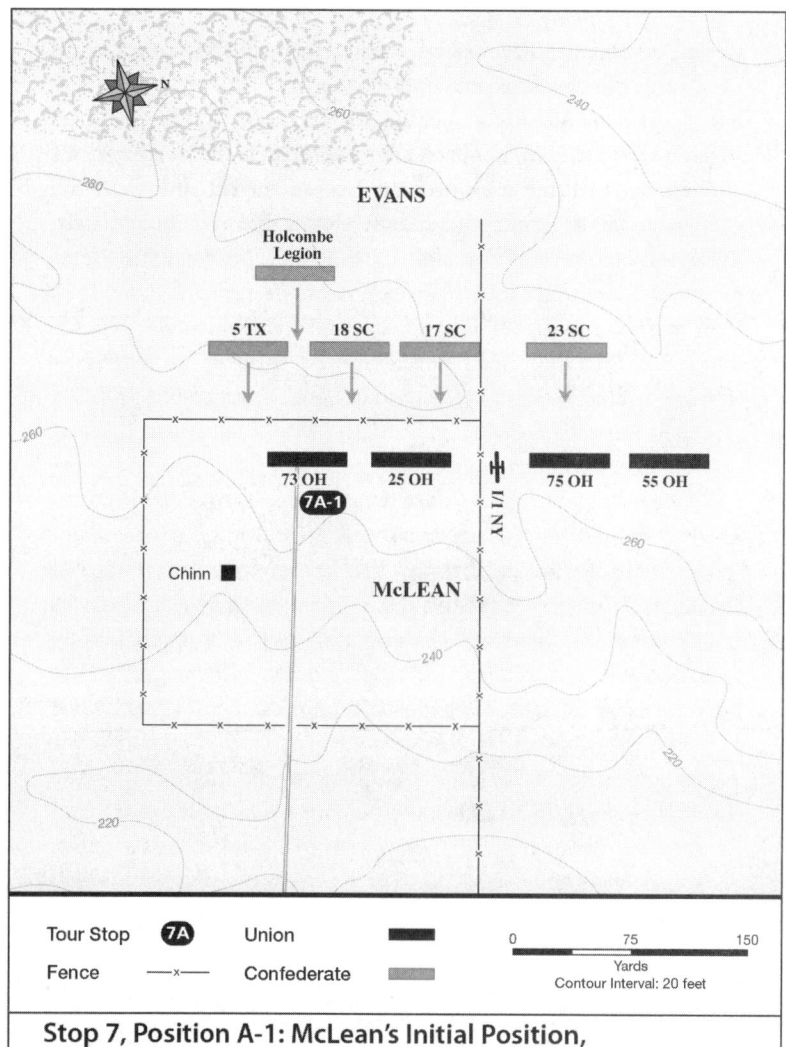

Stop 7, Position A-1: McLean's Initial Position, Late Afternoon, August 30, 1862

Report of Col. Nathaniel C. McLean, USA—continued

Soon after this a heavy force of the enemy, much superior to my own, marched out of the woods across the position formerly occupied by General Reynolds, in front of my left flank, and swept around, so as to come in heavy force both on the front and flank of

Appendix I

> my left wing. This force opened a heavy fire upon the Seventy-third Ohio, and the next moment the troops in my rear, supposed to be friends, also opened fire with musketry and artillery. Overpowered by such superiority in numbers, after a short time the Seventy-third and Twenty-fifth fell back over the crest of the hill, but were still exposed to the fire from both columns of the enemy. I immediately,

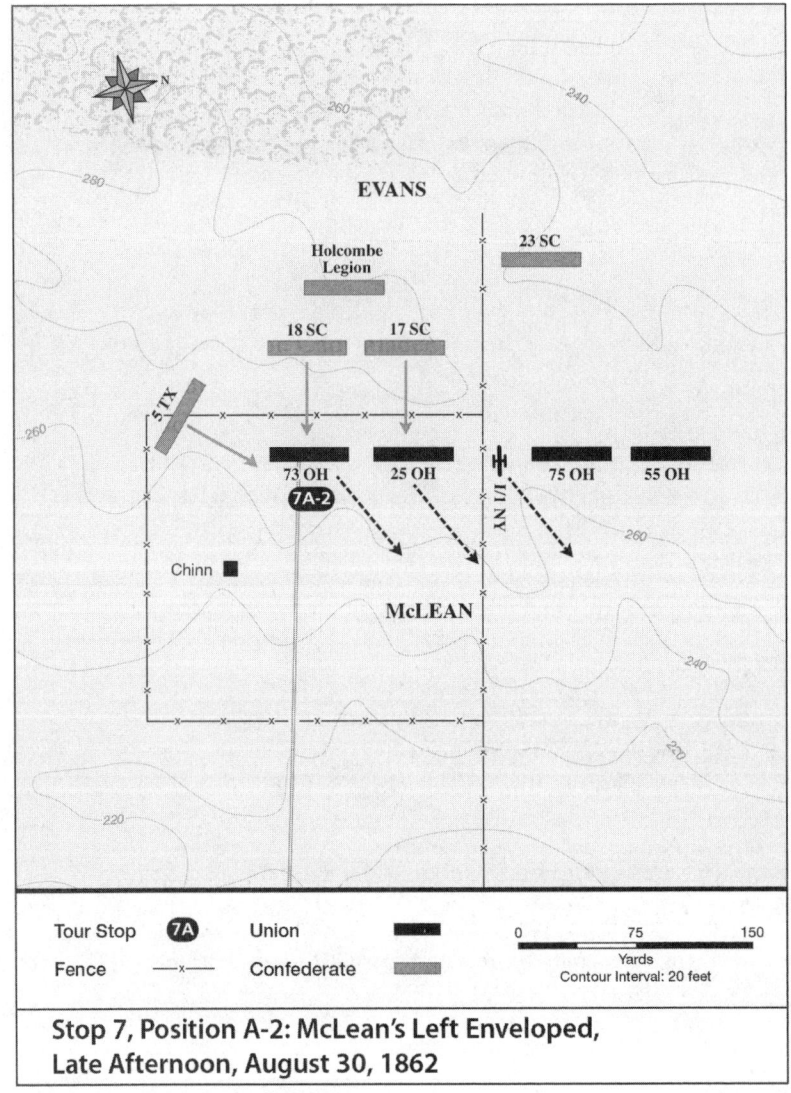

Stop 7, Position A-2: McLean's Left Enveloped, Late Afternoon, August 30, 1862

> when this attack was made, gave the order to change front, so as to repel it if possible, but the retreat of the battery at this moment interfered somewhat with the movement, as it passed through the Seventy-fifth in its retreat.[26]

From this position onward you will be provided directions to walk along the path on top of the ridge. This path is used to maintain your general direction of movement. Ground conditions permitting, you should also walk laterally left and right from the path to view each position from different perspectives and gain an appreciation of how the terrain influenced the fight.

Face right, and walk north on the path for seventy-five yards to a wooden fence. There is a Seventy-third Ohio marker at this location. Stop, turn around, and look southwest, back to where you came from.

Position B—McLean's Second Position

The three attacking Confederate regiments, having collapsed the left and center of McLean's defenses, now continued the attack toward the east side of the ridge. If successful this attack would flank the Union troops remaining on Chinn Ridge and make the position untenable. Also, the assault could possibly open an avenue of approach all the way to Henry Hill for the following Confederate units.

McLean ordered Col. John C. Lee to face his Fifty-fifth Ohio left and confront the Confederate attack. The unit advanced southwest along the ridge, halted where you are, and delivered staggering volleys into the left flank of the Seventeenth South Carolina. As that regiment faltered and fell back, the left flank of the Eighteenth South Carolina was exposed to heavy enfilading fire, and it also fell back. This same flanking fire was repeated with the Fifth Texas, which maneuvered to its right to a covered position on the ridge.

As the Fifty-fifth Ohio counterattacked, the Twenty-fifth and Seventy-fifth Ohio rallied on the east side of the ridge. The remnants of these regiments returned to the fight on the left of the Fifty-fifth Ohio. The Fifty-fifth Ohio had halted the attack of Hood's and Evans's regiments, but an even great threat was developing against McLean's southwest-facing position on Chinn Ridge.

When Hood's and Evans's Brigades attacked east, Brig. Gen. James L. Kemper's three-brigade division was on their right (south) flank. Kemper had deployed his division with two brigades in the first line, Col. Eppa Hunton's on

Appendix I

the left and Brig. Gen. Micah Jenkins's on the right, and Col. Montgomery D. Corse's troops in the second, supporting line. These brigades advanced east, arriving at a position south of where you are.

As Hunton's Brigade passed south of this area while moving east, he attempted to change direction and attack McLean's brigade. Because of command and control problems, Hunton he was unable to accomplish this task.

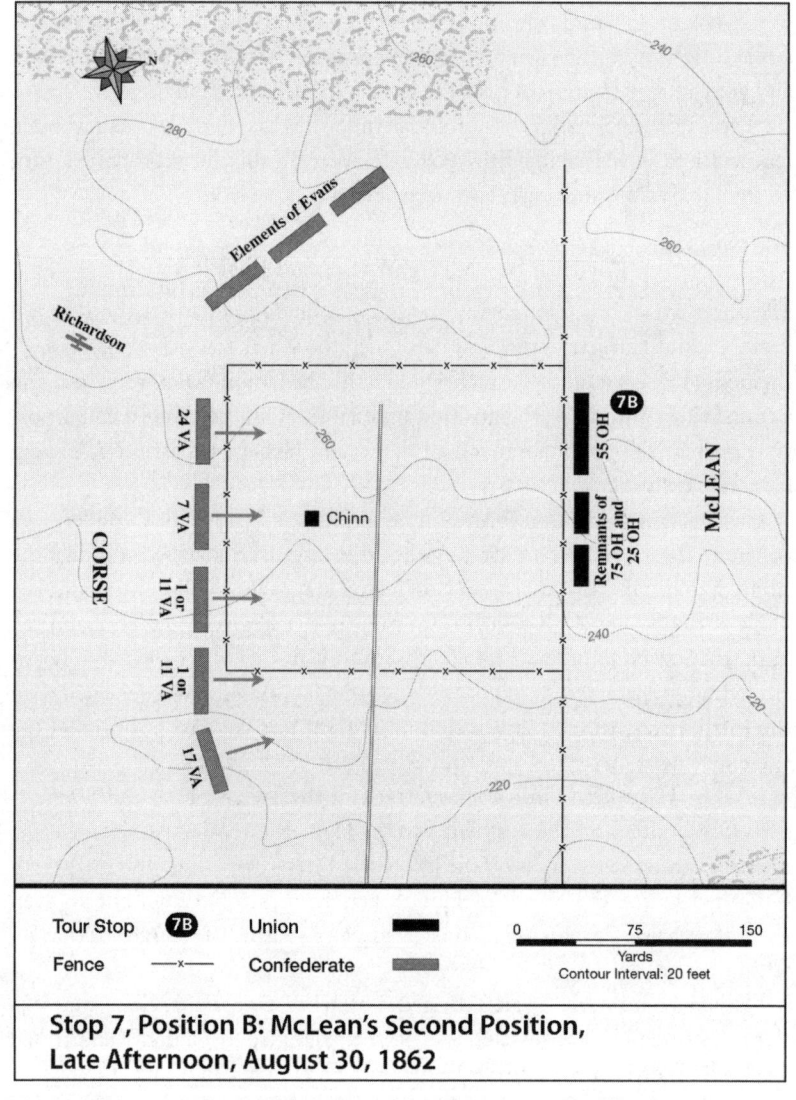

Stop 7, Position B: McLean's Second Position, Late Afternoon, August 30, 1862

He moved farther east before he could change his brigade's direction of attack. Jenkins's Brigade on Hunton's right was also unable to change direction of attack, and it continued on east, staying on Hunton's right flank. However, Corse's brigade followed and was able to wheel to the left and attack north along the southern end of Chinn Ridge.

Hunton and Jenkins would eventually change their direction of attack and join Corse in the assault on Chinn Ridge. However, for the overall success of Longstreet's attack it would have been better if these commanders had continued in the original direction of movement. They would then have come to the key terrain of Henry Hill, Longstreet's ultimate objective, which at this time still did not have a sufficient defensive force in place. The capture of Henry Hill at this point would have presented Pope with a severely adverse tactical situation. Lee might have been able to disperse or render Pope's army combat ineffective as a result.

However, this scenario did not develop. Corse's five-regiment brigade turned to the left (north) and attacked the Union defenders here. Corse was followed in the turn by Hunton's five-regiment brigade, and then Jenkins's five-regiment, one-battalion brigade.

Corse deployed all five of his regiments for the attack on this position. His right flank was in the low ground to your left, almost touching Chinn Branch, and his left flank was on the western portion of the ridge to your right. The assault was supported by Capt. John B. Richardson's Second Company (Battery) of the Washington Artillery (four guns). This battery was deployed to Corse's left rear so it could fire into this position. McLean's new battle line was positioned where you are standing and to your left. Your current location is the position of the Fifty-fifth Ohio. To these troops' left were the regrouped remnants of the Twenty-fifth and Seventy-fifth Ohio.

Report of Col. Montgomery D. Corse, CSA, Commanding Kemper's (Corse's) Brigade, Kemper's Division, Longstreet's Right Wing, Army of Northern Virginia

At 3 o'clock Colonel Hunton, commanding Pickett's brigade, brought the order that this brigade, with the others of [the division], were to occupy at 5 p.m. a wood near the Chinn house, in front of the line then occupied by Jenkins and Hunton [Brigades]. [This was probably the woods east of Chinn Ridge and along the west side of Sudley Road. From there, an attack could be launched to capture Henry Hill, which was on the east side of this road. Henry Hill had

> very few defenders at this point and was vulnerable to capture.] At 4.30 o'clock Captain *Flood* brought me an order to move forward in haste to the support of Jenkins and Hunton. I promptly obeyed, and overtook the two brigades advancing. I at once put my command in line about 250 yards in rear of the two advancing brigades, keeping my distance as [they] moved forward. Near the Chinn house, while under fire of the enemy's infantry and artillery, I pushed forward, changing front so as to cover the ground just before occupied by Hunton's (Pickett's) brigade. In passing the Chinn house it was necessary to face the Twenty-fourth Regiment (Col. William R. Terry's) to the left and file to the right. After passing this obstacle it [the brigade] came into line beautifully, and the whole line then became hotly engaged.[27]

Corse's first assault was stopped by the fire from this position. Pausing to regroup, his battle line again moved forward and was joined on his left (your right) by elements from Evans's Brigade. These regiments attacked this position obliquely and partially outflanked McLean's right.

Turn around and walk north for three hundred yards to the two artillery pieces. Stop, turn around, and face southwest.

Position C—Tower Reinforces McLean

Under heavy attacks from Corse's Brigade on his front and left flank and from elements of Evans's Brigade on his right flank, McLean's battle line fell back from its position along the fence to this location. By this time his regiments were in disarray and greatly weakened. When McLean's brigade fell back, its line shifted slightly to the right. The unit's left was then placed on the ridge, and its right extended off the ridge to your right.

You are at the position of Brig. Gen. Zealous B. Tower's Second Brigade, Second Division, Third Corps, Army of Virginia. This brigade was the first of four sent to reinforce the Union position on the ridge. It was followed by three other brigades dispatched from the north side of the Warrenton Turnpike. Tower had four regiments and the Fifth Maine Battery (five guns). When deployed, Tower's defensive position extended from McLean's left flank (to your right) into the low ground on your left.[28]

Corse's Brigade continued to lead the attack for Kemper's Division, and to Tower's right front, elements of Evans's Brigade also continued attacking.

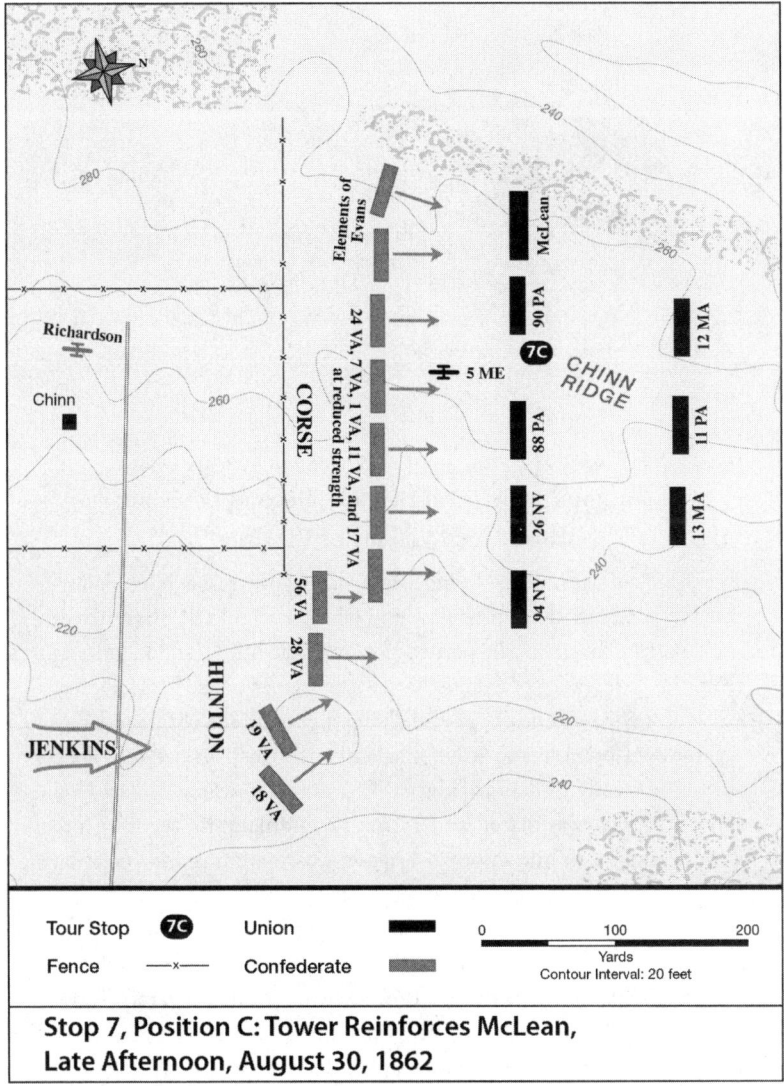

Stop 7, Position C: Tower Reinforces McLean, Late Afternoon, August 30, 1862

As these Confederate units renewed the attack, Col. Eppa Hunton's brigade, which had finally made the turn to the north, entered into the fight. The left of the brigade came up behind Corse's right, while the remainder extended the battle line to Corse's right. Hunton's regiments then moved forward and joined the attack.

Brigadier General Zealous B. Tower, USA, Commanding Second Brigade, Second Division, Third Corps, Army of Virginia. USAMHI.

Narrative of Brig. Gen. Zealous B. Tower, USA, Commanding Second Brigade, Second Division, Third Corps, Army of Virginia

Reaching the crest of [the] ridge, followed by my brigade I rode forward in person to determine how and where it should be placed. Seeing a battery firing nearby perpendicular to the hill crest and judging from the appearance of things that assistance was needed I decided to draw up my troops in the rear of this point and gave orders to bring up my own brigade and leave Hartsuff's [Stiles's] on the hill slope in column ready to deploy [Hartsuff's brigade, commanded by Col. John W. Stiles, was placed under Tower's command for the march to Chinn Ridge]. While my own brigade was marching into position the battery limbered up and dashed away through some of my troops furthest to the right. The cause was apparent they had been struck in flank and my own troops received the same attack while marching and were obliged to form under fire. The enemy were concealed mostly but they were quite near say 150 yards distant. A column attempted to form several times but was broken up. A Rebel regiment accompanied by a battery came forward. The fire came from the front and left and shells were bursting evidently from more distant batteries.[29]

Faced with a relentless Confederate attack, McLean and Tower were unable to hold this position and forced to fall back.

Turn around, and walk along the path for fifty yards, then stop, turn around, and again look southwest.

Position D—Stiles Reinforces; Jenkins Joins the Attack

This is the position where Col. John W. Stiles's Third Brigade, Second Division, Third Corps, Army of Virginia entered the fight. Stiles initially deployed his brigade approximately fifty to seventy-five yards behind you (to the north). McLean's and Tower's brigades were fighting from positions fifty yards in front of you.

Corse's, Hunton's, and units from Evans's Brigades continued their attack against McLean and Tower. They were reinforced by the arrival of Brig. Gen. Micah Jenkins's brigade.

The attacking battle line of Evans's, Corse's, Hunton's, and Jenkins's Brigades now extended from the western slope of Chinn Ridge, east across the ridge, and into the low ground where Chinn Branch is located. This battle line was long enough to extend beyond both McLean's and Tower's flanks as it attacked northward.

> ### Report of Col. Montgomery D. Corse, CSA—continued
> At this time, discovering a battery [Fifth Maine Battery] of the enemy to the left and rear of the Chinn house, I ordered a charge of the whole line. The order was gallantly responded to and brilliantly executed, the enemy being driven from their guns. Great gallantry was displayed by all engaged, Lieutenant-Colonel [Frederick G.] Skinner, First Virginia, dashing forward in advance of the whole line, was the first to reach the battery, and I saw him dealing deadly blows with his saber to the Yankee gunners. The steady veteran Terry, with the gallant Twenty fourth, delivered a destructive volley into the enemy's ranks on our left and pushed forward to the charge.[30]

Under increasing and sustained fire and greatly reduced in strength, the Union line fell back to where you are standing. Stiles then ordered his brigade forward to reinforce the position.

Tower's and Stiles's brigades had significant casualties among their senior officers: Brig. Gen. Zealous B. Tower was wounded, Col. Adrian Root (Ninety-fourth New York) was wounded, Lieut. Col. Joseph A. McLean (Eighty-eighth Pennsylvania) was killed, and Col. Fletcher Webster (Twelfth Massachusetts) was killed. Thus, the casualty rate for the two brigade and eight regimental commanders was 40 percent.

With the dissolving and retreat of Tower's and Stile's brigades, the southern part of Chinn Ridge fell into Confederate hands. However, the casualty

Appendix I

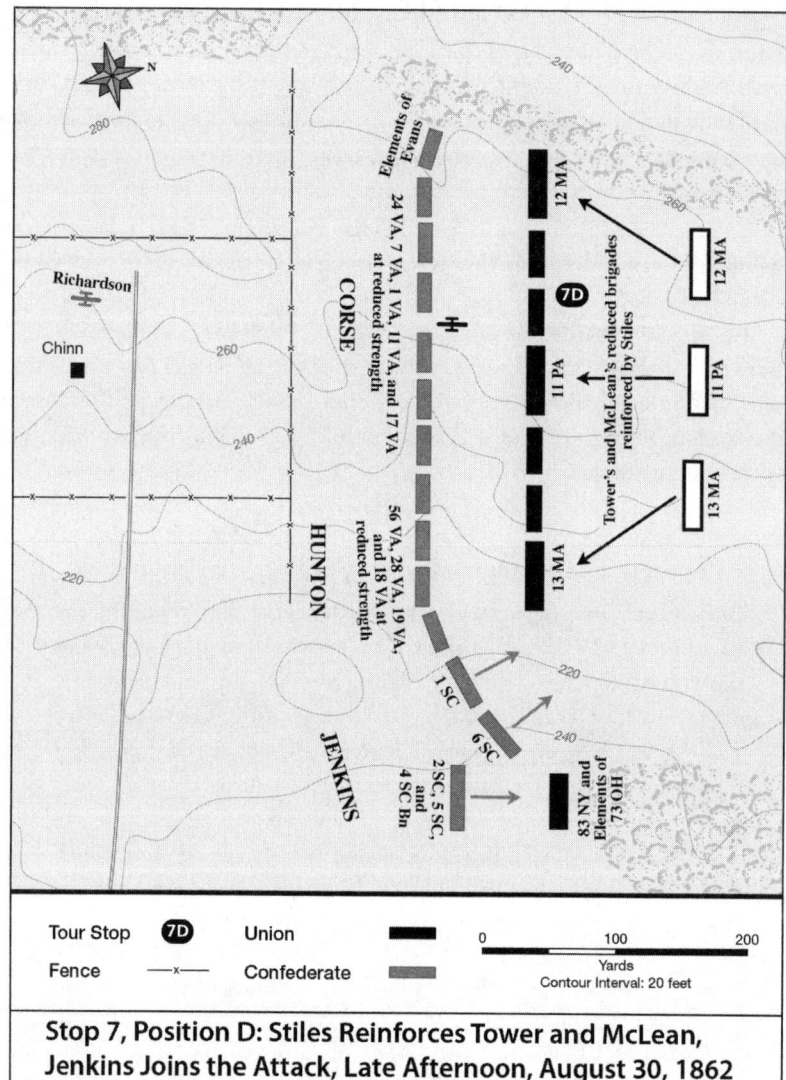

Stop 7, Position D: Stiles Reinforces Tower and McLean, Jenkins Joins the Attack, Late Afternoon, August 30, 1862

rate, expenditure of ammunition, and mingling of units significantly degraded the ability of the three brigades of Kemper's Division to continue the attack.

Turn around, and walk north on the path for fifty yards. Stop, turn around, and face south.

Position E—Koltes and Benning

As Stiles's brigade and the remnants of McLean's and Tower's were driven back, Col. John A. Koltes's three-regiment Second Brigade, Second Division, First Corps, Army of Virginia arrived and deployed just north of where you are. The Forty-first New York from the First Division's First Brigade had reached the ridge before Koltes's brigade and counterattacked to recapture the Fifth Maine Battery's guns. Koltes deployed, then moved forward to join the Forty-first New York.

The Confederate line facing Koltes's brigade included the three under-strength brigades of Kemper's Division and the remnants of Evans's Brigade. As you look at the Confederate line, elements from Evans's Brigade were deployed off the ridge to your right front. To their right (the left as you view it) were the intermingled brigades of Corse, Hunton, and Jenkins. Jenkins's right flank was off the ridge in the lower ground to your left.

In the three brigades composing Kemper's Division, senior leadership casualties included two brigade commanders and four regimental commanders. Among the three brigade and sixteen regimental commanders, this constituted a casualty rate of 31 percent.

After deploying his brigade in this location, Koltes attempted a counterattack to capture Richardson's guns. The Confederate battery had moved forward from a location near the Chinn House and were now two hundred yards away from Koltes and firing into his position. This attack was unsuccessful. Colonel Koltes was killed during the fighting, and Lieut. Col. Gustavus A. Muhleck assumed command of the brigade.

> **Report of Lieut. Col. Gustavus A. Muhleck, USA, Commanding First Brigade, Second Division, First Corps, Army of Virginia**
>
> I marched my regiment [the Seventy-third Pennsylvania] by the left flank, followed by the Twenty-ninth New York in the center and Sixty-eighth New York on the [left]. We reached the top of the hill under a terrific shower of shell [and] solid shot, I deployed at once. The enemy was right in front, advancing slowly but steadily in deep, dense masses. A galling fire commenced from both sides. To our left, where we found the De Kalb regiment [Forty-first New York] isolated from their brigade [and] a battery [which] had been abandoned. The enemy by this time had brought up two sections of artillery [Richardson's Battery], which, from a distance of scarcely 200

> yards, covered my own regiment as well as the others with a perfect shower of projectiles. It was at that supreme moment that the brave Colonel Koltes rode up to the front of his brigade, and swinging his sword high in the air, while ordering his command to take that rebel battery that a fragment of a shell killed both horse and rider. A rush was made toward the rebel cannons. Some of my men with Second Lieutenant [John] Kennedy, Company F, reached the pieces, but were unsupported, surrounded, and the lieutenant made a prisoner. He escaped a few moments afterward, a man of Company D, Seventy-third Pennsylvania volunteers, killing the rebel who had made him a prisoner.
>
> The combat here raged fierce and terrible for about half an hour, when our small regiments, exhausted and decimated and unsupported, had in their turn to fall back. The colors of my regiment had become rags. I had lost five of the color bearers and nearly one-half of the eight companies I brought into action.
>
> The loss of the Seventy-third was very heavy. Officers killed and wounded, 8; non-commissioned officers and privates killed, wounded, and missing, 138.[31]

The Confederate attack was strengthened by the arrival of Toombs's Brigade (commanded by Col. Henry Benning) of Jones's Division. Brig. Gen. David R. Jones's three-brigade division was initially deployed on the right (south) of Kemper's Division. When Kemper began his attack, Jones also moved forward with two of his brigades (Benning's and G. T. Anderson's). Jones's other brigade (Drayton's) protected the right flank. Initially moving in an easterly direction, Benning eventually turned his brigade to advance north and was drawn into the fight for Chinn Ridge.

Benning sent the Twentieth Georgia to reinforce the Confederate line's forward movement on the ridge. His other three regiments moved northward in the low ground east of the ridge (to your left). These regiments eventually arrived in a position where they could place devastating flanking fire into the left of the defenders. The combination of the frontal attack and the flanking fire caused Koltes's brigade to retreat.

The last Union brigade to fight on the ridge was the Second Brigade, Third Division, First Corps (Army of Virginia), commanded by Col. Wladimir Krzyzanowski. Krzyzanowski's brigade was deployed just north of your current location and engaged in a close-range firefight with the Confederates.

Battlefield Guide to the Critical Decisions at Second Manassas

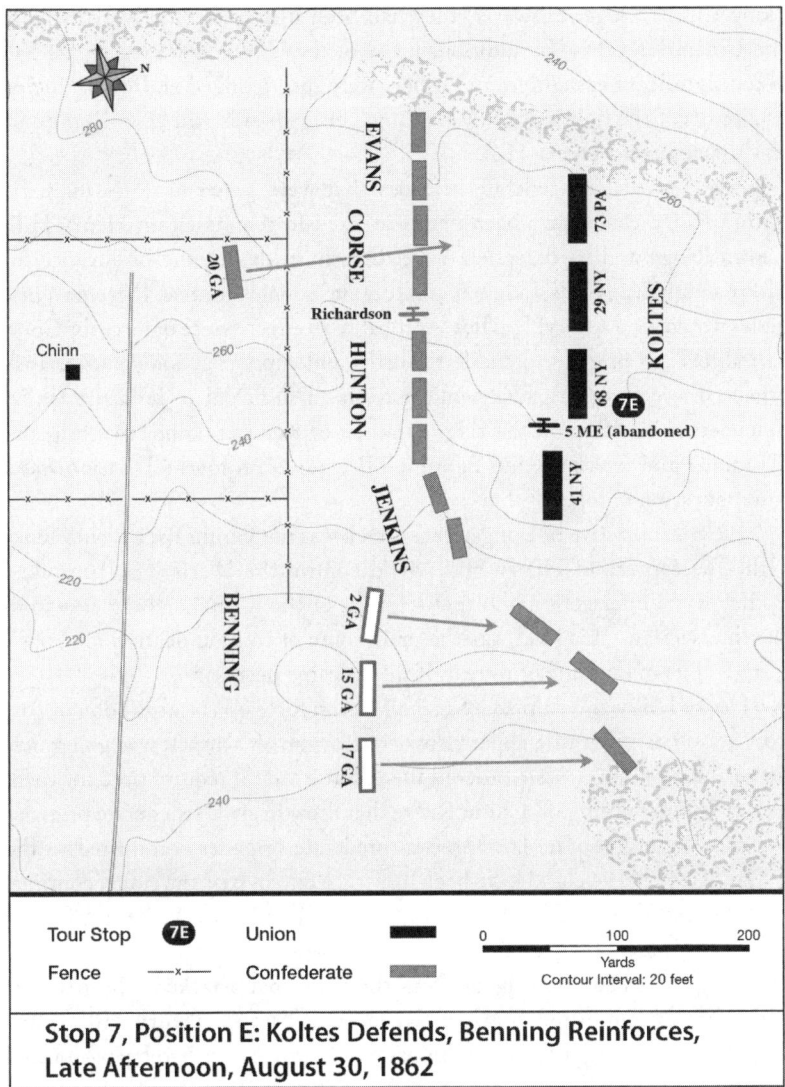

Stop 7, Position E: Koltes Defends, Benning Reinforces, Late Afternoon, August 30, 1862

As the overlapping battle line of Benning's Brigade and the remnants of Jenkins's, Hunton's, Corse's, and Evans's Brigades continued to press their attack, Krzyzanowski found his soldiers attacked from the front and both flanks. Consequently, he ordered a retreat off the ridge.

With the retreat of Krzyzanowski's brigade, Chinn Ridge was totally in Confederate hands. Regiments from six Confederate brigades had fought along Chinn Ridge. However, they had been unable to rapidly overwhelm the Union defenders. In addition, many of the Confederate regiments had taken significant casualties, and others were disorganized and intermingled as a result of the fighting. Only Benning's Brigade was still able to continue the attack toward Henry Hill.

Many of the Confederate brigades that were drawn into the fight on Chinn Ridge could have been better utilized in the attack on Henry Hill. Chinn Ridge and its defenders were directly in the avenue of advance for Hood's and Evans's Brigades. It is a forgone conclusion that these two brigades would attack the ridge. It was probably an effective use of force for Corse to redirect his brigade to the left (north) and support Hood's and Evans's attack. These three brigades would have been sufficient to hold the Union defenders in position on the ridge. The use of Kemper's other two brigades (Hunton's and Jenkins's) and Benning's Brigade from Jones's Division was a misapplication of force.

The true objective of Longstreet's attack was not Chinn Ridge, but Henry Hill. The capture of Henry Hill would control the Warrenton Turnpike–Sudley Road intersection and that segment of the turnpike going east from the intersection. This road was the main route of communication for Pope's force and its main route of retreat, if that became necessary.

Henry Hill was occupied by a small Union force on the afternoon of August 30. Once it became apparent where Longstreet's attack was going, additional Union forces were ordered there, but it would require time for them to arrive. The fighting on Chinn Ridge that drew in six Confederate brigades provided that time. The last three Confederate brigades committed to the Chinn Ridge battle could have been better used to bypass the ridge, continue moving east, cross the Sudley Road, turn north, and attack the insufficient defensive force on Henry Hill.

Longstreet had one brigade from the force that attacked Chinn Ridge and eight uncommitted brigades available to capture Henry Hill. Time would become a major factor in this assault. Chinn Ridge had been captured at approximately 6:00 p.m. Sunset on August 30, 1862, was at 6:43 p.m., and it would be dark at 7:11 p.m. Only a short period of time remained to capture Henry Hill and disrupt Pope's primary route of retreat.[32]

It was Colonel McLean's critical decision to remain and defend on Chinn Ridge that drew the Union and Confederate brigades into the fight there. This fight had provided the valuable time necessary for Union forces to occupy Henry Hill in sufficient strength, hold that piece of key terrain, and keep the vital route to the east under Union control.

Return to your car for the drive to Stop 8.

Depart the parking area, and drive east for 0.8 mile to the Sudley Road. At the Sudley Road turn left, and drive north 0.4 mile to the park entrance road to the Visitor Center. Turn right onto the park road, and drive to the visitor center parking area. Park, leave your car, and walk to the back (west) side of the visitor center.

Stop 8: Pope Decides to Retreat

You are again standing on Henry Hill. This piece of key terrain was vital to protecting the Warrenton Turnpike to the east from its intersection with the Sudley Road.

Stop 7, Position A on Chinn Ridge is 2,000 yards southwest of your location. The woods directly in front of you were not as extensive in 1862 as they are today. Directly in front of you at the western base of the hill is the south-to-north Sudley Road. To your right at the northern base of the hill is the Warrenton Turnpike. The intersection of these two vital roads is northwest of your present location (where the stoplight is). Buck Hill is 1,200 yards north of you; Matthews Hill is an additional 500 yards away. These three south to north hills provide a good defensive position parallel to the Sudley Road. This position protect the turnpike east from the intersection and the bridge and fords at Bull Run.

Five Union brigades' tenacious defense of Chinn Ridge had provided the time for the Henry Hill position to be strengthened. Chinn Ridge was eventually captured, which cleared the axis of advance to Henry Hill. The fight had lasted for about an hour and a half and had used up Hood's Texas Brigade, Evans's Brigade, and the three brigades (Corse's, Hunton's, and Jenkins's) of Kemper's Division. Plus, it had required the commitment of a brigade commanded by Col. Henry Benning from Jones's Division. But even more importantly, the time the fighting bought had allowed Pope to reinforce the defenses on Henry Hill.

When the fight for Chinn Ridge commenced, Henry Hill was only defended by Brigadier General Milroy's brigade, which was positioned in front of you and along the Sudley Road.

Maj. Gen. John F. Reynolds and two brigades of his Pennsylvania Reserves Division had earlier occupied a position west of the Warrenton Turnpike. These forces were subsequently ordered to move to the east side of the turnpike. When the danger of Longstreet's attack became apparent, Reynolds was sent to Henry Hill. Reynolds's two brigades occupied a double battle line on Milroy's right and just forward of the Henry House. These troops' position extended to the Warrenton Turnpike.

The next units to arrive were the two US Regular Brigades of Brig. Gen. George W. Sykes's division. Lieut. Col. William Chapman's Second US Regular Brigade occupied a position along the Sudley Road to Milroy's left. To Chapman's left was the Eighty-third New York, which had fought along Chinn Branch in the contest for Chinn Ridge. Lieut. Col. Robert C. Buchanan's First US Regular Brigade occupied a reserve position to your right. Brig. Gen. Abraham S. Piatt's two-regiment brigade was stationed to your right rear. Battery D, First Rhode Island (six guns), Second Maine Battery (four guns), and Battery C, Fifth US (six guns) supported Milroy and Reynolds. As the fighting progressed here, Col. Edward Ferrero's brigade and Battery K, First US Artillery (six guns) reinforced the defenses.

The first Confederate attacks against this position were by Toombs's (Benning's) and G. T. Anderson's Brigades of Brig. Gen. David R. Jones's division. These were frontal attacks, and although one of Benning's regiments penetrated the defenses, it was thrown back. The next assaults were by the three brigades (Wright's, Mahone's, and Armistead's) of Maj. Gen. Richard H. Anderson's division. These came against the front and left of the defenses. Although some success was achieved on the left, these attacks were stopped. Armistead's and Drayton's Brigades launched the final attacks.

North of Henry Hill, Jackson's Left Wing was exerting some offensive pressure on Pope's defenses along the Sudley Road.

With the approach of night, Pope had to decide what his army would do next. He could have decided to consolidate his defenses on the terrain along the Sudley Road. Alternatively, he could have pulled back to the defensible terrain on the other side of Bull Run. Pope did not choose either of these options, deciding instead to retreat east to the defensive works at Centreville.

Report of Maj. Gen. John Pope, USA, Commanding Army of Virginia

By dark our left had been forced back about half or three-quarters of a mile, but still remained firm and unbroken and still covered the turnpike in our rear.

About 6 o'clock in the afternoon, I heard accidentally that Franklin's corps had arrived at a point about 4 miles east of Centreville and 12 miles in our rear, and that it was only about 8,000 strong. The result of the battle of the 30th, the very heavy losses

> we had suffered, and the complete prostration of our troops from hunger and fatigue made it plain to me that we were no longer able, in the face of such overwhelming odds, to maintain our position so far to the front, nor would we have been able to do so under any circumstances, suffering as were the men and horses from fatigue and hunger and weakened by the heavy losses incident to the uncommon hardships which they had suffered.
>
> About 8 o'clock at night, therefore, I sent written instructions to the commanders of corps to withdraw leisurely toward Centreville, and stated to them what route each should pursue and where they should take post. The withdrawal was made slowly, quietly, and in good order, no pursuit whatever having been attempted by the enemy. I sent orders to General Banks, (Second Corps) at Bristoe Station, to destroy the railroad trains and such of the stores in them as he was unable to carry off, and rejoin me at Centreville.[33]

Pope's critical decision brought the Second Battle of Manassas to a close; however, it did not end the campaign. Pope's purpose in retreating was to rally his army in the Centreville defensive positions, five miles east of Bull Run. His army reached Centreville that night and the next day. However, it was soon forced to continue retreating east.

There is one more stop in the Manassas National Battlefield Park and three excursion stops away from the park. These stops take you to the Stone Bridge over Bull Run, the site of Porter's August 29 critical decision not to attack, to Thoroughfare Gap, and the route of Lee's second turning movement.

Directions to all of these stops start at the Henry Hill Visitor Center parking lot.

If you wish to visit the Stone Bridge, follow the directions below. If you wish to go to all or any of the excursion stops, go to those specific directions.

Directions to Stop 9: Depart the visitor center's parking area, and drive to the Sudley Road. Turn right on the Sudley Road, and drive north for 0.4 mile to the intersection with the Warrenton Turnpike (where the stoplight is). Turn right on to the Warrenton Turnpike, and drive east 1.4 miles to a parking area on your left. Turn left into the parking area, and park. Leave your car, and walk west on the path for one hundred yards to the Stone Bridge.

Appendix I

Stop 9: The Stone Bridge

You are at the Stone Bridge that played a predominant role in the movement of Union troops not only at Second Manassas in 1862, but also at First Manassas on July 21, 1861. The original bridge was built in 1825. The Stone Bridge survived First Manassas, but Confederates destroyed it as they withdrew from the Manassas area on March 9, 1862. Although the bridge's span sections had been destroyed, its abutments were in place during Second Manassas, and planking was put down to provide a roadway. In 1926 US Highway 29 (Warrenton Turnpike) was straightened out, and a different bridge was constructed. The current bridge, which you drove over, was constructed in the 1990s.

During the retreat of Pope's army across Bull Run, the Stone Bridge provided the crossing points for the majority of the Union forces.

The army's retreat was covered by Sigel's First Corps.

> **Report of Maj. Gen. Franz Sigel, USA, Commanding First Corps, Army of Virginia**
>
> Following the troops of Generals Porter and McDowell, my corps crossed Young's Branch, where it remained for two hours, until the commands of Generals McDowell, Reno, and Kearny had crossed Bull Run by the ford near the stone bridge, and the whole train had passed over the bridge. It was now between 9 and 10 p.m. I then marched to the turnpike, crossed the bridge over Bull Run, and took position on the left and right of the bridge, throwing my pickets out on the other side of the creek toward the battle-field. Soon afterward an officer of General McDowell's staff directed me to fall back. It was now after midnight, when I ordered my command to

Major General Franz Sigel, USA, Commanding First Corps, Army of Virginia. USAMHI.

> continue its march toward Centreville, first destroying the bridge across Bull Run. Our rear guard was composed of part of General Schurz's division, two pieces of Captain Dilger's battery, and a detachment of Colonel Kane's Bucktail Rifles, which had come up with several guns collected on their march of retreat.[34]

When you look at Bull Run, you can see how it and its steep banks form an obstacle to easy movement by any large force. This might bring up the question, "Why was Pope's army fighting west of Bull Run rather than east of it?"

Tactical doctrine calls for a defense to be positioned so that any major obstacle is in front of the defenders and not behind them. This arrangement provides a means to slow and channelize enemy movements. Today the area near Bull Run is more vegetated than in 1862, when it was fairly open terrain. The high ground on the east side would have provided positions with good fields of fire and observation

Time was on Pope's side; it was not on Lee's. Lee knew that he had to defeat Pope's army before McClellan's Army of the Potomac could provide significant reinforcement. Given time, these reinforcements would provide Pope with an overwhelming number of troops. Pope could afford to wait. Perhaps a better tactical plan would have been to occupy positions east of Bull Run, wait for more reinforcement, and force Lee to attack him across the water obstacle.

Return to your car. If you wish to visit any of the excursion stops, return to the Henry Hill Visitor Center parking lot, and follow the instructions for that specific excursion stop.

Excursion Stop 1: Porter Decides not to Attack

Depart the Henry Hill Visitor Center parking lot, and drive to the Sudley Road. Turn left onto the Sudley Road (Virginia Highway 234), and drive for 2.9 miles to Rixlew Lane. Turn right, and drive for 0.9 mile to the Wellington Road. Turn right again onto Wellington Road (Virginia Highway 674), and drive 2.8 miles to Dawkins Branch. There is no sign to identify the Dawkins Branch watercourse. Twenty yards after you cross Dawkin's Branch, there is a small area to pull into. BE EXTREMELY CAREFUL at this stop because of high-speed traffic.

This section of the Wellington Road is part of the historic Manassas Junction–Gainesville Road. Gainesville is 3.7 miles farther on.

Appendix I

You are on the extreme left flank of Pope's army on August 29. Groveton and the Warrenton Turnpike are 4,500 yards (2.5 miles) to your right (north). The Manassas Junction–Gainesville Road and the Warrenton Turnpike converge at Gainesville. A force moving on this road would intersect with the Warrenton Turnpike and be interposed between any enemy force to the east and west. A railroad is located 1,225 yards (0.7 mile) to your right. These modern tracks have replaced the historic 1862 Manassas Gap Railroad. Henry Hill and the visitor center are 5,275 yards (3.0 miles) to your right rear (northeast).

In 1862 the area to your right was wooded; the area to your left was open ground. The area in front of you on both sides of the road was open ground for 1,000 yards. At that distance, there was a wood on both sides of the road, where the higher ground is.

Mistakenly believing that Jackson was attempting to retreat west, Pope ordered Maj. Gen. Fitz John Porter to maneuver his Fifth Corps (Army of the Potomac) toward Gainesville. Accompanied by Maj. Gen. Irvin McDowell's Third Corps (Army of Virginia), Porter was charged with severing Jackson's supposed route of retreat. This combined force consisted of 4 divisions (14 brigades) and 14 artillery batteries (76 guns). Simultaneously, Pope ordered a series of attacks against Jackson's position along the unfinished railroad.

On the morning of August 29, Porter's lead division, Maj. Gen. George W. Morell's First Division, followed by Brig. Gen. George Sykes's Second Division, was marching on the road you just traveled. In late morning Morell's advance unit, Brig. Gen. Charles Griffin's Second Brigade, made contact with Confederate forces in front of you. Griffin deployed four regiments to your right and sent the Sixty-third Pennsylvania across Dawkin's Branch to form a skirmish line on the right of the road. The Sixty-third was shortly joined by the Thirteenth New York, which extended the skirmish line south of the road. The skirmish line was located five hundred yards in front of you. Capt. Augustus P. Martin's Third Massachusetts Battery (six Napoleons) went into position to your left on the other side of the road. Lieut. Charles E. Hazlett placed the six 10-pound Parrott Rifles of Battery D, Fifth US Artillery to the right of the infantry on this side of the road. Morell's other two brigades halted behind Griffin and remained in column of regiments.

Eight hundred yards in front of you was a Confederate skirmish line. Behind the skirmishers Col. Montgomery D. Corse's brigade was deployed on this side of the road. To Corse's right (south), your left, was Brig. Gen. Beverly Robertson's cavalry brigade. Additional Confederate units would reinforce this position and occupy terrain to the north.

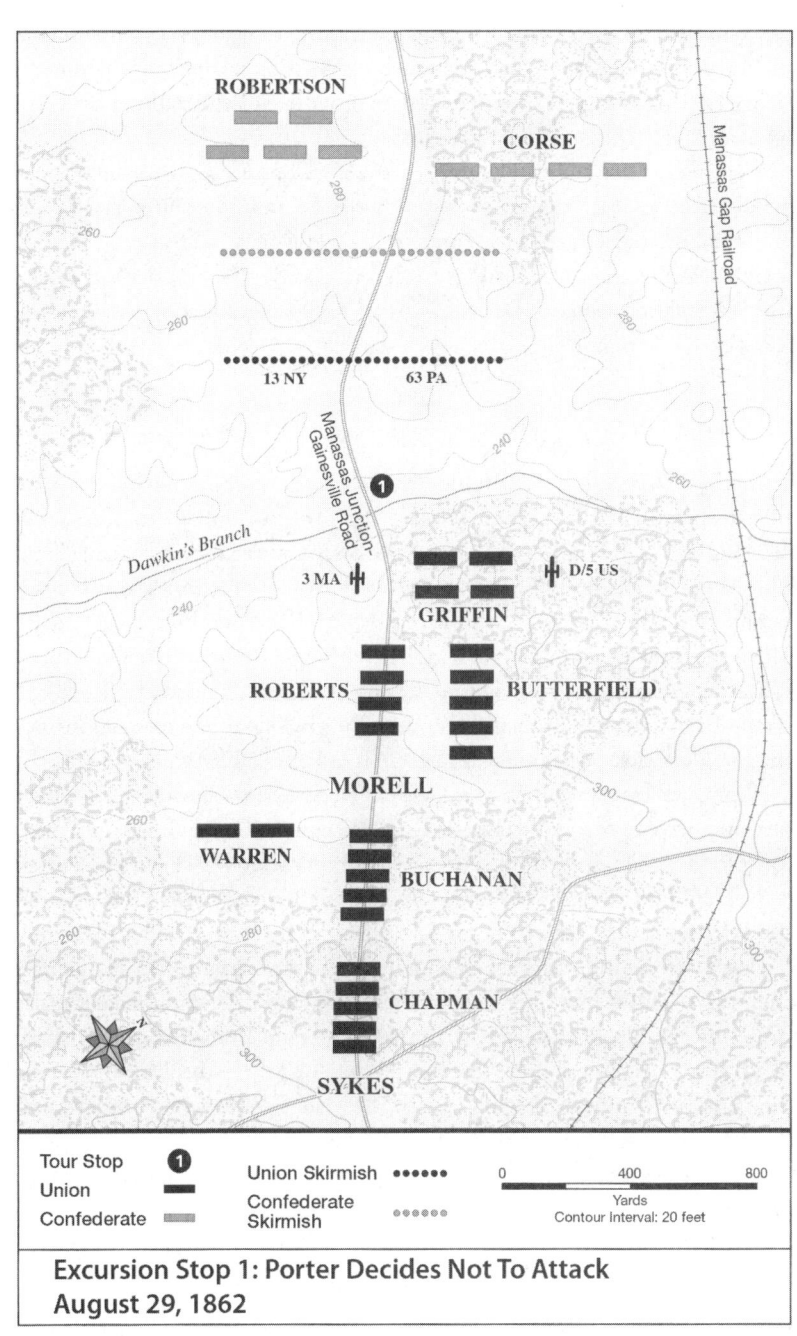

**Excursion Stop 1: Porter Decides Not To Attack
August 29, 1862**

Appendix I

This was as far as Porter's Corps advanced on August 29. Unsure of what was to his front, Porter kept trying to gain information, and the hours slipped by. In the afternoon McDowell marched his division north to the vicinity of Henry Hill. That night Porter received an order from Pope to bring his corps north and join the main body of the army.

Porter's critical decision prevented the development of a potentially favorable situation for Pope on his south flank. More importantly, had Porter continued on and engaged the force to his front, he would have developed irrefutable intelligence that Longstreet's Wing was in fact on the battlefield. This information would have had a direct influence on decisions made the next day.

Excursion Stop 2: Ricketts Fights Alone (Thoroughfare Gap)

From Excursion Stop 1: Continue driving on the Wellington Road for 3.6 miles to Linton Hall Road. Turn right, and drive 0.5 mile to an overpass at Lee Highway (US Highway 29). Continue on this overpass; the road becomes John Marshall Highway/Highway 55. Drive west for 6.4 miles to the intersection with Roads 674 and 628 (Trapp Branch Road and Bust Head Road). Along the route in 4.7 miles you will drive through Thoroughfare Gap. In 1.7 miles you will come to the road intersection. Turn left onto County Road 674 (Trapp Branch Road), immediately pull off to the side of the road, leave your car, and look back east to the gap. BE CAREFUL OF TRAFFIC.

From the Henry Hill Visitor Center: Depart the visitor center parking area, and drive to the Sudley Road. Turn right on the Sudley Road, and drive north for 0.4 mile to the intersection with the Warrenton Turnpike (located at the stoplight). Turn left onto the Warrenton Turnpike (US Highway 29–Lee Highway), and drive west for 4.7 miles to Highway 55 (John Marshall Highway). In 0.4 mile after driving under Interstate 66, take the right exit for Highway 55. Continue right onto Highway 55, and drive west for 6.4 miles to the intersection with Roads 674 and 628 (Trapp Branch Road and Bust Head Road). Along the route in 4.7 miles you will drive through Thoroughfare Gap. In 1.7 miles you will come to the road intersection. Turn left onto County Road 674 (Trapp Branch Road), immediately pull off to the side of the road, leave your car, and look back east to the gap. BE CAREFUL OF TRAFFIC.

Position A—Approaching the Gap

You are looking east and viewing Thoroughfare Gap as the Confederates saw it while they marched east. The high ground to the right (south) is Pond

Mountain (also called Biscuit Mountain). The high ground to the left (north) is Mother Leathercoat Mountain. These two terrain features extend 430 feet and 413 feet, respectively, above the floor of the gap. The gap itself is approximately 100 yards wide. In those 100 yards was a road (present-day Highway 55), the tracks of the Manassas Gap Railroad, and Broad Run.

Maj. Gen. Thomas J. "Stonewall" Jackson's Left Wing marched through the gap on August 26 on the way to Bristoe Station on the Orange and Alexandria Railroad. Arriving at Bristoe Station, Jackson had completed the turning movement ordered by Lee. Pope's main supply line was cut, and he was forced to retreat from his positions along the Rappahannock River on the morning of August 27. On the afternoon of August 26, Maj. Gen. James Longstreet began to march his Right Wing along Jackson's route to reunite the Army of Northern Virginia.

Longstreet began his march the day that Jackson captured Bristoe Station and then Pope's supply base at Manassas Junction. The next day Longstreet marched to the vicinity of White Plains, eight miles west of the gap. On August 28 Jackson moved his forces to the "Stony Ridge" overlooking the Warrenton Turnpike, and in the late afternoon he initiated the fight at Groveton against King's division (Stop 3).

On that same day Longstreet marched to the western edge of Thoroughfare Gap, where his units prepared to spend the night. As a precaution, a brigade commanded by Col. George T. Anderson was sent forward to secure the gap. Anderson sent Col. Benjamin Beck's Ninth Georgia into the gap, and the troops made contact with the First New Jersey Cavalry.

Maj. Gen. Irvin McDowell's Third Corps, Ricketts's, King's, and Reynolds's (attached) divisions were in the vicinity of Gainesville, while the First New Jersey Cavalry was at Thoroughfare Gap.

McDowell must have realized that he was in a position to completely disrupt Lee's maneuver plans and perhaps to inflict grave damage to the Confederate army. During the hour before midnight on August 27, McDowell chose a plan of action that would take advantage of his position near Gainesville. He ordered Sigel's First Corps and Reynolds's division to march through Gainesville to Haymarket. There, they would be in position to block and engage Longstreet's Right Wing as it emerged from Thoroughfare Gap. The two divisions of McDowell's Third Corps would turn southeast at Gainesville and march toward Manassas Junction to engage Jackson. When these moves were completed, McDowell would have isolated the two wings of Lee's army from each other. Doing so would have not only disrupted Lee's maneuver plan but also created conditions in which Lee's two wings could be attacked separately. Before McDowell's plan could be acted upon, he received an order from the army commander, Maj. Gen. John Pope, to march his corps, Sigel's corps, and Reynolds's division to Manassas Junction in a too-late attempt to trap Jackson. Still concerned about Longstreet, McDowell ordered Brig. Gen. James B. Ricketts's division to a position west of Haymarket with instructions to resist any attempt by Longstreet to march through the gap.[35]

Sigel's First Corps marched toward Manassas Junction. Reynolds's division marched from Gainesville, followed the Warrenton Turnpike east until it reached Pageland Lane, then turned southeast toward Manassas. King's division followed Reynolds's. While marching along the turnpike near Groveton, King's men made contact with Jackson's force, which resulted in the evening battle at the Brawner Farm (Stop 3). Ricketts, informed of the First New Jersey's contact at the gap, marched west to try and stop Longstreet.

As the initial contact developed in the gap, Jones sent the remainder of Anderson's Brigade into the opening and onto the high ground extending to the north. Two regiments of Col. Henry Benning's brigade were sent to the high ground to the right (Pond Mountain). Col. Evander Law's brigade of Hood's Division was sent to the higher ground to the left (Mother Leathercoat). Brig. Gen. Cadmus M. Wilcox's division was sent six miles north to pass through Hopewell Gap, turn south, and envelop the right flank of Ricketts's division.

Lee and Longstreet observed the deployment and fight from an elevation just west of the gap. Several historians believe that the high ground behind you, which is private property, is that location.

Return to your car for the drive to position B.

Reverse your route, and drive east back into the gap. In 0.6 mile pull over to your left near the site of several markers. Park, leave your car, and face in the direction you were driving.

Position B—Fight for the Gap

You are at the eastern end of the gap. Pond Mountain is to your right rear, and Mother Leathercoat is to your left rear. Across the interstate to your left are the railroad tracks and Broad Run. The ruins of the stone building were once Chapman Mill, which was here in 1862.

Moving into the gap, the Ninth Georgia made contact with the First New Jersey Cavalry and drove the Union troops east out of the opening.

Colonel George T. Anderson, CSA, Commanding Jones's (Anderson's) Brigade, Jones's Division, Longstreet's Right Wing, Army of Northern Virginia. USAMHI.

Report of Col. George T. Anderson, CSA, Commanding Jones's Brigade, Jones's Division, Longstreet's Right Wing, Army of Northern Virginia

Continuing our march, we reached Thoroughfare Gap August 28. My brigade was in front. I ordered Colonel [Benjamin] Beck, with his regiment (Ninth Georgia), in advance and to send forward two companies as skirmishers. Moving in this order, the brigade was halted by order of General Longstreet some half mile from the Gap and Colonel Beck ordered to proceed through the Gap on a reconnaissance. Proceeding cautiously, he drove a mounted picket before him, killing 3 of them, and cleared the pass, moving some quarter of a mile beyond, and held his position until attacked and driven back.[36]

As the Union cavalry retreated east, Ricketts's division progressed west along the road. The advance was led by Col. John W. Stiles's Third Brigade. Col. Joseph Thoburn's Fourth Brigade and Brig. Gen. Abram Duryea's First Brigade supported Stiles. Brig. Gen. Zealous B. Tower's Second Brigade was held in reserve. Two batteries of artillery deployed 1,200 yards in front of you. Capt. Ezra Matthews's Battery F, First Pennsylvania Artillery (six guns) deployed north of the road, and Capt. James Thompson's Battery C, Pennsylvania Artillery (four guns) deployed south of the road. Both batteries fired into the gap.

Report of Brig. Gen. James B. Ricketts, USA, Commanding Second Division, Third Corps, Army of Virginia

On the 28th, being ordered to "assist Colonel Wyndham, who at 10.15 a.m. reported the enemy passing through Thoroughfare Gap," marched through Hay Market, where the troops were relieved of their knapsacks to hasten the movement; but before reaching the Gap, about 3 p.m., met Colonel Wyndham's skirmishers retiring before the enemy, already in possession. Fully realizing the importance of gaining this point I pressed the division forward, although in a wearied condition, determined to effect the object if possible.

The road was entirely obstructed by felled timber, which delayed bringing the batteries into position; the Third Brigade in advance, then commanded by Colonel Stiles supported by the First and Fourth Brigades, the Second Brigade being held in reserve. The men moved forward gallantly, but owing to the nature of the ground, the strongest positions being already held by the enemy, we were subjected to severe loss, without any prospect of gaining the Gap.[37]

Stiles's Third Brigade deployed east of the gap. The Eleventh Pennsylvania, supported by the Eighty-third New York, was to the right (your left) of the road. The Thirteenth Massachusetts, with its right adjacent to the road, was to the left (your right) of the road. The Twelfth Massachusetts formed to the left of the Thirteenth. As Stiles's attack moved west, the Ninth Georgia fell back to where you are and occupied a position with the troops' left on Chapman Mill.

Report of Col. George T. Anderson, CSA—continued

The brigade was ordered forward, and moving rapidly to the front, I found Colonel Beck falling back very slowly before the large force of the enemy and caused him to form his regiment on the right of the railroad, and formed the other regiments on the left as fast as they came up. Having thus formed my line and advanced my skirmishers to the front, I ordered the line to advance which was done in the most gallant manner, the men climbing the rough mountain-side

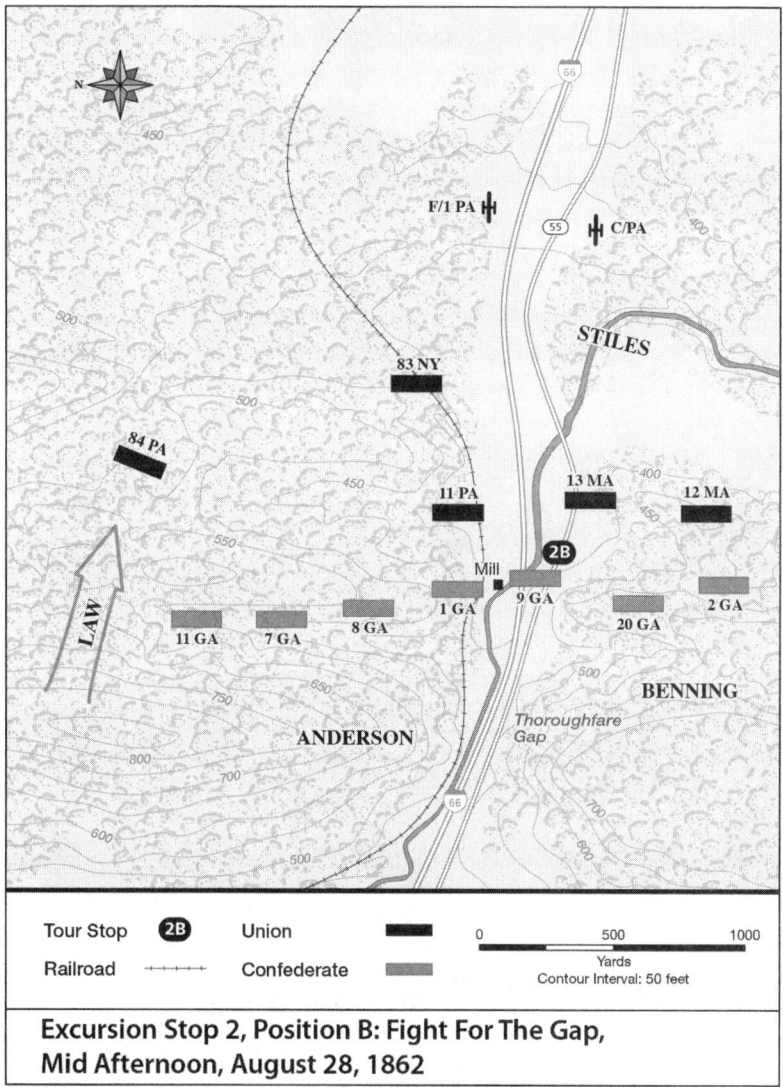

Excursion Stop 2, Position B: Fight For The Gap, Mid Afternoon, August 28, 1862

on their hands and knees to reach the enemy, occupying the crest of a hill [to your left], and delivering a murderous fire in their faces as they made the perilous ascent. From the nature of the ground and the impenetrable thickets of laurel and brush none of the regiments except the First Georgia obtained a favorable position.[38]

The Eleventh Pennsylvania was able to gain the high ground above Chapman Mill and engaged the right of Anderson's line. The Thirteenth Massachusetts pushed into the eastern end of the gap and occupied a position on the lower area of Pond Mountain. The Twelfth Massachusetts, on their left, climbed to a higher elevation. Both regiments fought the Twentieth Georgia and then the Second Georgia of Benning's Brigade.

> ### Report of Maj. James D. Waddell, CSA, Commanding, Twentieth Georgia, Toombs's (Benning's) Brigade, Jones's Division, Longstreet's Right Wing, Army of Northern Virginia
>
> On approaching Thoroughfare Gap, the Twentieth Georgia being the advance regiment of the brigade, I was ordered to proceed and take possession of the heights on our right, for which it was understood the enemy, already partially in position on the left, were making. The regiment advanced toward the position indicated subjected to a galling fire of artillery and infantry, in open view for some 200 yards, when we reached the cover of the hill. Immediately throwing forward a company of skirmishers, with orders to gain the summit with all possible expedition, I led the regiment to their support at a distance of less than 30 yards. On reaching the top the enemy's skirmishers were discovered advancing from the opposite side and distant from the crest not exceeding 40 yards. These were driven back precipitately by my skirmishers. On discovering that the enemy's skirmishers were supported by two full regiments of infantry I at once ordered forward all the men armed with guns of long range in the command numbering some 60, and directed such as were armed with the smoothbore musket to take shelter from the artillery fire of the enemy to which they were exposed behind the crest of the hill. I required but a few moments of well-directed fire to drive their infantry in wild disorder and rout from the base of the hill across the open plain until they gained the wood beyond the range of our guns.[39]

The Second Georgia also climbed the mountain and came into position on the right of the Twentieth Georgia. The soldiers were then in a position to outflank the Twelfth and Thirteenth Massachusetts, which caused these two regiments to withdraw from their exposed locations.

The Fight at Thoroughfare Gap, August 28, 1862; Confederate view. Library of Congress.

On the north side of the gap, the Eleventh Pennsylvania continued to engage the right of Anderson's line at Chapman Mill and on the rising terrain north of it. Eventually the left of Anderson's Brigade was able to climb to the higher part of the mountain and outflank the Eleventh Pennsylvania. With the Eighty-third New York, its supporting regiment, the Eleventh Pennsylvania retreated east.

Law's Brigade finally reached even higher terrain on Anderson's left. As they descended down the east side, they were engaged by the Eighty-fourth Pennsylvania from Thoburn's Fourth Brigade. Driving back the Eighty-fourth Pennsylvania and arriving at the lower ground, Law was in a position to outflank the entire Union position.[40]

With the retreat of Stiles's four regiments and with Law's Brigade on his flank, Ricketts gave up the fight and retreated east to Gainesville. The next morning (August 29) the division marched to Bristoe Station and then Manassas Junction. From Manassas Junction it marched to the battlefield and arrived there on the night of August 29.

The critical decision to only use one division to block the eastern egress from Thoroughfare Gap cost McDowell his last, most promising chance to keep Lee's army divided and gain additional time. Pope might have used the extra time McDowell gained to attack and defeat Jackson's and Longstreet's wings separately.

When Ricketts's division retreated, the advanced elements of Longstreet's Right Wing pushed through the gap and bivouacked on the east side. The next morning Longstreet resumed the march, and the remainder of his units passed through the gap. The column continued on to Gainesville, then followed the Warrenton Turnpike to the battlefield. At 10:00 a.m. the lead units began arriving and deploying on Jackson's right.

If you would like a view of the gap from higher ground where some of the fighting occurred, follow these directions.

Return to your car, and drive east on Highway 55 (John Marshall Highway) for 1.0 mile to the intersection with Turner Road (Road 723). Turn left onto Turner Road (#723), and drive north for 0.1 mile, crossing over Interstate 66, to the intersection with Beverley Mill Drive. Turn left onto Beverley Mill Drive, drive 0.8 mile, and park on the left of the road. Leave your car, cross the road to the trailhead, pick up a trail map, and walk on the Mountain Road Trail or the Quarry Trail to the overlook. BE CAREFUL as you cross the railroad tracks.

Excursion Stop 3: Lee Decides on Another Turning Movement

In this excursion, you will not only visit the area of the Battle of Chantilly (Ox Hill), but also follow Jackson's route.

Position A—Henry Hill

Pope's retreat left Gen. Robert E. Lee in possession of the battlefield and with a tactical victory. That triumph had moved the war in Virginia from Richmond and central Virginia to the vicinity of Washington, DC. However, Lee had not accomplished all that he intended. He decided to conduct another turning movement and once more bring Pope to battle. Jackson was again selected for the turning movement. Longstreet was to remain on the battlefield to keep Pope's attention focused on his wing, then follow Jackson.

> ### Report of Gen. Robert E. Lee, CSA, Commanding Army of Northern Virginia
>
> The obscurity of night and the uncertainty of the fords of Bull Run rendered it necessary to suspend operations until morning, when the cavalry, being pushed forward, discovered that the enemy had escaped to the strong position of Centreville, about 4 miles beyond Bull Run.

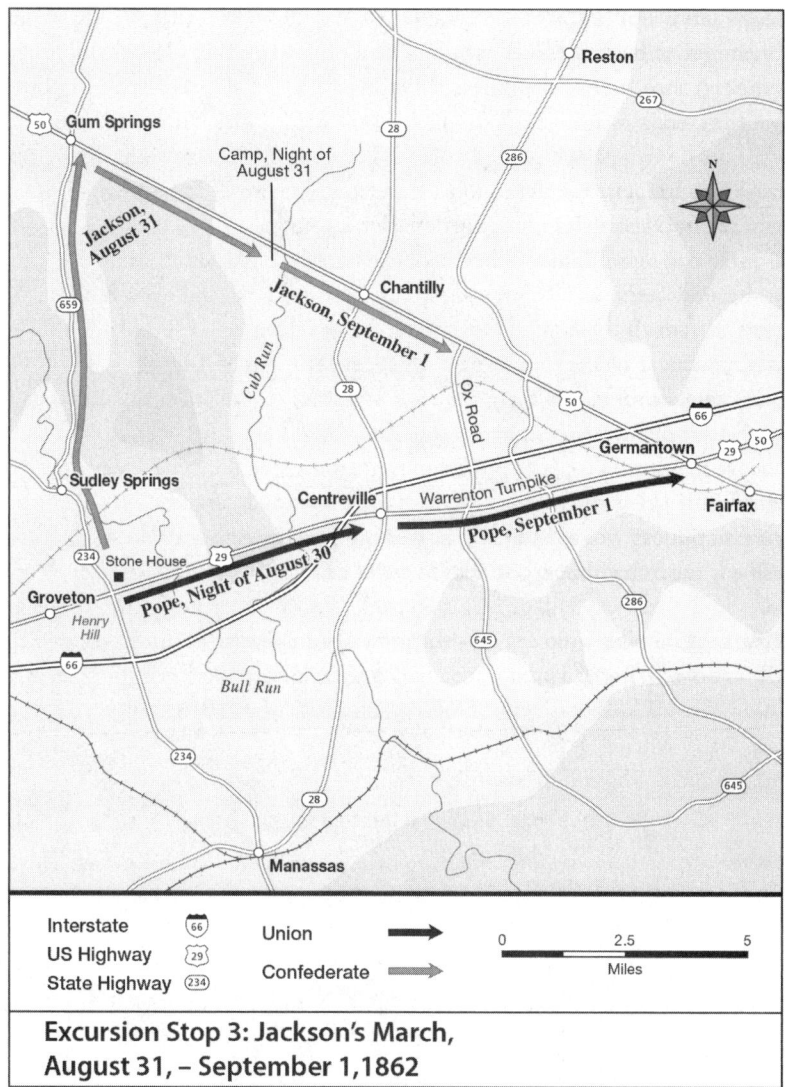

Excursion Stop 3: Jackson's March, August 31, – September 1, 1862

The prevalence of a heavy rain, which began during the night, threatened to render Bull Run impassable and impeded our movements. Longstreet remained on the battlefield to engage the attention of the enemy and cover the burial of the dead and the removal of the wounded, while Jackson proceeded by Sudley Ford to the Little River turnpike to turn the enemy's right and intercept his retreat to Washington.[41]

Appendix I

You will now follow Jackson's march.

Depart the visitor center parking area, and drive to the Sudley Road. Turn right on the Sudley Road (Virginia Highway 234). Drive north, through the stoplight intersection, on the Sudley Road for 2.7 miles. At the intersection with the Gum Springs Road (Virginia Highway 659), turn right. Drive 6.6 miles on Gum Springs Road to the intersection with US Highway 50–John Mosby Highway (in 1862 the Little River Turnpike).

You are in the vicinity of the 1862 small village of Gum Springs.

Turn right on to US Highway 50 and drive for 10.1 miles to the exit for West Ox Road. In 4.2 miles you will cross Cub Run.

Cub Run is where Jackson's troops spent the night of August 31. The Civil War canteen held about forty-six ounces of water—just under one and a half quarts. Unlike today, the transportation of large amounts of water was not feasible in 1862. Whenever possible, commanders would halt the day's march next to a major water source, usually a large stream or a river.

Continue to drive, and take the exit ramp to the right. At West Ox Road follow the ramp to the right onto West Ox Road. Stay in the right through lane. Drive for 0.24 mile (425 yards) to the entrance for Ox Hill Battlefield Park. It is on your right, 75 yards past the West Ox Road intersection with Monument Drive. Turn right into the parking area, park, leave your car, and follow the walking path to the other side of the park. There, you will find what appear to be grave markers.

Position B—Battle of Ox Hill

These two markers give the impression that Maj. Gen. Philip Kearny (Third Division, Third Corps, Army of the Potomac) and Brig. Gen. Isaac I. Stevens (First Division, Ninth Corps, Army of the Potomac), who were both killed in this battle, are buried here. They are not; these are memorial markers to the two generals. Kearny is buried in Arlington National Cemetery, and Stevens is buried in Island Cemetery in Newport, Rhode Island.[42]

Look south across the park toward the parking lot.

> ### Report of Maj. Gen. John Pope, USA, Commanding Army of Virginia
>
> I directed General Sumner, on the morning of the 1st of September, to push forward a reconnaissance of two brigades toward the Little River turnpike, to ascertain if the enemy were making any move-

> ments in the direction of Germantown or Fairfax Court-House. The enemy was found moving again slowly toward our right, heavy columns of his force being in march toward Fairfax along Little River turnpike.[43]

This small park is all that remains of the Chantilly, or, if you prefer, the Ox Hill battlefield.

The John Mosby Highway that you traveled was here in 1862 as the Little River Turnpike. West Ox Road that you drove on to the parking area was also here in 1862. It was a narrow farm road and was just called Ox Road.

The area around you looks very different today than at the time of the battle. To your right and right front was a large cornfield. Except for the Reid House one-half mile to your right front, there were no structures in this vicinity. There was a wooded area behind you.

Jackson was tasked with a turning movement that would take him to the intersection of the Little River Turnpike and the Warrenton Turnpike at Germantown (sometimes spelled Jermantown), located another two and one-half miles farther on. Capturing and controlling this intersection would cut Pope's line of communication and retreat farther east from Centreville.

Report of Maj. Gen. Thomas J. Jackson, CSA, Commanding Left Wing, Army of Northern Virginia

> It being ascertained next morning that the Federal Army had retreated in the direction of Centreville, I was ordered by the commanding general to turn that position, crossing Bull Run at Sudley Ford thence pursuing a country road until we reached the Little River turnpike, which we followed in the direction of Fairfax Court-House until the troops halted for the night.
>
> Early the next morning (September 1) we moved forward, and late in the evening, after reaching Ox Hill, came in contact with the enemy, who were in position on our right and front, covering his line of retreat from Centreville to Fairfax Court-House. Our line of battle was formed, General Hill's division on the right, Ewell's division, General Lawton commanding, in the center, and Jackson's division, General Starke commanding, on the left, all on the right [south] of the turnpike road. Artillery was posted on an eminence to the left of the road.[44]

Appendix I

At 4:00 p.m. on September 1, 1862, Jackson's wing was halted along the Little River Turnpike, six hundred yards behind you. Skirmishers reported the presence of Union troops south of the turnpike, and Jackson ordered Maj. Gen A. P. Hill to investigate. Two of Hill's brigades moved to this location and to your right. Skirmishers from these brigades soon began to make contact with an advanced element of Stevens's division that was deploying eight hundred yards in front of you. Jackson immediately began to deploy additional units. When this deployment was completed, the right of his position was the two brigades from A. P. Hill that were deployed to your right rear. Starting behind you and going east through the present-day intersection were two brigades from Ewell's (Lawton's) Division. Three brigades from Jackson's (Stark's) Division extended the line north to the turnpike. Other brigades were held just south of the turnpike as a reserve.

> ### Report of Maj. Gen. Thomas J. Jackson, CSA—continued
>
> The brigades of Branch and Field, Col. [J. M.] Brockenbrough commanding the latter, were sent forward to feel and engage the enemy. A cold and drenching thunder-shower swept over the field at this time, striking directly into the faces of our troops. These two brigades gallantly engaged the enemy, but so severe was the fire in front and flank of Branch's brigade as to produce in it some disorder and falling back. The brigades of Gregg, Thomas, and Pender were then thrown into the fight. Soon a portion of Ewell's [Lawton's] division became engaged. The conflict now raged with great fury, the enemy obstinately and desperately contesting the ground until their generals (Kearny and Stevens) fell in front of Thomas' brigade, after which they retired from the field.[45]

Stevens's division moved forward and, in a driving thunderstorm, attacked the defenders where you are and to your right rear. During this attack Stevens was killed; he fell just to your immediate right. Stevens's division continued the assault, crossing the road behind you, but the soldiers were eventually stopped. The division fell back through this location to a position nine hundred yards south of you and astride the Ox Road.

Shortly after 5:00 p.m. Kearny's division arrived on the field and deployed 1,100 yards to your right front. These Union units then attacked that portion of Jackson's defenses to your right. Kearny was also killed during this attack, approximately where the road intersection is located sixty yards to your right rear. The fighting continued in this area until nightfall, when both sides drew apart.

Battlefield Guide to the Critical Decisions at Second Manassas

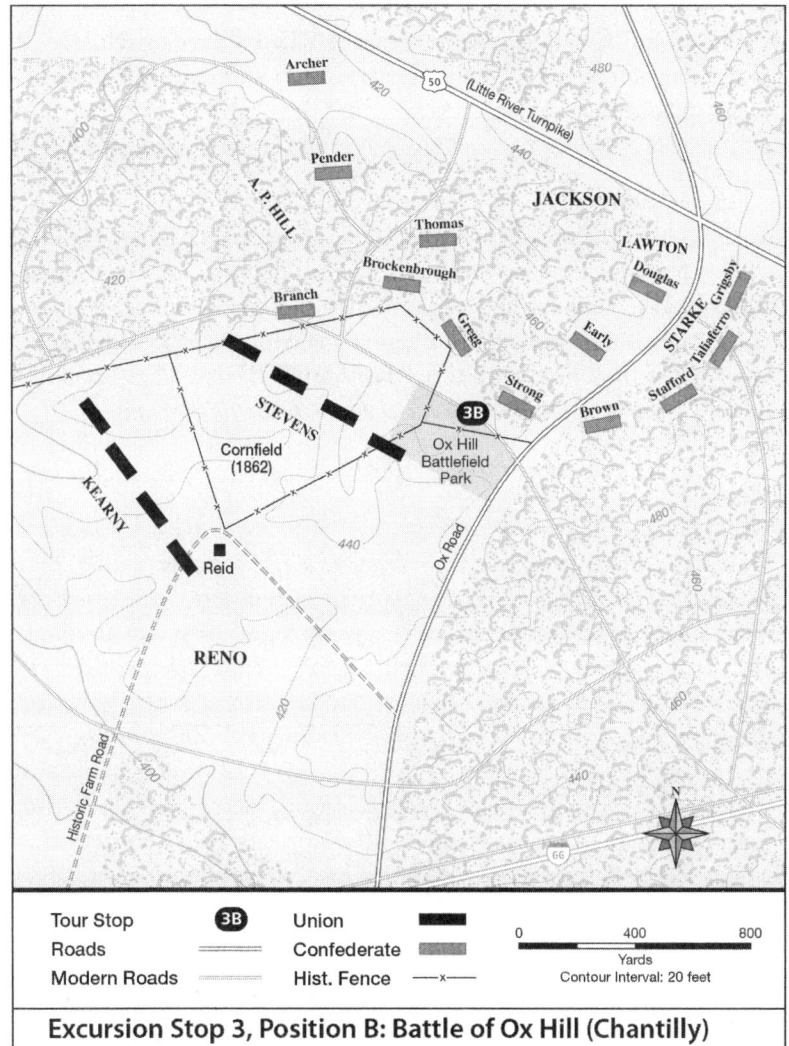

**Excursion Stop 3, Position B: Battle of Ox Hill (Chantilly)
Late Afternoon, September 1, 1862**

Report of Gen. Robert E. Lee, CSA—continued

Longstreet's command arrived after the action was over, and the next morning it was found that the enemy had conducted his retreat so rapidly that the attempt to intercept him was abandoned. The proximity of the fortifications around Alexandria and Washington rendered their pursuit useless, and our army rested during

> the 2d near Chantilly, the enemy being followed only by the cavalry, who continued to harass him until he reached the shelter of his intrenchments.[46]

Jackson had failed to cut Pope's route of retreat. The Union troops continued moving east, passed through the key intersection, and marched on to the Washington-Alexandria area. Lee marched his army to Leesburg, then crossed the Potomac River and commenced the Maryland Campaign of 1862.

This completes your battlefield tour of the critical decisions. For an in-depth tour of the entire battle, see Matt Spruill III and Matt Spruill IV, *Summer Lightning: A Battlefield Guide to the Second Battle of Manassas*.

APPENDIX II

UNION ORDER OF BATTLE

ARMY OF VIRGINIA
    Maj. Gen. John Pope

FIRST ARMY CORPS
    Maj. Gen. Franz Sigel

First Division
    Brig. Gen. Robert C. Schenck (w)
    Brig. Gen. Julius Stahel
First Brigade
    Brig. Gen. Julius Stahel
    Col. Adolphus Buschbeck
    8th New York
    41st New York
    45th New York
    27th Pennsylvania
    2d Battery, New York Artillery
Second Brigade
    Col. Nathaniel C. McLean
    25th Ohio
    55th Ohio
    73d Ohio
    75th Ohio
    Battery K, 1st Ohio Artillery

SECOND DIVISION
    Brig. Gen. Adolph von Steinwehr
FIRST BRIGADE (attached to Third Division)
    Col. John A. Koltes (k)
    Lieut. Col. Gustavus A. Muhleck
    29th New York
    68th New York
    73d Pennsylvania

THIRD DIVISION
    Brig. Gen. Carl Schurz
FIRST BRIGADE
    Brig. Gen. Henry Bohlen (k)
    Col. Alexander Schimmelfennig
    61st Ohio
    74th Pennsylvania
    8th West Virginia
    Battery F, Pennsylvania Artillery
SECOND BRIGADE
    Col. Wladimir Krzyzanowski
    54th New York
    58th New York
    75th Pennsylvania
    Battery L, 2d New York Artillery
UNATTACHED
    Company C, 3d West Virginia Cavalry
    Battery I, 1st Ohio Artillery

INDEPENDENT BRIGADE
    Brig. Gen. Robert H. Milroy
    2d West Virginia
    3d West Virginia
    5th West Virginia
    82d Ohio
    Companies C, E, and L, 1st West Virginia Cavalry
    12th Ohio Battery

CORPS RESERVE ARTILLERY
    Capt. Frank Buell (k)
    Capt. Louis Schirmer

Battery I, 1st New York Artillery
13th New York Battery
Battery C, West Virginia Artillery

CORPS CAVALRY BRIGADE
    Col. John Beardsley
    1st Connecticut Cavalry Battalion
    1st Maryland Cavalry
    4th New York Cavalry
    9th New York Cavalry
    6th Ohio Cavalry

SECOND ARMY CORPS
    Maj. Gen. Nathaniel P. Banks

FIRST DIVISION
    Brig. Gen. Alpheus S. Williams
FIRST BRIGADE
    Brig. Gen. Samuel W. Crawford
    5th Connecticut
    10th Maine
    28th New York
    46th Pennsylvania
THIRD BRIGADE
    Brig. Gen. George H. Gordon
    27th Indiana
    2d Massachusetts
    3d Wisconsin

SECOND DIVISION
    Brig. Gen. George H. Green
FIRST BRIGADE
    Col. Charles Candy
    Col. John H. Patrick
    5th Ohio
    7th Ohio
    29th Ohio
    66th Ohio
    28th Pennsylvania

SECOND BRIGADE
    Col. M. Schlaudecker
    Col. Thomas B. Van Buren
    3d Maryland
    102d New York
    109th Pennsylvania
    111th Pennsylvania

THIRD BRIGADE
    Col. James A. Tait
    3d Delaware
    1st District of Columbia
    60th New York
    78th New York
    Purnell Legion, Maryland

CORPS ARTILLERY
    Capt. Clermont L. Best
    4th Maine Battery
    Battery M, 1st New York Artillery
    10th New York Battery
    Battery E, Pennsylvania Artillery
    Battery F, 4th US Artillery

CORPS CAVALRY BRIGADE
    Brig. Gen. John Buford
    1st Michigan Cavalry
    5th New York Cavalry
    1st Vermont Cavalry
    1st West Virginia Cavalry

THIRD ARMY CORPS
    Maj. Gen. Irvin McDowell

FIRST DIVISION
    Brig. Gen. Rufus King
    Brig. Gen. John P. Hatch (w)
    Brig. Gen. Abner Doubleday

FIRST BRIGADE
    Brig. Gen. John P. Hatch
    Col. Timothy Sullivan

22d New York
24th New York
30th New York
84th New York (14th NYSM)
2d US Sharpshooters

SECOND BRIGADE
Brig. Gen. Abner Doubleday
Col. William P. Wainwright
76th New York
95th New York
56th Pennsylvania

THIRD BRIGADE
Brig. Gen. Marsena R. Patrick
21st New York
23d New York
35th New York
80th New York (20th NYSM)

FOURTH BRIGADE
Brig. Gen. John Gibbon
19th Indiana
2d Wisconsin
6th Wisconsin
7th Wisconsin

DIVISION ARTILLERY
Capt. Joseph B. Campbell
1st New Hampshire Battery
Battery L, 1st New York Artillery
Battery D, 1st Rhode Island Artillery
Battery B, 4th US Artillery

SECOND DIVISION
Brig. Gen. James B. Ricketts

FIRST BRIGADE
Brig. Gen. Abram Duryea
97th New York
104th New York
105th New York
107th Pennsylvania

Second Brigade
Brig. Gen. Zealous B. Tower (w)
Col. William H. Christian
26th New York
94th New York
88th Pennsylvania
90th Pennsylvania

Third Brigade
Brig. Gen. George L. Hartsuff
Col. John W. Stiles
12th Massachusetts
13th Massachusetts
83d New York (9th NYSM)
11th Pennsylvania

Fourth Brigade
Col. Joseph Thoburn (w)
7th Indiana
84th Pennsylvania
110th Pennsylvania
1st West Virginia

Division Artillery
2d Maine Battery
5th Maine Battery
Battery F, 1st Pennsylvania Artillery
Battery C, Pennsylvania Artillery

Pennsylvania Reserves Division (attached to Third Corps, Army of Virginia)
Brig. Gen. John F. Reynolds

First Brigade
Brig. Gen. George G. Meade
3d Pennsylvania Reserves
4th Pennsylvania Reserves
7th Pennsylvania Reserves
8th Pennsylvania Reserves
13th Pennsylvania Reserves (6 companies)

Second Brigade
Brig. Gen. Truman Seymour
1st Pennsylvania Reserves
2d Pennsylvania Reserves

   5th Pennsylvania Reserves
   6th Pennsylvania Reserves
  THIRD BRIGADE
   Brig. Gen. Conrad F. Jackson
   Col. Martin D. Hardin (w)
   Col. James T. Kirk (w)
   Lieut. Col. Robert Anderson
   9th Pennsylvania Reserves
   10th Pennsylvania Reserves
   11th Pennsylvania Reserves
   12th Pennsylvania Reserves
  DIVISION ARTILLERY
   Capt. Dunbar R. Ransom
   Battery A, 1st Pennsylvania Artillery
   Battery B, 1st Pennsylvania Artillery
   Battery G, 1st Pennsylvania Artillery
   Battery C, 5th US Artillery

  CORPS CAVALRY BRIGADE
   Brig. Gen. George D. Bayard
   1st Maine Cavalry
   1st New Jersey Cavalry
   2d New York Cavalry
   1st Pennsylvania Cavalry
   1st Rhode Island Cavalry

  CORPS UNATTACHED
   3d Maine Battery (Pontonniers)
   16th Indiana Battery
   3d Indiana Cavalry (detachment)
   Companies C, G, H, and I, 13th Pennsylvania Reserves

ARMY OF THE POTOMAC (units attached to Army of Virginia)

THIRD ARMY CORPS
  Maj. Gen. Samuel P. Heintzelman

  FIRST DIVISION
   Maj. Gen. Philip Kearny (k)
   Brig. Gen. David B. Birney

FIRST BRIGADE
    Brig. Gen. John C. Robinson
    20th Indiana
    30th Ohio (6 companies)
    63d Pennsylvania
    105th Pennsylvania
SECOND BRIGADE
    Brig. Gen. Davis B. Birney
    Col. J. H. Hobart Ward
    3d Maine
    4th Maine
    1st New York
    38th New York
    40th New York
    101st New York
    57th Pennsylvania
THIRD BRIGADE
    Col. Orlando M. Poe
    2d Michigan
    3d Michigan
    5th Michigan
    37th New York
    99th Pennsylvania
DIVISION ARTILLERY
    6th Maine Battery
    Battery E, 1st Rhode Island Artillery (attached)
    Battery K, 1st US Artillery

SECOND DIVISION
    Maj. Gen. Joseph Hooker
FIRST BRIGADE
    Brig. Gen. Cuvier Grover
    1st Massachusetts
    11th Massachusetts
    16th Massachusetts
    2d New Hampshire
    26th Pennsylvania
SECOND BRIGADE
    Col. Nelson Taylor
    70th New York

71st New York
72d New York
73d New York
74th New York

THIRD BRIGADE
Col. Joseph B. Carr
5th New Jersey
6th New Jersey
7th New Jersey
8th New Jersey
2d New York
115th Pennsylvania

DIVISION ARTILLERY
Battery E, 4th US Artillery (attached)

FIFTH ARMY CORPS
Maj. Gen. Fitz John Porter

FIRST DIVISION
Maj. Gen. George W. Morell

FIRST BRIGADE
Col. Charles W. Roberts
2d Maine
18th Massachusetts
22d Massachusetts
1st Michigan
13th New York
25th New York

SECOND BRIGADE
Brig. Gen. Charles Griffin
9th Massachusetts
32d Massachusetts
4th Michigan
14th New York
62d Pennsylvania

THIRD BRIGADE
Brig. Gen. Daniel Butterfield (commanded First and Third Brigades on August 30, 1862)
Col. Henry S. Lansing
Col. Henry A. Weeks (w)

Col. James C. Rice
16th Michigan
12th New York
17th New York
44th New York
83d Pennsylvania

SHARPSHOOTERS
1st US Sharpshooters

DIVISION ARTILLERY
3d Massachusetts Battery
Battery C, 1st Rhode Island Artillery
Battery D, 5th US Artillery

SECOND DIVISION
Brig. Gen. George Sykes

FIRST BRIGADE
Lieut. Col. Robert C. Buchanan
3d United States
4th United States
1st Battalion, 12th United States
1st Battalion, 14th United States
2d Battalion, 14th United States

SECOND BRIGADE
Lieut. Col. William Chapman
Company G, 1st United States
2d United States
6th United States
10th United States
11th United States
17th United States

THIRD BRIGADE
Col. Gouverneur K. Warren
5th New York
10th New York

DIVISION ARTILLERY
Capt. Stephen H. Weed
Batteries E and G, 1st US Artillery
Battery I, 5th US Artillery
Battery K, 5th US Artillery

RESERVE CORPS
STURGIS'S DIVISION
    Brig. Gen. Samuel D. Sturgis
PIATT'S BRIGADE (attached to Fifth Corps, Army of the Potomac)
    Brig. Gen. Abram S. Piatt
    63d Indiana (4 companies)
    86th New York
UNATTACHED CORPS ARTILLERY
    2d New York Heavy Artillery
    11th New York Battery
    Detachment, Battery C, 1st New York Artillery

SIXTH ARMY CORPS
FIRST DIVISION
    Brig. Gen. Henry W. Slocum
FIRST BRIGADE
    Brig. Gen. George W. Taylor (mw)
    Col. Henry W. Brown
    1st New Jersey
    2d New Jersey
    3d New Jersey
    4th New Jersey

NINTH ARMY CORPS
    Maj. Gen Jesse L. Reno

FIRST DIVISION
    Brig. Gen. Isaac I. Stevens (k)
    Col. Benjamin C. Christ
FIRST BRIGADE
    Col. Benjamin C. Christ
    Lieut. Col. Frank Graves
    8th Michigan
    50th Pennsylvania
SECOND BRIGADE
    Col. Daniel Leasure (w)
    Lieut. Col. David A. Leckey
    46th New York
    100th Pennsylvania

THIRD BRIGADE
    Col. Addison Farnsworth (w)
    Lieut. Col. David Morrison
    28th Massachusetts
    79th New York
DIVISION ARTILLERY
    8th Massachusetts Battery
    Battery E, 2d US Artillery

SECOND DIVISION
    Maj. Gen. Jesse L. Reno
FIRST BRIGADE
    Col. James Nagle
    6th New Hampshire
    48th Pennsylvania,
    2d Maryland
SECOND BRIGADE
    Col. Edward Ferrero
    21st Massachusetts
    51st New York
    51st Pennsylvania
    Battery D, Pennsylvania Artillery (attached)

KANAWHA DIVISION (detachment of) FIRST BRIGADE
    Col. E. Parker Scammon
    11th Ohio
    12th Ohio
    30th Ohio (6 companies)
    36th Ohio

k—killed
w—wounded mw—mortally wounded
c—captured

[*OR*, vol. 12, pt. 2, 250–545; *B&L*, vol. 2, pp. 497–99; Hennessy, *Second Manassas Battlefield Map Study*, 452–463.]

APPENDIX III

CONFEDERATE ORDER OF BATTLE

ARMY OF NORTHERN VIRGINIA
    Gen. Robert E. Lee

LONGSTREET'S RIGHT WING
    Maj. Gen. James Longstreet

ANDERSON'S DIVISION
    Maj. Gen. Richard H. Anderson
ARMISTEAD'S BRIGADE
    Brig. Gen. Lewis A. Armistead
    9th Virginia
    14th Virginia
    38th Virginia
    53d Virginia
    57th Virginia
    5th Virginia Battalion
MAHONE'S BRIGADE
    Brig. Gen. William Mahone (w)
    Col. David A. Weisiger (w)
    6th Virginia
    12th Virginia
    16th Virginia

41st Virginia
49th Virginia

WRIGHT'S BRIGADE
Brig. Gen. Ambrose R. Wright
44th Alabama
3d Georgia
22d Georgia
48th Georgia

DIVISION ARTILLERY
Maj. John S. Saunders
Huger's (Virginia) Battery
Moorman's (Virginia) Battery

JONES'S DIVISION
Brig. Gen. David R. Jones

TOOMBS'S BRIGADE
Col. Henry L. Benning
Brig. Gen. Robert A. Toombs
2d Georgia
15th Georgia
17th Georgia
20th Georgia

DRAYTON'S BRIGADE
Brig. Gen. Thomas F. Drayton
50th Georgia
51st Georgia
15th South Carolina
Phillips's Legion
Leake's (Virginia) Battery

JONES'S BRIGADE
Col. George T. Anderson
1st Georgia (Regulars)
7th Georgia
8th Georgia
9th Georgia
11th Georgia
Wise (Virginia) Battery

Wilcox's Division
   Brig. Gen. Cadmus M. Wilcox
Wilcox's Brigade
   Brig. Gen. Cadmus Wilcox
   8th Alabama
   9th Alabama
   10th Alabama
   11th Alabama
   Thomas's (Grimes's) (Virginia) Battery
Pryor's Brigade
   Brig. Gen. Roger A. Pryor
   14th Alabama
   2d Florida
   5th Florida
   8th Florida
   3d Virginia
   Maurin's Donaldsonville (Louisiana) Battery
Featherston's Brigade
   Brig. Gen. Winfield S. Featherston
   Col. Carnot Posey
   12th Mississippi
   16th Mississippi
   19th Mississippi
   2d Mississippi Battalion
   Chapman's Dixie (Virginia) Battery

Hood's Division
   Brig. Gen. John B. Hood
Hood's Brigade
   Brig. Gen. John B. Hood
   18th Georgia
   Hampton (SC) Legion
   1st Texas
   4th Texas
   5th Texas
Whiting's Brigade
   Col. Evander M. Law
   4th Alabama
   2d Mississippi

11th Mississippi
6th North Carolina

DIVISION ARTILLERY
Maj. Bushrod W. Frobel
Bachman's German (South Carolina) Battery
Garden's Palmetto (South Carolina) Battery
Reilly's Rowan (North Carolina) Battery

KEMPER'S DIVISION
Brig. Gen. James L. Kemper

KEMPER'S BRIGADE
Col. Montgomery D. Corse (w)
Col. William R. Terry
1st Virginia
7th Virginia
11th Virginia
17th Virginia
24th Virginia
Rogers's Loudoun (Virginia) Battery

JENKINS'S BRIGADE
Brig. Gen. Micah Jenkins (w)
Col. Joseph Walker
1st South Carolina Volunteers
2d South Carolina Rifles
5th South Carolina
6th South Carolina
4th South Carolina Battalion
Palmetto (South Carolina) Sharpshooters
Stribling's Fauquier (Virginia) Battery

PICKETT'S BRIGADE
Col. Eppa Hunton
8th Virginia
18th Virginia
19th Virginia
28th Virginia
56th Virginia

EVANS'S INDEPENDENT BRIGADE
Brig. Gen. Nathan G. Evans (on August 30 also commanded Hood's Division)

Col. P. F. Stevens
17th South Carolina
18th South Carolina
22d South Carolina
23d South Carolina
Holcombe (South Carolina) Legion
Boyce's Macbeth (South Carolina) Battery

LONGSTREET'S RIGHT WING'S ARTILLERY

WASHINGTON ARTILLERY
Col. James B. Walton
Eshleman's (4th) Company
Miller's (3d) Company
Richardson's (2d) Company
Squires's (1st) Company

LEE'S BATTALION
Col. Stephen D. Lee
Eubank's (Virginia) Battery
Grimes's (Virginia) Battery
Jordan's Bedford (Virginia) Battery
Parker's (Virginia) Battery
Rhett's (South Carolina) Battery
Taylor's (Virginia) Battery

JACKSON'S LEFT WING
Maj. Gen. Thomas J. Jackson

JACKSON'S DIVISION
Brig. Gen. William B. Taliaferro (w)
Brig. Gen. William E. Starke

FIRST BRIGADE
Col. William S. H. Baylor (k)
Col. Andrew J. Grigsby (w)
2d Virginia
4th Virginia
5th Virginia
27th Virginia
33d Virginia

SECOND BRIGADE
   Col. Bradley T. Johnson
   21st Virginia
   42d Virginia
   48th Virginia
   1st Virginia (Irish) Battalion

THIRD BRIGADE
   Col. Alexander G. Taliaferro
   47th Alabama
   48th Alabama
   10th Virginia
   23d Virginia
   37th Virginia

FOURTH BRIGADE
   Brig. Gen. William E. Starke
   Col. Leroy A. Stafford
   1st Louisiana
   2d Louisiana
   9th Louisiana
   10th Louisiana
   15th Louisiana
   Coppen's (Louisiana) Battalion

DIVISION ARTILLERY
   Maj. Lindsay M. Shumaker
   Brockenbrough's (Maryland) Battery
   Carpenter's (Virginia) Battery
   Caskie's Hampden (Virginia) Battery
   Cutshaw's (Virginia) Battery
   Poague's Rockbridge (Virginia) Battery
   Raine's Lee (Virginia) Battery
   Rice's (Virginia) Battery
   Wooding's Danville (Virginia) Battery

HILL'S LIGHT DIVISION
   Maj. Gen. Ambrose P. Hill

BRANCH'S BRIGADE
   Brig. Gen. Lawrence O'B. Branch
   7th North Carolina
   18th North Carolina

28th North Carolina
33d North Carolina
37th North Carolina

PENDER'S BRIGADE
Brig. Gen. William D. Pender
16th North Carolina
22d North Carolina
34th North Carolina
38th North Carolina

GREGG'S BRIGADE
Brig. Gen. Maxcy Gregg
1st South Carolina (Provisional Army)
1st South Carolina Rifles
12th South Carolina
13th South Carolina
14th South Carolina

ARCHER'S BRIGADE
Brig. Gen. James J. Archer
5th Alabama Battalion
19th Georgia
1st Tennessee (Provisional Army)
7th Tennessee
14th Tennessee

FIELD'S BRIGADE
Brig. Gen. Charles W. Field (w)
Col. John M. Brockenbrough
40th Virginia
47th Virginia
55th Virginia
22d Virginia Battalion

THOMAS'S BRIGADE
Brig. Gen. Edward L. Thomas
14th Georgia
35th Georgia
45th Georgia
49th Georgia

DIVISION ARTILLERY
Lieut. Col. Reuben L. Walker

Braxton's Fredericksburg (Virginia) Artillery
Crenshaw's (Virginia) Battery
Davidson's Letcher (Virginia) Battery
Fleet's Middlesex (Virginia) Battery
Latham's Branch (North Carolina) Battery
McIntosh's Pee Dee (South Carolina) Battery
Pegram's Purcell (Virginia) Battery

EWELL'S DIVISION
Maj. Gen. Richard S. Ewell (w)
Brig. Gen. Alexander R. Lawton

LAWTON'S BRIGADE
Brig. Gen. Alexander R. Lawton
Col. Marcellus Douglass
13th Georgia
26th Georgia
31st Georgia
38th Georgia
60th Georgia
61st Georgia

TRIMBLE'S BRIGADE
Brig. Gen. Isaac R. Trimble (w)
Capt. William F. Brown
15th Alabama
12th Georgia
21st Georgia
21st North Carolina
1st North Carolina Battalion

EARLY'S BRIGADE
Brig. Gen. Jubal A. Early
13th Virginia
25th Virginia
31st Virginia
44th Virginia
49th Virginia
52d Virginia
58th Virginia

HAYS'S BRIGADE
Col. Henry Forno (w)

Col. Henry B. Strong
5th Louisiana
6th Louisiana
7th Louisiana
8th Louisiana
14th Louisiana

DIVISION ARTILLERY
Balthis's Staunton (Virginia) Battery
Brown's Chesapeake (Maryland) Battery
D'Aquin's Louisiana Guard Battery
Dement's (Maryland) Battery
Johnson's Virginia Battery
Latimer's Courtney (Virginia) Battery

CAVALRY
Maj. Gen. J. E. B. Stuart

ROBERTSON'S BRIGADE
Brig. Gen. Beverly H. Robertson
2d Virginia Cavalry
6th Virginia Cavalry
7th Virginia Cavalry
12th Virginia Cavalry
17th Virginia Cavalry Battalion

LEE'S BRIGADE
Brig. Gen. Fitzhugh Lee
1st Virginia Cavalry
3d Virginia Cavalry
4th Virginia Cavalry
5th Virginia Cavalry
9th Virginia Cavalry

ARTILLERY
Pelham's (Virginia) Battery

k—killed
w—wounded
mw—mortally wounded

[*OR*, vol. 12, pt. 2, 546–761; *B&L*, vol. 2, pp. 499–500; Hennessy, *Second Manassas Battlefield Map Study*, 464–72.]

NOTES

Introduction

1. Mark Boatner III, *The Civil War Dictionary* (New York: David McKay, 1959), 394–97, 752–57; Timothy B. Smith, *Shiloh: Conquer or Perish* (Lawrence: University Press of Kansas, 2014), 401–2.
2. Jerry Korn, ed. *War on the Mississippi: Grant's Vicksburg Campaign* (Alexandria, VA: Time-Life Books, 1985), 20; Virgil Carrington Jones, *The Civil War at Sea*, vol. 2, *The River War: March 1862–July 1863* (New York: Holt, Rinehart, Winston, 1961; repr., Wilmington, NC: Broadfoot, 1990), 2–58, 2–176.
3. Mark Boatner, *Civil War Dictionary*, 591–92, 627–28.
4. U.S. War Department, *The War of Rebellion: A Compilation of the Official Records of the Union and Confederate Armies* (Washington, DC, 1880–1901), ser. 1, vol. 9:506–12, 530–35, 540–45, 551. (Hereafter cited as *OR*, followed by appropriate volume, part, and page numbers. All citations are from series 1 unless otherwise noted.)
5. *OR*, vol. 4:566; *OR* vol. 9:351–53, 354–58, 362–63, 365–66.
6. Stephen W. Sears, *To the Gates of Richmond: The Peninsula Campaign* (New York: Ticknor & Fields, 1992), 6, 106; Nevins, *War for the Union*, vol. 2, *War Becomes Revolution*, 2–118, 2–131; *OR*, vol. 11, pt. 1:8–50.
7. *OR*, vol. 16, pt. 1:1088–94; *OR*, vol. 20, pt. 1:184–85, 188–00, 663–72.
8. *OR*, vol. 11, pt. 3:405, 408–9, 419–20, 568; *OR*, vol. 11, pt. 1:934.

9. *OR,* vol. 11, pt. 2:490–91, 493, 496–97; William F. Fox, *Regimental Losses in the American Civil War, 1861–1865,* (Albany, 1889).
10. Jeffry D. Wert, *A Glorious Army: Robert E. Lee's Triumph, 1862–1863* (New York: Simon & Schuster, 2011), 65–66, 71–72.
11. *OR,* vol. 12, pt. 2:729; Joseph T. Glatthaar, *General Lee's Army: From Victory to Collapse* (New York: Free Press, 2008), 146, 157.

Chapter 1

1. Thomas E. Griess, ed. *The American Civil War,* The West Point Military History Series (Wayne, NJ: Avery, 1987), 50.
2. Griess, *American Civil War,* 50; Nevins, *War for the Union,* vol. 2, *War Becomes Revolution,* 58–59; Clifford Dowdey, *The Seven Days: The Emergence of Robert E. Lee* (New York: Little, Brown, 1964; repr., Wilmington, NC: Broadfoot, 1988), 70–71. Lenoir Chambers, *Stonewall Jackson* (New York: William Morrow, 1959; repr., Wilmington, NC: Broadfoot, 1988), 1:471–72, 554; Matthew F. Steele, *American Campaigns* (Washington, DC: Byron S. Adams, 1909), 1:220.
3. Griess, *American Civil War,* 50.
4. "Edwin M. Stanton," http://www.ohiohistorycentral.org/w/Edwin_M._Stanton. Accessed March 17, 2017.
5. Matt Spruill III and Matt Spruill IV, *Summer Lightning: A Guide to the Second Battle of Manassas* (Knoxville: University of Tennessee Press, 2013), 2.
6. Ezra J. Warner, *Generals in Blue: Lives of the Union Commanders* (Baton Rouge: Louisiana State University Press, 1964), 18, 299, 448. After Second Manassas all three were reassigned. Siegel went to the Department of West Virginia, where he was again defeated in 1864 at the Battle of New Market. Bank went to the Department of West Mississippi, where he, too, continued to be defeated, most notably in the Red River Campaign. McDowell was transferred to the Department of the Pacific, about as far away from the fighting as possible.
7. Warner, *Generals in Blue,* 376; John J. Hennessy, *Return to Bull Run: The Campaign and Battle of Second Manassas* (New York: Simon & Schuster, 1993), 4–5; *OR* vol. 12, pt. 3:435.
8. Warner, *Generals in Blue,* 376; John J. Hennessy, *Return to Bull Run,* 4–5; *OR* vol. 12, pt. 3:435.
9. *OR* vol. 12, pt. 3:435; Peter Cozzens, *General John Pope: A Life for the Nation* (Urbana: University of Illinois Press, 2000), 75–76.

10. Warner, *Generals in Blue*, 291.
11. Sears, *To the Gates of Richmond*, 12–14; James M. McPherson, *Battle Cry of Freedom: The Civil War Era* (New York: Oxford University Press, 1988), 423.
12. Matt Spruill III and Matt Spruill IV, *Echoes of Thunder: A Guide to the Seven Days Battles* (Knoxville: University of Tennessee Press, 2006), 3–5.
13. Ibid., 19, 273, 277.
14. David Herbert Donald, *Lincoln* (London: Jonathan Cape, 1995), 359–61.
15. Warner, *Generals in Blue*, 195–97; Mark M. Boatner, *The Civil War Dictionary* (New York: David McKay Company, Inc., 1959), 353, 367.
16. Stephen E. Ambrose, *Halleck: Lincoln's Chief of Staff* (Baton Rouge: Louisiana State University Press, 1962), 67; Sears, *To the Gates of Richmond*, 351–52.
17. William C. Davis, *Death in the Trenches: Grant at Petersburg* (Alexandria, VA: Time-Life Books, 1986), 2–3.18.
18. The Army of the Potomac and Army of Virginia had a combined strength of 130,000. George Constable, ed., *Lee Takes Command: From Seven Days to Second Bull Run* (Alexandria: Time-Life Books, 1986), 124.
19. Ambrose, *Halleck*, 66–69.
20. Judkin Browning, *The Seven Days' Battles: The War Begins Anew* (Santa Barbara: Praeger, 2012), 156; *OR*, vol. 11, pt. 1:80–8; Ambrose, *Halleck*, 66–69.
21. A turning movement avoids an enemy's main defensive position by seizing objectives deep in the opponent's rear area. Doing so causes the enemy to move out of his current position or divert major forces against the new threat. The presence of a friendly force in an opponent's rear area turns him out of his position.
22. *OR*, vol. 11, pt. 1:80–81; William F. Miller, comp., "The Grand Campaign: A Journal of Operations on the Peninsula, March 17–August 26, 1862," in *The Peninsula Campaign of 1862: Yorktown to the Seven Days*, ed. William J. Miller (Campbell, CA: Savas-Woodbury, 1993), 1:205.
23. *OR*, vol. 12, pt. 3:435; *OR*, vol. 12, pt. 2:176–78.
24. David G. Martin, *The Second Bull Run Campaign: July–August 1862* (Cambridge, MA: Perseus Books Group, 1997; repr., Cambridge, MA: Da Capo, 2003), 59, 83; *OR*, vol. 12, pt. 2, 324.
25. *OR*, vol. 12, pt. 2:551–52; Constable, *Lee Takes Command*, 124.
26. Ezra J. Warner, Generals in Gray: Lives of the Confederate Commanders (Baton Rouge: Louisiana State University Press, 1959), 180-83.

27. Ibid.
28. *OR*, vol. 12, pt. 2:552.
29. *OR*, vol. 12, pt. 2:552; The Army of the Potomac and Army of Virginia had a combined strength of 130,000. Constable, *Lee Takes Command*, 124.
30. *OR*, vol. 12, pt. 2:552–53.
31. *OR*, vol. 12, pt. 3:942.
32. Warner, *Generals in Gray*, 151–52; Jack D. Welsh, *Medical Histories of Confederate Generals* (Kent, OH: Kent State University Press, 1995), 113.
33. *OR*, vol. 12, pt. 2:554–55, 642–43. Although Longstreet and Jackson commanded what appeared to be corps, the units were not defined as such. The Confederate Congress did not authorize corps organizations until September 18, 1862. Lee formally organized his army into corps on November 6, 1862. Prior to that time the group of divisions commanded by Longstreet and Jackson were designated as Longstreet's Command and Jackson's Command. During the Second Manassas Campaign, with the reorganization of the Army of Northern Virginia, the terminology used was Longstreet's Right Wing and Jackson's Left Wing, sometimes shortened to Longstreet's Wing and Jackson's Wing.
34. *OR*, vol. 12, pt. 2:13–14, 555, 564.
35. Ibid., 642–43.
36. Ibid., 13–14; Spruill and Spruill, *Summer Lightning*, 15.
37. Hennessy, *Return to Bull Run*, 123–26, 134–35.
38. *OR*, vol. 12, pt. 2:644; Joseph W. A. Whitehorne, *The Battle of Second Manassas: Self-Guided Tour* (Washington, DC: Center of Military History), 1989.

Chapter 2

1. *OR*, vol. 12, pt. 2:554–55, 642–43, 644; Whitehorne, *Battle of Second Manassas: Self-Guided Tour*, 23, 25; Spruill and Spruill, *Summer Lightning*, 11–14.
2. *OR*, vol. 12, pt. 2:13–14.
3. Ibid., 359–360; John Hennessy, *Second Manassas Battlefield Map Study* (Lynchburg: H. E. Howard, 1991), 1
4. Warner, *Generals in Blue*, 297–99.
5. Spruill and Spruill, *Summer Lightning*, 300; *OR*, vol. 12, pt. 2:555, 564.

6. *OR*, vol. 12, pt. 2:69; Stephan Z. Starr, *The Union Cavalry in the Civil War* (Baton Rouge: Louisiana State University Press, 1979), 1:302–3; Edward Longacre, *General John Buford: A Military Biography* (Conshohocken, PA: Combined Books, 1995), 99; *OR*, vol. 12, pt. 2:335.
7. *OR*, vol. 12, pt. 3:688; *OR*, vol. 12, pt. 2:35, 38; Hennessy, *Return to Bull Run*, 139.
8. *OR*, vol. 12, pt. 2:36, 335.
9. Ibid., 336.
10. Ibid., 584; Hennessy, *Battlefield Map Study*, 70–71.
11. *OR*, vol. 12, pt. 2:556.
12. Ibid., 642–44.
13. Spruill and Spruill, *Summer Lightning*, 16. *Key terrain* is defined as follows: Any locality, or area, the seizure or retention of which offers a marked advantage to either combatant. [*US Army Field Manual*, 3-21.10, *The Infantry Rifle Company* (Washington: Department of the Army, 2006), chapter 2.]
14. Hennessy, *Second Manassas Battlefield Map Study*, 1; Spruill and Spruill, *Summer Lightning*, 17.
15. Hennessy, *Second Manassas Battlefield Map Study*, 2.
16. *OR*, vol. 12, pt. 2:360, 383–84; Hennessy, *Second Manassas Battlefield Map Study*, 3, 15; Spruill and Spruill, *Summer Lightning*, 17–19.
17. Hennessy, *Second Manassas Battlefield Map Study*, 30.
18. Spruill and Spruill, *Summer Lightning*, 22–40.
19. Hennessy, *Second Manassas Battlefield Map Study*, 41; *OR*, vol. 12, pt. 3:717–18.

Chapter 3

1. Spruill and Spruill, *Summer Lightning*, 44–45.
2. *OR*, vol. 12, pt. 2:564–65, 571; Hennessy, *Second Manassas Battlefield Map Study*, 76, 110–11, 113.
3. *OR*, vol. 12, pt. 2:577; Hennessy, *Return to Bull Run*, 108, 309; Martin, *Second Bull Run Campaign*, 113.
4. Hennessy, *Second Manassas Battlefield Map Study*, 61.
5. *OR* vol. 12, pt. 2:324–25.

6. Hennessy, *Second Manassas Battlefield Map Study*, 70–71; Martin, *Second Bull Run Campaign*, 161.

7. *OR*, vol. 12, pt. 2:412; Hennessy, *Second Manassas Battlefield Map Study*, 19, 50, 73.

8. Hennessy, *Second Manassas Battlefield Map Study*, 20, 74; *OR*, vol. 12, pt. 2:481; Timothy J. Reese, *Sykes' Regular Infantry Division, 1861–1864: A History of Regular United States Infantry Operations in the Civil War's Eastern Theater* (Jefferson, NC: McFarland, 1990), 112.

9. Hennessy, *Second Manassas Battlefield Map Study*, 21, 50, 74.

10. *OR*, vol. 12, pt. 2:266, 279, 393.

11. Ibid., 266, 296.

12. Ibid., 266, 319.

13. Martin, *Second Bull Run Campaign*, 169, 172; Hennessy, *Second Manassas Battlefield Map Study*, 72, 103–4, 109.

14. Spruill and Spruill, *Summer Lightning*, 46, 65; *OR*, vol. 12, pt. 2:16, 324–25.

15. Brig. Gen. Rufus King commanded the First Division, Third Corps (Army of Virginia) during the fighting on August 28 at Groveton. Suffering from the effects of an epileptic seizure, the next morning he relinquished command of the division to Brig. Gen. John P. Hatch. Henceforth the First Division, Third Corps, Army of Virginia will be referred to as Hatch's division.

16. *OR*, vol. 12, pt. 2:40, 42, 76; Peter Cozzens, *General John Pope*, 139.

17. *OR*, vol. 11, pt. 2:96–98; Lawrence A. Kreiser Jr., *Defeating Lee: A History of the Second Corps, Army of the Potomac* (Bloomington: Indiana University Press, 2011), 43. Franklin was promoted to major general on July 4, 1862.

18. Hennessy, *Return to Bull Run*, 233–34; Cozzens, *General John Pope*, 144; Hennessy, *Second Manassas Battlefield Map Study*, 75; Longacre, *General John Buford*, 101; *OR*, vol. 12, pt. 2 (Supplement), 1010–11.

19. The main attack is the attack that the commander has designed to capture the enemy position or key terrain to achieve the overall objective. Usually it has the majority of troops assigned to it and has priority of supporting artillery fire. The reserve is normally placed so as to be able to reinforce the main attack or exploit success.

20. Supporting attacks are designed to assist the main attack by causing the enemy to disperse his forces and fight in several locations. These as-

saults also pin enemy forces in position, cause a premature or incorrect commitment of enemy reserve, and confuse the enemy as to which is the main attack.

21. *OR*, vol. 12, pt. 2:604, 630.
22. Ibid., 736.
23. Ibid., 36, 335; Longacre, *General John Buford*, 99.
24. *OR*, vol. 12, pt. 2:335, 360, 383–84; Hennessy, *Second Manassas Battlefield Map Study*, 3.
25. *OR*, vol. 12, pt. 2:367, 369, 381; Hennessy, *Second Manassas Battlefield Map Study*, 70-71.
26. *OR*, vol. 12, pt. 2:75; *OR*, vol. 12, pt. 3:729; John C. Ropes, *The Army Under Pope* (New York: Charles Scribner's Sons, 1881; repr., Wilmington, NC: Broadfoot, 1989), 86.
27. Cozzens, *General John Pope*, 137–38; Hennessy, *Second Manassas Battlefield Map Study*, 97.
28. *OR*, vol. 12, pt. 2:76.
29. *Ibid.*
30. *OR*, vol. 12, pt. 2:736.
31. Ibid., 565, 579, 598, 625–26; James Longstreet, *From Manassas to Appomattox: Memoirs of the Civil War in America* (Philadelphia, 1896; repr., Secaucus, NJ: Blue & Grey Press, 1984), 180–81; Jeffry D. Wert, *General James Longstreet: The Confederacy's Most Controversial Soldier* (New York: Simon & Schuster, 1993), 169–70.
32. Warner, *Generals in Blue*, 378-80.
33. Ibid.
34. *OR*, vol. 12, pt. 2:338, 565.
35. Rickett's division had marched from Bristoe Station to Manassas Junction, and it was ordered to join McDowell and Hatch just a few miles northwest on the road to Gainesville.
36. John Hennessy, Second Battle of Manassas, Troop Movement Maps 1–16 (Eastern National Park and Monument Association, 1985), Maps 4, 5, 6, and 7. Hereafter cited as Hennessy, Map(s) with map number(s).
37. *OR*, vol. 12, pt. 2:338, 367; Spruill and Spruill, *Summer Lightning*, 127.
38. Hennessy Map 5.
39. Hennessy Maps 4, 5, 6, 7.

Chapter 4

1. Hennessy, *Second Manassas Battlefield Map Study*, 248, 253.
2. Spruill and Spruill, *Summer Lightning*, 140–41; *OR*, vol. 12, pt. 1:652; William T. Poague, *Gunner With Stonewall: Reminiscences of William Thomas Pogue . . .* (written in 1903; Jackson, TN: McCowat-Mercer Press, 1957; repr., Wilmington, NC: Broadfoot, 1987), 37–38.
3. Hennessy, Maps 8 and 9; *OR*, vol. 12, pt. 2:325.
4. *OR*, vol. 12, pt. 2:267–68, 341, 412–13, 416; Hennessy, *Second Manassas Battlefield Map Study*, 245–46; Hennessy, Maps 9 and 10.
5. *OR* vol. 12, pt. 2:76.
6. Hennessy, *Second Manassas Battlefield Map Study*, 286–90, 294–97; *OR* vol. 12, pt. 2:472, 473–74, 482, 577–78, 666–67, 668–69.
7. Rufus R. Dawes, *Service with The Sixth Wisconsin Volunteers* (Marietta, 1890; repr., Dayton: Press of Morningside Bookshop, 1996), 71; *OR*, vol. 12, pt. 2:488; Hennessy, *Second Manassas Battlefield Map Study*, 291, 299.
8. Spruill and Spruill *Summer Lightning*, 185; Hennessy, Map 11.
9. *OR*, vol. 12, pt. 2:286, 394.
10. Longstreet, *From Manassas to Appomattox*, 188; Wert, *General James Longstreet*, 177.
11. Data from the US Naval Observatory's Astronomical Applications Department reports that sunset was at 6:43 p.m. It was dark at 7:11 p.m.
12. *OR*, vol. 12, pt. 2:394; Hennessy, *Second Manassas Battlefield Map Study*, 236, 268–69.
13. *OR*, vol. 12, pt. 2:286; Hennessy, *Second Manassas Battlefield Map Study*, 263. Wiedrich's two 12-pound howitzers had been previously detached and were elsewhere on the battlefield.
14. *OR*, vol. 12, pt. 2:321, 503; Hennessy, Map 10.
15. Spruill and Spruill *Summer Lightning*, 140; Donald B. Sanger and Thomas Robson Hay, *James Longstreet: Soldier, Politician, Officeholder, and Writer* (Baton Rouge: Louisiana State University Press, 1952; repr., Gloucester, MA: Peter Smith, 1968), 88.
16. *OR*, vol. 12, pt. 2:504, 565; William Garrett Piston, *Lee's Tarnished Lieutenant: James Longstreet and His Place in Southern History* (Athens: University of Georgia Press, 1987), 24; Alfred Davenport, *Camp and Field Life of the Fifth New York Volunteer Infantry* (New York, 1879), 273–86.

17. *OR*, vol. 12, pt. 2:256; *OR*, vol. 51, pt. 1:130–31; US Department of the Interior, Manassas National Battlefield Park, "Union Artillery at Second Manassas."
18. Spruill and Spruill, *Summer Lightning*, 186–87; Scott C. Patchan, *Second Manassas: Longstreet's Attack and the Struggle for Chinn Ridge* (Washington, DC: Potomac Books, 2011), 42–43.
19. Warner, *Generals in Blue*, 304–5; Jack D. Welsh, *Medical Histories of Union Generals*, 217.
20. *OR*, vol. 12, pt. 2:626; Spruill and Spruill, *Summer Lightning*, 194–95; Patchan, *Second Manassas*, 17–18.
21. *OR*, vol. 12, pt. 2:286–87; Spruill and Spruill, *Summer Lightning*, 195–96, 201–2, 212.
22. John Gibbon, *Personal Recollections of the Civil War* (New York: G. P. Putnam's Sons, 1928; repr., Dayton: Press of Morningside Bookshop, 1988), 69; The reinforcing column coming from Richmond consisted of Maj. Gen. Daniel H. Hill's, Maj. Gen. LaFayette McLaws's, and Brig. Gen. John G. Walker's infantry divisions, Brig. Gen. William N. Pendleton's four-battalion Artillery Reserve, and Brig. Gen. Wade Hampton's cavalry brigade. Depending upon the source, between 23,900 and 25,415 troops were marching to join Lee. Joseph L. Harsh, *Taken at the Flood: Robert E. Lee and Confederate Strategy in the Maryland Campaign of 1862* (Kent, OH: Kent State University Press, 1999), 34–37, 39; John Owen Allen, "The Strengths of the Union and Confederate Forces at Second Manassas" (master's thesis, George Mason University, 1993), 186–209.
23. *OR*, vol. 12, pt. 2:323, 483; Patchan, *Second Manassas*, 106.
24. Douglas Southall Freeman, ed., *Lee's Dispatches: Unpublished Letters of General Robert E. Lee, C.S.A., to Jefferson Davis and the War Department of the Confederate States of America 1862–65* (New York: G. P. Putnam's Sons, 1957; repr. with additional dispatches and foreword by Grady McWhiney, Baton Rouge: Louisiana State University Press, 1994), 59–60.

Chapter 5

1. *OR*, vol. 12, pt. 2:43; Vincent J. Esposito, ed., Map 64, in *The West Point Atlas of American Wars, vol. 1, 1689–1900* (New York: Praeger, 1959; rev. ed., New York: Henry Holt, 1995).

2. Harsh, *Taken at the Flood*, 34–37, 39; Allen, "Strengths of the Union and Confederate Forces at Second Manassas, 186–209.
3. *OR*, vol. 12, pt. 2:557–58.
4. Ibid., 558; George B. Davis, Leslie J. Perry, Joseph W. Kirkley, and Calvin D. Cowles, Maps 111-1, 117, in *Atlas to Accompany the Official Records of the Union and Confederate Armies* (Washington, DC, 1891–95; repr., New York: Fairfax, 1983).
5. *OR*, vol. 12, pt. 2:647. George F. R. Henderson, *Stonewall Jackson and the American Civil War* (New York: Longmans, Green, 1900; modern abridgment with an introduction by E. B. Long, Gloucester, MA: Peter Smith, 1968), 399–401; Chambers, *Stonewall Jackson*, 2:173–74.
6. *OR*, vol. 11, pt. 3:569; Brian K. Burton, *Extraordinary Circumstances: The Seven Days Battles* (Bloomington: Indiana University Press, 2001), 397–98; *OR*, vol. 12, pt. 2:176–78, 511–52.
7. *OR*, vol. 12, pt. 2:552, 554–55, 558; Spruill and Spruill, *Summer Lightning*, 8–11.
8. D. Scott Hartwig, *To Antietam Creek: The Maryland Campaign of September 1862* (Baltimore: Johns Hopkins University Press, 2012), 49–50; Harsh, *Taken at the Flood*, 22; Robert E. Lee, "Letter to William M. McDonald," *Southern Historical Society Papers*, 7 (1879). A six-mule or six-horse supply wagon could carry about 2,500 pounds of ammunition, rations, or other supplies. Its sustained rate of travel varied between 2½ and 4 miles per hour. Under ideal conditions a team and wagon could carry supplies from the Rappahannock River to the army in one day—12 hours of travel. Another day would be required to return. Not counting the time to unload the wagons and then reload them upon completing the return trip, it would take 2 days under ideal conditions to bring supplies and return for more. A more realistic round-trip time would be 3 to 4 days. Logistical planning in the Civil War held that 25 wagons could support every 1,000 troops. Lee's strength after Second Manassas was approximately 50,000—other estimates are lower and higher. For 50,000 troops Lee would need 1,250 wagons and from 5,000 to 7,500 horses or mules, which he apparently did not have.
9. Hartwig, *To Antietam Creek*, 51.

Appendix I

1. *OR*, vol. 12, pt. 2:644–45.

2. The restored house on the Brawner farm is a postwar structure that sits on the approximate site of the wartime home. The existing house neither resembles the original house nor sits on the original foundation. The Brawner family never lived in the present-day house.
3. *OR*, vol. 12. pt. 2:644–45.
4. Ibid., 377–78.
5. Ibid., 382.
6. Ibid., 369.
7. Ibid., 372–73.
8. Ibid., 378.
9. Ibid., 311–12.
10. Ibid., 685–86.
11. Ibid., 692–93.
12. Ibid., 686.
13. Ibid., 310.
14. Ibid., 693.
15. Ibid., 310.
16. Joseph Gould, *The Story of the Forty-Eighth*, (Philadelphia: Alfred M. Slocum, 1908), 66–67.
17. Quick Time was a 28-inch step done at the rate of 110 steps per minute. Double-Quick Time was a 33-inch step done at 165 steps per minute and was only done for a brief period of time. (Silas Casey, *Infantry Tactics for the Instruction, Exercise, and Maneuvers of the Soldier, A Company, Line of Skirmishers, Battalion, Brigade, or Corps D'Armee.* School of the Soldier, vol. 1. [New York: 1862. Reprint, Dayton: Press of Morningside Bookshop, 32.]
18. *OR*, vol. 12, pt. 2:471–72.
19. Ibid., 473–74.
20. George C. Hopper, "The Battle of Groveton," in *Military Order of the Loyal Legion of the United States, Michigan* (Detroit: 1893; repr., Wilmington, NC: Broadfoot, 1993), 448–50.
21. *OR* vol. 12, pt. 2:668–69.
22. Ibid., 577–78.
23. Ibid., 395.
24. Wiedrich's two 12-pouund howitzers had been previously detached and were elsewhere on the battlefield.

25. *OR*, vol. 12, pt. 2:286.

26. Ibid., 286-87.

27. Ibid., 626.

28. The Fifth Maine Battery had five guns at Second Manassas. A sixth gun was disabled along the Rappahannock River on August 23.

29. Letter of Zealous B. Tower, dated Nashville, Tenn. June 6, 1865. In archives of Manassas National Battlefield Park, Manassas, VA.

30. *OR*, vol. 12, pt. 2:626.

31. Ibid., 307–8.

32. These brigades were: Benning's, Drayton's and G. T. Anderson's from Jones's Division; Armistead's, Mahone's, and Wright's from R. H. Anderson's Division; Wilcox's, Pryor's, and Featherston's from Wilcox's Division.

33. *OR*, vol. 12, pt. 2:43. The Sixth Corps, Army of the Potomac arrived Centreville at 6:00 p.m.

34. Ibid., 269–70.

35. Ibid., 383–84. Ricketts's route was from Buckland to Gainesville, then to Haymarket, and finally to a position west of Haymarket.

36. Ibid., 594.

37. Ibid., 383–84.

38. Ibid., 594.

39. Ibid., 591.

40. In several accounts historians have misidentified this regiment as the Eighty-fourth New York. The Eighty-fourth New York was part of Hatch's First Brigade of King's First Division of the Third Corps. At the time of the fight for Thoroughfare Gap, it was located in the vicinity of Groveton and the Brawner farm.

41. *OR*, vol. 12, pt. 2:557–58.

42. Warner, *Generals in Blue*, 259, 476.

43. *OR*, vol. 12, pt. 2:45.

44. Ibid., 647.

45. Ibid., 647.

46. Ibid., 558.

BIBLIOGRAPHY

Allen, John Owen. "The Strengths of the Union and Confederate Forces at Second Manassas." master's thesis, George Mason University, 1993.

Ambrose, Stephen E. *Halleck: Lincoln's Chief of Staff.* Baton Rouge: Louisiana State University Press, 1962.

Astronomical Applications Department of the US Naval Observatory website. Last modified December 19, 2011. http://aa.usno.navy.mil/index.php.

Boatner, Mark M., III. *The Civil War Dictionary.* New York: David McKay, 1959.

Browning, Judkin. *The Seven Days' Battles: The War Begins Anew.* Santa Barbara: Praeger, 2012.

Burton, Brian K. *Extraordinary Circumstances: The Seven Days Battles.* Bloomington: Indiana University Press, 2001.

Casey, Silas. *Infantry Tactics for the Instruction, Exercise, and Maneuvers of the Soldier, A Company, Line of Skirmishers, Battalion, Brigade, or Corps D'Armee.* School of the Soldier, vol. 1. 1862. Reprint, Dayton: Press of Morningside Bookshop.

Chambers, Lenoir. *Stonewall Jackson.* 2 vols. New York: William Morrow, 1959. Reprint, Wilmington, NC: Broadfoot, 1988.

Constable, George, ed. *Lee Takes Command: From Seven Days to Second Bull Run.* Alexandria, VA: Time-Life Books, 1986.

Cozzens, Peter. *General John Pope: A Life for the Nation*. Urbana: University of Illinois Press, 2000.

Davenport, Alfred. *Camp and Field Life of the Fifth New York Volunteer Infantry*. New York, 1879.

Davis, George B., Leslie J. Perry, Joseph W. Kirkley, and Calvin D. Cowles. *Atlas to Accompany the Official Records of the Union and Confederate Armies*. Washington, DC, 1891–95. Reprint, New York: Fairfax, 1983.

Davis, William C. *Death in the Trenches: Grant at Petersburg*. Alexandria, VA: Time-Life Books, 1986.

Dawes, Rufus R. *Service with The Sixth Wisconsin Volunteers*. Marietta, 1890. Reprint, Dayton: Press of Morningside Bookshop, 1996.

Donald, David Herbert. *Lincoln*. London: Jonathan Cape, 1995.

Dowdey, Clifford. *The Seven Days: The Emergence of Robert E. Lee*. New York: Little, Brown, 1964. Reprint, Wilmington, NC: Broadfoot, 1988.

Esposito, Vincent J., ed. *1689–1900*. Vol. 1 of *The West Point Atlas of American Wars*. New York: Praeger, 1959. rev. ed. New York: Henry Holt, 1995.

Fox, William F. *Regimental Losses in the American Civil War, 1861–1865*. Albany, 1889.

Freeman, Douglas Southall, ed. *Lee's Dispatches: Unpublished Letters of General Robert E. Lee, C.S.A., to Jefferson Davis and the War Department of the Confederate States of America 1862–65*. New York: G. P. Putnam's Sons, 1957. Reprinted with additional dispatches and foreword by Grady McWhiney. Baton Rouge: Louisiana State University Press, 1994.

Gibbon, John. *Personal Recollections of the Civil War*. New York: G. P. Putnam's Sons, 1928. Reprint, Dayton: Press of Morningside Bookshop, 1988.

Glatthaar, Joseph T. *General Lee's Army: From Victory to Collapse*. New York: Free Press, 2008.

Gould, Joseph. *The Story of the Forty-Eighth*. Philadelphia: Alfred M. Slocum, 1908.

Griess, Thomas E., ed. *The American Civil War. The West Point Military History Series*. Wayne, NJ: Avery, 1987.

Harsh, Joseph L. *Sounding the Shallows: A Confederate Companion for the Maryland Campaign of 1862*. Kent, OH: Kent State University Press, 2000.

———. *Taken at the Flood: Robert E. Lee and Confederate Strategy in the Maryland Campaign of 1862*. Kent, OH: Kent State University Press, 1999.

Hartwig, D. Scott. *To Antietam Creek: The Maryland Campaign of September 1862.* Baltimore: Johns Hopkins University Press, 2012.

Henderson, George F. R. *Stonewall Jackson and the American Civil War.* 2 vols. New York: Longmans, Green, 1900. Modern abridgment with an introduction by E. B. Long. Gloucester, MA: Peter Smith, 1968.

Hennessy, John J. *Return to Bull Run: The Campaign and Battle of Second Manassas.* New York: Simon & Schuster, 1993.

———. Second Battle of Manassas, *Troop Movement Maps 1–16.* Eastern National Park and Monument Association, 1985.

———. *Second Manassas Battlefield Map Study.* Lynchburg: H. E. Howard, 1991.

Hopper, George C. "The Battle of Groveton, "in *Military Order of the Loyal Legion of the United States, Michigan.* Detroit, 1893. Reprint, Wilmington, NC: Broadfoot, 1993.

Johnson, Robert U., and Clarence C. Buel, eds. *Battles and Leaders of the Civil War: Being for the Most Part Contributions by Union and Confederate Officers. Vol. 2.* New York, 1884–89. Reprint, Secaucus, NJ: Castle Books, 1982.

Jones, Virgil Carrington. *The River War: March 1862–July 1863.* Vol. 2 of *The Civil War at Sea.* New York: Holt, Rinehart, Winston, 1961. Reprint, Wilmington, NC: Broadfoot, 1990.

Korn, Jerry, ed. *War on the Mississippi: Grant's Vicksburg Campaign.* Alexandria, VA: Time-Life Books, 1985.

Kreiser, Lawrence A., Jr. *Defeating Lee: A History of the Second Corps, Army of the Potomac.* Bloomington: Indiana University Press, 2011.

Lee, Robert E. "Letter to William M. McDonald." *Southern Historical Society Papers* 7 (1879): 445–56.

Longacre, Edward. *General John Buford: A Military Biography.* Conshohocken, PA: Combined Books, 1995.

Longstreet, James. *From Manassas to Appomattox: Memoirs of the Civil War in America.* Philadelphia, 1896. Reprint, Secaucus, NJ: Blue & Grey Press, 1984.

Martin, David G. *The Second Bull Run Campaign: July–August 1862.* New York: Perseus Books Group, 1997. Reprint, Cambridge, MA: Da Capo, 2003.

McPherson, James M. *Battle Cry of Freedom: The Civil War Era.* New York: Oxford University Press, 1988.

Miller, William F., comp. "The Grand Campaign: A Journal of Operations on the Peninsula, March 17–August 26, 1862." In *The Peninsula Campaign of 1862: Yorktown to the Seven Days*, edited by William J. Miller. 3 vols. Campbell, CA: Savas Woodbury, 1993.

Nevins, Allen. *The War for the Union*. 5 vols. New York: Charles Scribner's Sons, 1960.

Patchan, Scott C. *Second Manassas: Longstreet's Attack and the Struggle for Chinn Ridge*. Washington, DC: Potomac Books, 2011.

Piston, William Garrett. *Lee's Tarnished Lieutenant: James Longstreet and His Place in Southern History*. Athens: University of Georgia Press, 1987.

Poague, William T. *Gunner With Stonewall: Reminiscences of William Thomas Pogue. . . . Written in 1903*. Jackson, TN: McCowat-Mercer Press, 1957. Reprint, Wilmington, NC: Broadfoot, 1987.

Reese, Timothy J. *Sykes' Regular Infantry Division, 1861–1864: A History of Regular United States Infantry Operations in the Civil War's Eastern Theater*. Jefferson, NC: McFarland, 1990.

Ropes, John C. *The Army Under Pope*. New York: Charles Scribner's Sons, 1881. Reprinted with an introduction by William Alan Blair, Wilmington, NC: Broadfoot, 1989.

Sanger, Donald B., and Thomas Robson Hay. *James Longstreet: Soldier, Politician, Officeholder, and Writer*. Baton Rouge: Louisiana State University Press, 1952. Reprint, Gloucester, MA: Peter Smith, 1968.

Sears, Stephen W. *To the Gates of Richmond: The Peninsula Campaign*. New York: Ticknor & Fields, 1992.

Smith, Timothy B. *Shiloh: Conquer or Perish*. Lawrence: University Press of Kansas, 2014.

Spruill, Matt, III, and Matt Spruill IV. *Summer Lightning: A Guide to the Second Battle of Manassas*. Knoxville: University of Tennessee Press, 2013.

———. *Echoes of Thunder: A Guide to the Seven Days Battles*. Knoxville: University of Tennessee Press, 2006.

Stanton, https://en.wikipedia.org/wiki/Edwin_Stanton.

Starr, Stephen Z. *The Union Cavalry in the Civil War*. 3 vols. Baton Rouge: Louisiana State University Press, 1979–85.

Steele, Matthew F. *American Campaigns*. 2 vols. Washington, DC: Byron S. Adams, 1909.

US Army Field Manual, 3–21.10, *The Infantry Rifle Company*. Washington: Department of the Army, 2006.

US Department of the Interior. Manassas National Battlefield Park, "Union Artillery at Second Manassas."

US War Department. *The War of the Rebellion: A Compilation of the Official Records of the Union and Confederate Armies*. 128 vols. Washington, DC, 1880–1901.

Warner, Ezra J. *Generals in Blue: Lives of the Union Commanders*. Baton Rouge: Louisiana State University Press, 1964.

———. *Generals in Gray: Lives of the Confederate Commanders*. Baton Rouge: Louisiana State University Press, 1959.

Welsh, Jack D. *Medical Histories of Confederate Generals*. Kent, OH: Kent State University Press, 1995.

———. *Medical Histories of Union Generals*. Kent, OH: Kent State University Press, 1996.

Wert, Jeffry D. *A Glorious Army: Robert E. Lee's Triumph, 1862–1863*. New York: Simon & Schuster, 2011.

———. *General James Longstreet: The Confederacy's Most Controversial Soldier*. New York: Simon & Schuster, 1993.

Whitehorne, Joseph W. A. *The Battle of Second Manassas: Self-Guided Tour*. Washington, DC: Center of Military History, United States Army, 1990.

INDEX

Abbreviations:
ANV–Army of Northern Virginia
AP–Army of the Potomac
Arty–Artillery
AV–Army of Virginia
Bn–Battalion
Bde–Brigade
Btry–Battery
Cav–Cavalry
Cmdr–Commander
Div–Division
PA–Provisional Army

Alcott, Russell H., Capt., USA (1st MI, AP), 164, 165
Aldie, VA, 28, 38, 39, 121
Alexandria, VA, 27
Allen, Thomas S., Maj., USA (2nd WI, AV), 133
Amisville, VA, 31
Anderson, George T., Col., CSA (Bde Cmdr, ANV): at Thoroughfare Gap, 195, 201; attacks Henry Hill, 188; brigade of, 184; reports of, 197, 198–99
Anderson, Richard H., Maj. Gen., CSA (Div Cmdr, ANV): attacks Henry Hill, 188; division of, xvi, 46, 71, 72, 151–52; division's position, 152
Antietam, Battle of, s113
Archer, James J., Brig. Gen., CSA (Bde Cmdr, ANV): brigade of, 138; brigade position, 138
Arlington National Cemetery, 204
Armistead, Lewis A., Brig. Gen., CSA (Bde Cmdr, ANV): attacks Henry Hill, 188; brigade of xvi
Armstrong, James, Lieut., CSA (1st SC-PA, ANV), 142
Army of Kentucky (CSA), 2
Army of Northern Virginia (CSA), 3, 7, 10, 26, 40, 94, 107; created, 10; moves to Gordonsville, 19; positions of, 71–72, 122, 152; supply routes, 16
Army of Northern Virginia, artillery battalions and batteries
—Louisiana: Richardson's 2nd Company, 177, 183; Washington Artillery Battalion, 46, 66
—Virginia: Carpenter's Virginia, 124; Crenshaw's Virginia, 147; Eubank's Virginia, 167; Garber's Staunton, 122; Jordan's Bedford,

Army of Northern Virginia, artillery battalions and batteries (*cont.*) 167; Parker's Virginia, 167; Pelham's Virginia, 127; Poague's Rockbridge, 124; S. D. Lee's Battalion, 46, 71, 72, 77, 124, 152; Taylor's Virginia, 167
—South Carolina: Rhett's South Carolina, 167

Army of Northern Virginia, infantry regiments and battalions
—Alabama: 15th, 148, 158, 165
—Georgia: 1st (**Regulars**), 199; 2nd, 200; 9th, 195, 196, 197, 198; 12th, 148; 18th, 171; 20th, 184, 200; 21st, 148
—Louisiana: 1st 165; 15th, 165
—North Carolina: 1st **Battalion,** 148; 21st, 148
—South Carolina: 1st, 139, 142; 1st **Rifles,** 142, 143, 144, 145; 12th, 142, 143, 144, 145; 13th 141, 142, 143; 17th, 172, 175; 18th, 172, 175; 23rd, 172; Hampton Legion, 172; Holcombe Legion, 172
—Texas: 5th, 171, 172, 175
—Virginia: 1st, 181; 24th, 181

Army of the Mississippi (CSA), 2
Army of the Ohio (USA), 1
Army of the Potomac (USA), 2, 4, 7, 14, 15, 16, 94, 99, 107, 113; evacuates the Peninsula, 18, 117; moving to join Army of Virginia, 21, 22, 27, 40, 153

Army of the Potomac, corps
—Second (Sumner), 50, 51, 68, 72, 94–95
—Third (Heintzelman), 39, 41, 48, 55, 60, 66, 137, 153, 169
—Fifth (Porter), 41, 48, 57, 58, 63, 64, 66, 69, 72, 73, 77, 137, 152, 153, 192
—Sixth (Franklin), 26, 50, 51, 68, 72, 75, 94, 95
—Ninth (Reno), 46, 49, 55, 60, 101, 137

Army of the Potomac, artillery batteries
—Massachusetts: 3rd, 192
—U.S: K/1st, 188; D/5th, 192

Army of the Potomac, infantry Regiments
—Maine: 2nd, 157
—Maryland: 2nd, 148, 149, 150
—Massachusetts: 18th, 157, 160, 162, 200
—Michigan: 1st, 157, 161, 163; 16th, 157
—New Hampshire: 6th, 148, 149, 150
—New York: 12th, 157, 161; 13th, 157, 161, 164, 192; 17th, 157, 161; 25th, 156; 44th, 157, 161
—Pennsylvania: 63rd, 192; 83rd, 157
—U.S: 1st **Sharpshooters,** 156

Army of the Tennessee (USA), 1
Army of Virginia (USA), 3, 4, 7, 21, 23, 94; assigned missions, 13; created, 12, 19; organization, 11; Pope repositions, 32; positions, 72–73, 135–37, 152; withdraws to the Rappahannock River, 20

Army of Virginia, corps
—First (Sigel), 32, 35, 39, 46–47, 48, 50, 51, 55, 58, 59, 60, 72, 113
—Second (Banks), 10, 19, 47, 72, 75, 95, 113, 189, 195
—Third (McDowell), 31, 40, 47–48, 57, 58, 63, 64, 68, 69, 72, 113, 137, 192

Army of Virginia, artillery batteries
—Maine: 2nd, 188; 5th, 178, 181, 183
—New York: I/1st, 83, 170, 171, 175; L/1st, 122
—Ohio: I/1st, 191
—Pennsylvania: F/1st, 197; G/1st, 84, 169; C/PA, 197
—Rhode Island: D/1st, 188
—U.S: B/4th, 123, 128, 132; C/5th, 188

Army of Virginia, cavalry regiments
—New Jersey: 1st, 195, 196

Army of Virginia, infantry regiments
—Indiana: 19th, 124, 125, 127, 128, 134
—Massachusetts: 12th, 181, 198; 13th 198, 200
—New York: 22nd, 157; 24th, 157, 161; 29th, 183; 30th, 157; 41st, 161, 183; 54th, 138; 58th, 138; 68th, 183; 76th, 128, 130, 131, 132; 83rd, 188,

198, 201; 84th (14th NYSM), 157, 201; 94th, 181; 95th 132
—Ohio: 25th, 83, 171, 174, 175, 177; 55th, 83, 171, 172, 175, 177; 61st, 147; 73rd, 83, 171, 172, 174; 75th, 83, 85, 171, 172, 175, 177
—Pennsylvania: 11th, 198, 200, 201; 13th Reserves, 191; 48th, 148, 149, 150; 56th, 128, 130, 131, 132; 73rd 183, 184; 74th, 144, 145, 147; 75th, 138, 88th, 181
—U.S: 2nd Sharpshooters, 156
—West Virginia: 8th, 144
—Wisconsin: 2nd, 124, 125, 127, 133; 6th, 127, 128, 132, 133; 7th, 124, 125, 127, 128, 133, 134
Arnold, Henry C., Lieut., USA (1st MI, AP), 164

Bald Hill, 170
Baltimore, MD, 104
Banks, Nathaniel P., Maj. Gen., USA (Corps Cmdr, ANV), 8; appointed to corps command, 10; corps of, 19; corps' positions, 47, 72, 75, 95
Bardstown, KY, 2
Barnes, Dixon, Col., CSA (12th SC, ANV), 142, 143; regiment of, 142, 143, 144, 145
Baylor, William S. H., Col., CSA (Bde Cmdr, ANV), 156; brigade of, 125, 128, 156, 165
Beaver Dam Creek (Mechanicsville), Battle of, 14
Beck, Benjamin, Col., CSA (9th GA, ANV), 195, 197, 198; regiment at Thoroughfare Gap, 195, 198
Benning, Henry L., Col., CSA (Bde Cmdr, ANV): at Thoroughfare Gap, 196; attacks Chinn Ridge, 89, 184; attacks Henry Hill, 90, 188; brigade of, 89
Berdan, Hiram, Col., USA (1st U.S. Sharpshooters, AP), 159
Beverly Mill Drive, 202
Bill, George, Maj., USA (7th WI, AV), wounded, 133

Biscuit Mountain. *See* Pond Mountain
Blackburn's Ford, 29
Blessing, Franz, Maj., USA (74th PA, AV), 145, 147; regiment of, 144, 145, 147; report of, 144–45, 147
Blue Ridge Mountains, 105
Bragg, Braxton, Gen., CSA (Army Cmdr), invades Kentucky, 2–3
Bragg, Edward S., Lieut., Col., USA (6th WI): regiment of, 127, 128, 132; report of, 128–29
Branch, Lawrence O'B., Brig. Gen., CSA (Bde Cmdr, ANV): brigade of, 138, 147; brigade's position, 138
Brawner Farm, 121, 152
Bristoe Station, 4, 48, 58, 95; Jackson captures, 24, 25, 32, 119
Broad Run, 195
Brockenbrough, John M., Col. CSA (40th VA and Bde Cmdr, ANV), 206
Brown, W. F., Capt., CSA (Bde Cmdr, ANV), 148; brigade of, 165
Buchanan, Robert C., Lieut. Col., USA (Bde Cmdr, AP), brigade on Henry Hill, 188
Buck Hill, 118, 134; as a defensive position, 50, 135, 187; importance of, 118
Buckland, VA, 40, 58
Buell, Don Carlos, Maj. Gen., USA (Army Cmdr), 1
Buford, John, Brig. Gen., USA (Cav Bde Cmdr, AV), 33; performs reconnaissance, 33, 52; reports Longstreet's movements, 52, 58, 73
Bull Run, 29, 32, 38, 39, 62, 81, 96, 100, 202, 203; potential defensive positions along, 75, 95
Bull Run Mountains, 27, 28, 105, 121
Burnside, Ambrose E., Brig. Gen., USA (Expedition Cmdr), 2
Bust Head Road (#628), 194
Butterfield, Daniel, Brig. Gen., USA (Bde and Div Cmdr, AP), 77, 154, 160; division's position, 155; ordered to attack, 77

Cairo, IL, 1
Campbell, Joseph B., USA (Btry B, 4th US Arty. AV), 125; battery of, 123, 128, 132
Carpenter, Joseph, Capt., CSA (Carpenter's Btry, ANV), battery of, 124
casualties: Confederate, 98, 108; Union 108
Cedar Mountain, Battle of, 4, 19, 97
Centreville, VA, 2, 5, 13, 31, 32, 39, 48, 62, 81; Pope retreats to, 96, 97
Chancellorsville, Battle of, 3, 18
Chantilly (Ox Hill), Battle of, 5, 101, 202, 205
Chantilly, VA, 101, 102
Chapman, William, Lieut. Col., USA (Bde Cmdr, AP), brigade on Henry Hill, 188
Chapman Mill, 196, 200
Charlottesville, VA, 13
Chattanooga, TN, 2
Chesapeake Bay, 13, 19,
Chinn Branch, 170
Chinn House, 168, 170, 177, 178
Chinn Ridge, 79, 83, 118, 170; importance of, 170, 171, 175, 186
Cleveland, Grover, President, USA, 62
Columbus, KY, 1
Congdon, George R., Lieut., CSA (1st SC-PA, ANV), 142
Corman, George, Capt., USA (56th PA, AV), 132
Corse, Montgomery D., Col., CSA (Bde Cmdr, ANV), 177; attacks Chinn Ridge, 89, 177–81, 183; brigade of, 60, 4, 88, 91, 176, 178, 192; reports of, 177–78, 181
Crenshaw, William G., Capt., CSA (Crenshaw's Btry, ANV), battery of, 147
critical decisions: criterion, xiii–xiv; hierarchy of, xiii–xiv; how presented, xvi; importance of, xiii–xiv; list of, xiv-xv; summary of, 108–12; types, xiv
Cub Run, 204
Culpeper, VA, 19

Cumberland River, 1
Cutler, Lysander, Col., USA (6th WI, AV), 128; regiment of, 127, 132; wounded, 129, 133

Davis, Jefferson, President, CSA, replaces Johnston with Lee, 14
Dawkins Branch, 58, 60, 62, 191
decision hierarchy, xiii, xiv
"Deep Cut," 151, 157
Department of the East (USA), 33
Department of the Northwest (USA), 113
Department of the Pacific (USA), 13, 33
Department of the South (USA), 14
Department of the Trans-Mississippi (CSA), 1
Dilger, Hubert, Capt., USA (Btry I, 1st OH, AV), battery of, 191
Dogan House, 93
Dogan's Ridge, 73, 152; as a Union artillery position, 92, 171, 172
Doubleday, Abner, Brig. Gen., USA (Bde and Div Cmdr, AV), 126, 130; fight at Brawner Farm 41, 130–32; report of 131–32
Douglass, Marcellus, Col., CSA (13th GA and Bde Cmdr, ANV), 148; brigade's deployment, 148
Drayton, Thomas, Brig. Gen., CSA (Bde Cmdr, ANV), 184; attacks Henry Hill, 188; brigade of 148
Duryea, Abram, Brig. Gen., USA (Bde Cmdr, AV), 153; at Thoroughfare Gap, 197; brigade of 153

Edwards, Oliver E., Col., CSA (13th SC, ANV), 143; regiment of 142, 143
Elliot, William, Lieut., CSA (Rhett's Btry, ANV), 167
Emancipation Proclamation, 113
Eubanks, John L., Capt., CSA (Eubank's Btry ANV), battery of, 167
Evans, Nathan G., Brig. Gen., CSA (Bde Cmdr, ANV): attacks Chinn Ridge, 85, 87, 171, 172, 178, 181; brigade of, 46, 57, 72, 84, 91; brigade's position, 152

Index

Ewell, Richard S., Maj. Gen., CSA (Div Cmdr, ANV), 131; division of, 46, 119, 122, 138; division's defensive position, 46, 121, 135, 148, 152

Fair Oaks, Battle of. *See* Seven Pines
Fairfax Court House, VA, 101, 205; Pope retreats to, 101
Featherbed Lane (Road 622), 135
Fellers, J. B., Lieut., CSA (13th SC, ANV), 141
Ferrero, Edward, Col, USA (Bde Cmdr, AP), brigade of on Henry Hill, 188
Fields, Charles W., Brig. Gen, CSA (Bde Cmdr, ANV), 206; brigade of, 138, 148; brigade's position, 138
First Manassas (Bull Run), Battle of, 4, 13, 27, 39
Fitzhugh, Norman, Maj., CSA (Cav Staff Officer, ANV), 20
Flood, Joel, Capt., CSA (Staff Officer, ANV), 178
Foote, Andrew, Cmdr., USN (Flotilla Cmdr), 1
Fort Donelson, TN, 1
Fort Henry, TN, 1
Fort Monroe, VA, 13, 16, 18
Franklin, William B., Maj. Gen., USA (Corps Cmdr AP): corps of, 26, 50, 51; marching to join Pope, 72, 94
Fredericksburg, VA, 7, 19, 113
Fremont, John C., Maj. Gen., USA (Dept. Cmdr), 8; resigns as corps commander, 10

Gainesville, VA, 27, 32, 34, 46, 58, 191; as a road hub, 32
Garber, Asher W., Lieut., CSA (Staunton Btry, ANV) battery of, 122
Garrison, Irwin L., Lieut., USA (1st MI, AP), 164
Germantown, VA, 100, 205
Gibbon, John, Brig. Gen., USA (Bde Cmdr, AV), 123, 131; brigade of, 41; fight at Brawner Farm, 41, 123–34; reports of, 125–27, 133–34
Glorieta Pass, NM, 2

Gordonsville, VA, 13, 19
Gould, Joseph, Sgt., USA (48th PA, AP), 150; narrative of, 150–51
Grant, Ulysses S., Brig. Gen., USA (Army Cmdr), 1
Grant, Ulysses S., Lieut. Gen., USA (General-in-Chief), 14, 15
Gregg, Maxcy, Brig. Gen., CSA (Bde Cmdr, ANV), 141, 143, 145; at Ox Hill, 206; brigade deployment, 139; brigade of, 137, 144; brigade's position, 138
Griffin, Charles, Brig. Gen., USA (Bde Cmdr, AP), 154; brigade of, 60, 192
Grover, Cuvier, Brig. Gen., USA (Bde Cmdr, AP), attack by, 53, 148
Groveton, VA, 41, 48, 122, 135, 154, 192
Groveton Woods, 153
Groveton-Sudley Road, 48, 73, 135, 152, 153; importance of, 135
Gum Springs, VA, 204
Gum Springs Road (VA 659), 100, 204

Halleck, Henry W., Maj. Gen., USA (General-in-Chief), 12, 26; appointed general-in-chief, 14; biography of, 14; critical decision, 13–18, 109, 116; orders McClellan to evacuate the Peninsula, 18, 117; visits McClellan, 18
Hamilton, Charles A., Lieut. Col. (7th WI, AV), 133; wounded, 133
Hardin, Martin D., Col., USA (Bde Cmdr, AV), 84; brigade of 169, 170; brigade overrun, 171
Harper's Ferry, VA, 104
Harrison's Landing, VA, 3, 7, 14, 15, 19
Hatch, John G., Lieut., USA (1st MI, AP), 164
Hatch, John P., Brig. Gen., USA (Bde and Div Cmdr, AV), 55, 160; attacks by, 55, 66; brigade of, xvi, 41; division of 48, 49, 51, 73, 151, 154; ordered to "pursue" on Warrenton Turnpike, 151, 154
Haymarket, VA, 27, 34, 39, 40, 58, 198
Hazlett, Charles E., Lieut., USA (Btry D, 5th US Arty, AP), 192

Index

Heartland, The, 2

Heintzelman, Samuel P., Maj. Gen., USA (Corps Cmdr, AP), 55, 62; corps of, 39, 153, 169; corps' positions 60, 72, 137

Henry Hill, 39, 48, 79, 81, 170, 175, 177–78, 192; as a defensive position, 50, 87, 137; importance of, 81, 92, 118, 177, 187

Hill, Ambrose P., Maj. Gen., CSA (Div Cmdr, ANV), 26; at Ox Hill, 205, 206; division of, 29, 72, 76, 119, 120, 122, 137; division's defensive position, 45, 55, 121, 135, 138, 152; reinforces Jackson, 19

Hoffman, J. William, Lieut. Col., USA (56th PA, AV): regiment of, 128, 130, 131, 132; report of, 132

Hood, John B., Brig. Gen., CSA (Div Cmdr, ANV), 60; attacks by, 55, 170, 171; attacks Chinn Ridge, 85, 87, 171; division of, 46, 57, 68, 151; division's position, 66, 72, 84, 152

Hooker, Joseph, Maj. Gen., USA (Div Cmdr, AP): division of, 48, 51, 55; division's position, 137

Hopewell Gap, 196

Hopper, George C., Capt., USA (1st MI, AP), 163; narrative of, 163–65

Hunton, Eppa, Col., CSA (Bde Cmdr, ANV), 176, 177, 178; attacks Chinn Ridge, 88–89, 179, 181, 183; brigade of, 88, 91, 175, 177

Island Cemetery, Newport, RI, 204
Island Number 10, TN, 12

Jackson, Thomas J. "Stonewall", Maj. Gen., CSA (Wing Cmdr, ANV), xvi, 3, 4, 8, 18, 20, 26, 40, 105, 134; attacks King's division, 41, 58; biography of, 23–24; critical decisions, 25–29, 38–43, 109, 110; departs Manassas Junction, 29, 31, 39; report of, 119, 124–25, 205, 206; turning movement, 18, 31–32, 117, 119

Jackson's Left Wing, 3, 4, 38, 45, 188; attacks against, 53–55; conducts a turning movement, 23, 24, 31, 38–39, 107; conducts a second turning movement, 100, 117, 195, 203–4, 205; defensive position, 45–46, 57, 71–72; moves to Stony Ridge, 29, 39, 117, 119; positions of, 121, 122, 135, 152; sent to Gordonsville, 19, 107

James River, 3, 7, 14, 15, 107

Jeffersonton, VA, 24

Jenkins, Micah, Brig. Gen. CSA (Bde Cmdr, ANV), 177, 178; attacks Chinn Ridge, 89, 181, 183; brigade of, 88, 91, 176, 177

John Marshall Highway (US 55), 194, 202

John Mosby Highway (US 50), 204, 205

Johnson, Bradley T., Col., CSA (Bde Cmdr, ANV), 156; brigade defensive position, 157; brigade of, 156, 165

Johnson, Charles A., Col., USA (25th NY, AP), 159; regiment of, 156

Johnson, Jerome B., Lieut., USA (6th WI, AV), 129

Johnston, Albert S., Gen., CSA (Army Cmdr), 1

Johnston, Joseph E., Gen., CSA (Army Cmdr), 2, 3; at Seven Pines, 14; retreat from Centreville, 13; wounded, 3, 14, 20

Joint Order, 50, 59–60, 62, 75; implied task, 62; stated task, 62

Jones, Caldwalader, Lieut. Col., CSA (12th SC, ANV), 142, 143; reports of, 142, 145–46

Jones, David R., Brig. Gen., CSA (Div Cmdr, ANV): division of, 46, 60, 64, 66, 72, 84; division's positions, 152, 184

Jordan, Tyler, Capt., CSA (Bedford Btry, ANV), 167

Kane, Thomas L., Lieut. Col., USA (13th PA Reserves, AV), 191

Kearny, Philip, Maj. Gen., USA (Div Cmdr, AP), 204; at Ox Hill, 206; attacks by, 148; division of, 48, 51, 55, 73; division's position, 137; killed, 101, 206

Kemper, James L., Brig. Gen., CSA (Div Cmdr, ANV): division deployed for attack, 87–88, 175–76; division of, 46, 60, 66, 68; division's positions, 66, 72, 84, 152
Kennedy, John, Lieut., USA (73rd PA, AV), 184
Kentucky, invasion of, potential Confederate advantages, 2–3
Kerns, Mark, Capt., USA (Btry G, 1st PA Arty), battery of, 84, 169
King, Rufus, Brig. Gen., USA (Div Cmdr, AV), 122, attacked by Jackson, 41, 58, 122; division of, xvi, 32, 40, 47, 58, 134
Knoxville, TN, 2
Koltes, John A., Col., USA (Bde Cmdr, AV), 183; brigade of, 89; defends Chinn Ridge, 89, 183
Krzyzanowski, Wladimir, Col., USA (Bde Cmdr, AV), 138; attacks by, 53, 138, 148; brigade deployment, 138; brigade of, 89, 144, 185; defends Chinn Ridge, 89, 184–85; report of, 138–39

Law, Evander, Col., CSA (Bde Cmdr, ANV), at Thoroughfare Gap, 196, 201
Lawton, Alexander R., Brig. Gen., CSA (Bde and Div Cmdr, ANV), 46, 135, 138, 148, 152; at Ox Hill, 205, 206; brigade deployment, 148; brigade of, 127, 128, 148; defensive position, 121, 135; division of, 55, 72, 137
Leasure, Daniel, Col., USA (Bde Cmdr, AV), attacks by, 53, 148
Lee, John C., Col., USA (55th OH, AV), 175; counterattack of, 175; regiment of, 83, 171, 172, 177
Lee, Robert E., Gen. (Army Cmdr, ANV), xv, 3, 4, 7, 9, 15, 22, 40, 45, 63, 68, 95, 97, 98; advisor to President Davis, 20; appointed to army command, 14, 20, 107; at Thoroughfare Gap, 196; attempts to trap Pope, 20; biography of, 19–20; critical decisions, 18–25, 97–102, 102–6, 109, 112; exterior line, 73; mover focus of the war, 24; operational intention, 41, 51, 75, 99, 102, 103, 108, 113, 122, 153, 202; orders a turning movement, 23, 107; orders a second turning movement, 99, 202; reports of, 202–3, 207–8; sends Jackson's Wing to Gordonsville, 19, 107; threatens Washington, 99, 103, 107
Lee, Stephen D., Col., CSA (Arty. Bn Cmdr, ANV), 159, 166; battalion of, 46, 71, 72, 77, 124, 152, 156; report of 166–68
Leesburg, VA, 5, 105, 112, 208
Lewis Lane, 48, 73, 135, 169
Lexington, KY, 2
Lincoln, Abraham, President, USA, 8, 9, 18, 105; critical decision, 7–13, 108, 116; issues Emancipation Proclamation, 113; visits McClellan, 14
Linton Hall Road, 194
Little River Turnpike, 100, 101, 203, 204, 205
Longstreet, James, Maj. Gen., CSA (Wing Cmdr, ANV), 3, 18, 20, 26 29, 60, 63, 81, 99, 107, 121, 202; at Thoroughfare Gap, 196, 197
Longstreet's Right Wing, xvi, 3, 4, 27, 32, 40, 60; attacks August 30, 81, 84, 170; fights at Thoroughfare Gap, 37, 202; follows Jackson's Wing, 23, 24, 26, 117, 196; marches through Thoroughfare Gap, 37; marches to join Jackson's Wing, 31, 33, 37, 40, 41, 45, 46, 50, 57, 58; positions, 60–61, 64, 66, 68, 72, 84, 122, 152; reunites with Jackson's Wing, 46, 52, 57, 66

Mahler, Francis, Lieut. Col., USA (75th PA, AV), 139; regiment of, 138
Mahone, William, Brig. Gen., CSA (Bde Cmdr, ANV), attacks Henry Hill, 188
Malvern Hill, Battle of, 3, 14
Manassas, VA, 13
Manassas Gap Railroad, 192, 195

Index

Manassas Gap Railroad, Independent Line of. *See* unfinished railroad
Manassas Gap Road, 46
Manassas Junction, VA, 26, 27, 29, 32, 40, 48, 58; as a supply depot, 4; Jackson captures and destroys, 24, 25, 32, 119
Manassas Junction-Gainesville Road, 59, 61, 62, 63, 66, 72, 191
Marsh, John F., Capt., USA (6th WI, AV), 129
Marshall, Elisha G., Col., USA (13th NY, AP), 161; regiment of, 157, 161, 192; report of, 161–63
Marshall, J. Foster, Col., CSA (1st SC Rifles, ANV), 143; regiment of, 143, 144
Marshall, VA. *See* Salem
Martin, Augustus P., Capt., USA (3rd MA Btry, AP), 192
Maryland, 5, 105, 106
Maryland Campaign, 113, 208
Matthews, Ezra, Capt., USA (Btry F, 1st PA Arty, AV), battery of, 197
Matthews Hill, 118, 119; as a defensive position, 50, 135, 187; importance of, 118
Matthews House (Stone House), 118, 134
May, Isaac M., Maj., USA (19th IN, AV), wounded, 134
McClellan, George B., Maj. Gen., USA (Army Cmdr, AP), 2, 3, 7, 9, 13, 18, 22, 23, 107, 113, 153; ordered to evacuate the Peninsula, 18; request reinforcements, 18; visited by Halleck, 18; visited by Lincoln, 14
McCorkle, William H., Maj., CSA (12th SC, ANV), 142
McCrady, Edward, Lieut. Col., CSA (1st SC-PA, ANV), 142; regiment of, 139, 142; report of 139–42, 143
McDowell, Irving, Maj. Gen., USA (Corps Cmdr AV), 10, 31, 35, 62, 63, 66, 68, 79, 169, 194; appointed corps commander, 10; at First Manassas (Bull Run), 33; biography of, 32–33; corps composition, 32; corps of, xvi, 7, 8, 40, 57, 58, 63, 64, 66, 68, 69, 72, 192, 195; corps' positions, 47–48, 72; critical decisions, 31–38, 78–83, 110, 111; does not forward Buford's sighting report, 52; first plan to stop Longstreet at Thoroughfare Gap, 34, 35, 195; orders from Pope, 137, 195–96; orders Reynolds to move north of turnpike, 80, 81, 84, 169
McLean, Joseph A., Lieut. Col., USA (88th PA, AV), 181
McLean, Nathaniel C., Col., USA (Bde Cmdr, AV), 93, 170, 180; brigade of, 183; brigade positions 79, 83, 171, 178; critical decision, 83–93; defends on Chinn Ridge, 85, 170; ordered to Chinn Ridge, 85, 170; reports of, 171–72, 173–75
Meade, George G., Brig. Gen., USA (Bde Cmdr, AV), 169; brigade of, 169
Memphis, TN, 1, 12
Meredith, Solomon, Col, USA (19th IN, AV), 128; regiment of, 124, 125, 127, 128
Meredith, Sullivan A., Col., USA (56th PA, AV), 131, 132; regiment of, 128, 130, 131, 132; wounded, 132
Milroy, Robert H., Brig. Gen., USA (Bde Cmdr, AV), 96; attacks by, 53, 138, 148; brigade of, 48, 55, 187; brigade positions, 72, 79, 83, 136
Mississippi River, 1, 12
Monument Drive, 204
Morell, George W., Maj. Gen., USA (Div Cmdr, AP), 68; division of, 60, 154, 192; ordered to attack, 154
Mother Leathercoat Mountain, 195, 196
Mountain Department (USA), 10
Mountain Road Trail, 202
Muhleck, Gustavus, Lieut. Col., USA (73rd PA and Bde Cmdr, AV), 183; report of 183–84

Nagle, James, Col., USA (Bde Cmdr, AP), 148; attacks by, 53, 148–50; brigade deployment, 148; brigade of, 148
New Madrid, TN, 12
New Orleans, capture of, 1
Norfolk and Petersburg Railroad, 13

Index

O'Connor, Edgar, Col., USA (2nd WI, AV): regiment of 124, 125, 127; wounded, 133
Ohio River, importance of, 2
Orange and Alexandria Railroad, 4, 19, 25, 32; as Lee's supply line, 22, 104; as Pope's supply line, 4, 20, 22, 23, 24, 26, 117
Orleans, VA, 31
Ox Hill (Chantilly), Battle of, 5, 101, 202, 205
Ox Hill Battlefield Park, 204

Pageland Lane, 46, 124, 134, 152
Parker, Michael P, Capt., CSA (1st SC-PA, ANV), 142
Parker, William W., Capt., CSA (Parker's Btry, ANV), battery of, 167
Patrick, Marsena R., Brig. Gen., USA (Bde Cmdr, AV), 41; brigade of, 166
Pea Ridge (Elk Horn Tavern), Battle of, 1, 10
Pelham, John, Capt., CSA (Pelham's Btry, ANV), battery of, 127, 128
Pender, William D., Brig. Gen., CSA (Bde Cmdr, ANV): at Ox Hill, 206, brigade of, 138; brigade position 138
Peninsula Campaign, 2, 9, 10, 14, 16
Peninsula, The, 2, 7, 13, 14, 107
Pennsylvania, 105, 106
Perkins, Henry W., Lieut., USA (Aide to Brig. Gen. Butterfield, AP), 160
Perryville, Battle of, 3
Petersburg, VA, 14, 15; railroad hub, 16
Piatt, Abraham S., Brig. Gen., USA (Bde Cmdr, AP), brigade of 188
Poague, William T., Capt., CSA (Rockbridge Btry, ANV), battery of, 124
Pomeroy, Edward, Capt., USA (1st MI, AP), 165
Pond Mountain, 194, 196
Pope, John, Maj. Gen., USA (Army Cmdr AV), xv, 3, 4, 20, 22, 26, 51, 151; appointed army commander, 12; believes Jackson is at Manassas Junction, 34; believes Jackson is retreating, 45, 50, 52, 60, 76, 137, 151, 154, 192; biography of, 11–12; critical decisions, 45–57, 71–78, 94–96, 110, 111, 112; interior line, 73; misunderstands Longstreet's location, 50, 60, 76–77, 151, 154; orders army to Manassas Junction, 34, 39; orders a retreat, 96, 97; orders attacks on August 29th, 52, 137, 151, 153; orders attacks on August 30th, 76, 153; orders to Porter, 58, 59, 62, 66; relieved of command, 113; reports of, 188–89, 204–5; retreats to Centreville, 107, 189, 202; retreats to Washington-Alexandria, 107, 208; withdraws from the Rappahannock River, 24, 26
Porter, Fitz John, Maj. Gen., USA (Corps Cmdr, AP), 62, 63, 68, 192, 194; corps of, 57, 58, 63, 64, 66, 69, 72, 73, 153; corps positions, 48 72, 73, 152; court martialed, 61–62; critical decision, 57–69, 110; ordered to attack, 77, 153; orders from Pope, 58, 59, 62, 66, 72, 77, 137
Post, James B., Lieut. Col., USA (95th NY, AV), 132; regiment of, 132
Potomac River, 5, 7, 69, 104, 106; Lee crosses, 113, 208
Powers, Charles J., Capt., USA (Staff Officer, AP), 160

Quarry Trail, 202

Rapidan River, 4, 19; bridges destroyed, 23, 104
Rappahannock River, 2, 3, 4, 13, 19, 22, 46, 195; bridges destroyed, 20; crossing over, 20
Reid House, 205
reinforcing column, 98, 104, 112; composition of 98, 112
Reno, Jesse L., Maj. Gen., USA (Corps Cmdr, AP), 62; corps' positions, 48, 60, 72, 137; division of, 48, 51, 53, 73
Reynolds, John A., Capt., USA (Btry L, 1st NY Arty, AV), battery of, 122
Reynolds, John F., Brig. Gen., USA (Div Cmdr, AV), 169; division of, 32, 35,

257

Index

Reynolds, John F., Brig. Gen., USA (Div Cmdr, AV) (*cont.*) 40, 50, 55, 68, 73, 153, 154; division's positions, 48, 79, 137, 152, 169; ordered to move north of the turnpike, 80, 84, 169; report of, 169

Richardson, John B., Capt. (2nd Company, Washington Arty, ANV), 183; battery of, 177, 183

Richmond, VA, 2, 3, 4, 7, 13, 15, 105, 107

Richmond and Danville Railroad, 16

Richmond and Petersburg Railroad, 16

Ricketts, James B., Brig. Gen., USA (Div Cmdr, AV), 153, 201; at Thoroughfare Gap, 37, 197–98, 200–201; division of, 32, 40, 47, 52, 59, 73; ordered to Thoroughfare Gap, 37, 58; report of, 198

Rixlew Lane, 191

Roberts, Charles W., Col., USA (Bde Cmdr, AP), 77, 155; brigade of, 155, 157, 161, 166; report of 159–61

Roberts, Horace, Col., USA (1st MI, AP), 164

Robertson, Beverly H., Brig. Gen., CSA (Cav Bde Cmdr, ANV), brigade of, 57, 58, 60, 64, 66, 192

Robinson, John C., Brig. Gen., USA (Bde Cmdr, AP), attacks by, 15

Robinson, William, Col., USA (7th WI, AV): regiment of, 124, 125, 127; wounded, 133

Root, Adrian, Col., USA (94th NY, AV), 181

Salem (Marshall), VA, 24, 31

Santa Fe, NM, 2

Schimmelfenning, Alexander, Col., USA (Bde Cmdr, AV), 144; attacks by, 53, 144–45, 148; brigade of, 144; deployment, 144

School House Branch, 156, 157, 163

Schurz, Carl, Brig. Gen., USA (Div Cmdr, AV), 144; division of, 48, 55, 73, 191; division's position, 136

Second Manassas (Bull Run), Battle of, xiii, 3, 4, 29, 45, 96, 102, 107

Second Manassas (Bull Run) Campaign, xiii, 4, 99, 105, 107

Seven Days Battles, 3, 7, 14, 24, 107

Seven Pines (Fair Oaks), Battle of, 3, 20

Seymour, Truman, Brig. Gen., USA (Bde Cmdr, AV), 169

Shenandoah Valley, 3, 8, 13, 15, 104

Shiloh, Battle of, 1, 3

Shooter, William P., Capt., CSA (1st SC, ANV), 141, 142

Shumaker, Lindsay M., Maj., CSA (Arty. Jackson's Div, ANV), 72, 124, 152, 156, 159, 166

Sibley, Henry H., Brig. Gen., CSA (Army Cmdr), 2

Sickles, Daniel E., 8

Sigel, Franz, Maj. Gen., USA (Corps Cmdr, AV), 62, 96; appointed to corps command, 10; corps of, 32, 35, 39, 51, 55, 58, 59; corps' positions, 46, 48, 60, 72, 136; report of, 190–91

Skinner, Frederick G., Lieut. Col., CSA (1st VA, ANV), 181

Smith, Edmund Kirby, Maj. Gen., CSA (Army Cmdr), invades Kentucky, 2–3

Smith, L. A., Sgt., CSA (1st SC-PA, ANV), 143

Southside Railroad, 16

Spencer, Clinton, Capt., USA (1st MI, AP), 164

Stafford, Leroy, Col., CSA (19th LA and Bde Cmdr, ANV), 156, 157; brigade of, 156; defensive position, 157; report of, 165–66

Stanton, Edwin M., Secretary of War, USA, 8, 9; biography of, 8–9

Starke, William E., Brig. Gen., CSA (Bde And Div Cmdr, ANV), 135, 156; at Ox Hill, 205, 206; defensive position, 46–47, 121, 135, 152; division of, 46

Stevens, Isaac I., Brig. Gen., USA (Div Cmdr, AP), 204; at Ox Hill, 206; division of, 48, 51, 53, 73, 154; division position, 137; killed, 101, 206

Stiles, John W., Col., USA (Bde Cmdr, AV), 198; at Thoroughfare Gap, 197, 198; brigade of, 89, 180, 181, 193; defends Chinn Ridge, 89; reinforces Tower and McLean, 181

Stone Bridge, 81, 96, 189–90
Stone House. *See* Matthews House
Stony Ridge, 32, 38; as a defensive position, 39, 45; Jackson moves to, 29, 39, 117, 119, 195
Stuart, J. E. B., Maj. Gen., CSA (Cav Cmdr, ANV), 22, 57, 60, 124
Sudley Church, 152
Sudley Ford, 100, 203, 205
Sudley Road, 29, 191, 204; importance of, 118
Sudley Springs, VA, 135
Sullivan, Timothy, Col., USA (24th NY and Bde Cmdr, AV), 77, 157; brigade of, 161, 166
Sumner, Edwin V., Maj. Gen., USA (Corps Cmdr, AP): corps of, 50, 51; marching to join Pope, 72, 75, 94–95
Sykes, George W., Brig. Gen., USA (Div Cmdr, AP), 96; division of, 68, 154, 192; ordered to attack, 77, 154

Taliaferro, Alexander G., Col., CSA (Bde Cmdr, ANV), 156; brigade of, 128, 156
Taliaferro, William B., Brig. Gen., CSA (Div Cmdr, ANV), xvi, 131; defensive position of 121, 131; division of, 29, 119, 122
Taylor, James S., Capt., CSA (Taylor's Btry, ANV), 167
Tennessee River, 1
Terry, William R., Col., CSA (24th VA, ANV), 181
Thoburn, Joseph, Col., USA (Bde Cmdr, AV), at Thoroughfare Gap, 197
Thomas, Edward L., Brig. Gen., CSA (Bde Cmdr, ANV): at Ox Hill, 206; brigade of, 138; brigade position, 138
Thompson, James, Capt., USA (Btry C, PA Arty, AV), battery of, 197
Thoroughfare Gap, 4, 27, 32, 36, 58, 194, 197; Jackson marches through, 24, 32; Longstreet at, 24, 31, 121
Tower, Zealous B., Brig. Gen., USA (Bde Cmdr, AV), 181; at Thoroughfare Gap, 197; brigade of, 89, 181, 183; defends Chinn Ridge, 89, 178; reinforces McLean, 178; report of, 180
Trapp Branch Road (#674), 194
Trimble, Isaac R., Brig. Gen., CSA (Bde Cmdr, ANV): brigade of, 128, 148, 165; brigade's deployment, 148
Turner Road (#723), 202

unfinished railroad, 120, 135, 137, 139, 141, 153; as a defensive position, 122, 141, 156
Union Mills, VA, 48

Virginia Central Railroad, 13, 16; as Lee's supply line, 22, 104

Waddell, James D., Maj., CSA (20th Ga, ANV), regiment of, 200; report of, 200
Wainwright, William P., Col., USA (76th NY, AV), 131; regiment of, 128, 130, 131, 132
Walton, James B., Col., CSA (Arty. Bn Cmdr, ANV), 46, 66
Warren, Gouverneur K., Col., USA (Bde Cmdr, AP), brigade of, 73; brigade overrun, 119; brigade position 79, 84, 170
Warrenton, VA, 32
Warrenton Turnpike, 28, 32, 134, 135, 152, 180, 192, 195; importance of, 118, 121, 135
Warrenton Turnpike-Sudley Road Intersection, 29, 39, 46, 48, 66, 72, 135, 151, 187; importance of, 118, 121, 135
Washington (LA) Artillery Battalion, 46, 66
Washington, DC, 4, 13, 16, 27, 97; threatened by Lee, 25, 99, 103
Washington College (Washington and Lee University), 20
Webster, Fletcher, Col., USA (12th MA, AV), 181
Weeks, Henry A., Col., USA (12th NY and Bde Cmdr, AP), 77, 155, 157; brigade of, 155, 157, 161, 166
Weldon Railroad, 16
Wellington Road, 191, 194

Wendell, Charles E., Capt., USA (1st MI, AP), 164
West Ox Road, 204, 205
White Plains, VA, 26, 33, 195
Whittlesey, Eben T., Capt., USA (1st MI, AP), 164
Wiedrich, Michael, Capt., USA (Btry I, 1st NY Arty.), battery of, 83, 170, 171, 175
Wilcox, Cadmus M., Brig. Gen., CSA (Div Cmdr, ANV): at Thoroughfare Gap, 196; division of, 46, 61, 64, 66, 68, 72, 84, 152
Winchester, VA, 104, 105
Wooding, George, Capt., CSA (Danville Btry, ANV), battery of, 123
Wright, Ambrose R., Brig. Gen., CSA (Bde Cmdr, ANV), attacks Henry Hill, 188
Wyndham, Percy, Col, USA (1st NJ Cav, AV), 198; regiment of, 195, 196

Young's Branch, 170